MA

A Colour Guidebook

Edited by Marilyn Morton

Formac Publishing Company Limited
Halifax

CONTENTS

CONTENTS

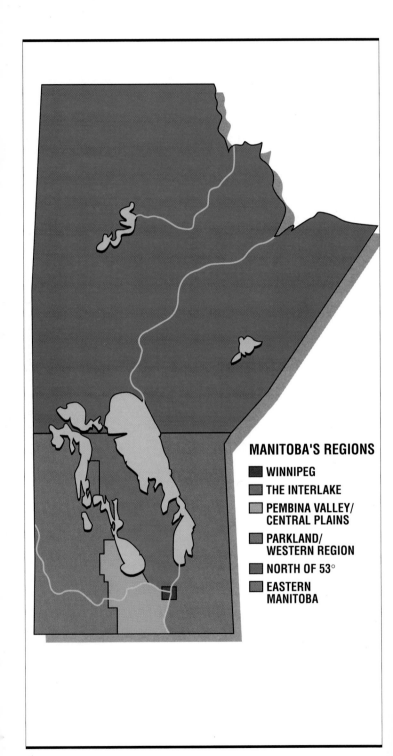

MANITOBA'S REGIONS

■ WINNIPEG

■ THE INTERLAKE

■ PEMBINA VALLEY/
CENTRAL PLAINS

■ PARKLAND/
WESTERN REGION

■ NORTH OF 53°

■ EASTERN
MANITOBA

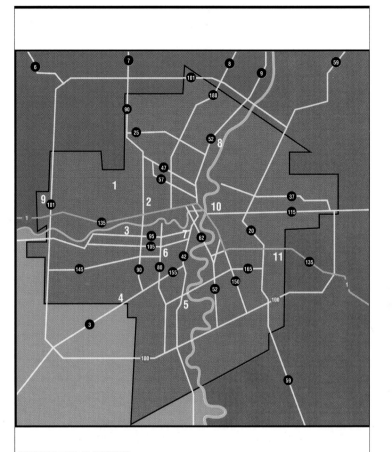

WINNIPEG ROUTES

Points of Interest
1   Winnipeg International Airport
2   Winnipeg Arena
3   Assiniboine Park Zoo
4   Fort Whyte Nature Centre
5   University of Manitoba
6   Pan-Am Pool
7   Corydon Village
8   Rainbow Stage
9   Assiniboia Downs
10 St. Boniface Musuem
11 The Winnipeg Mint

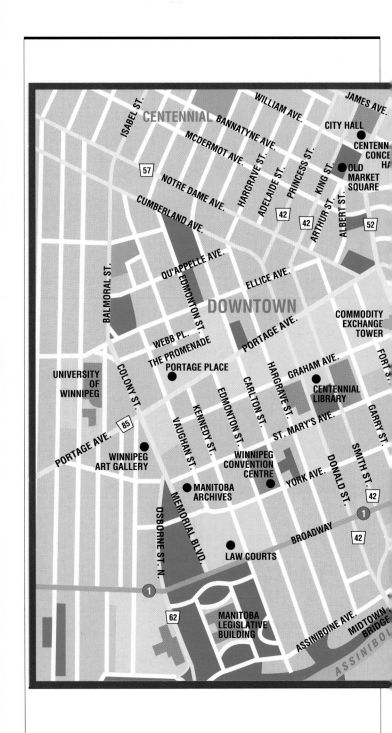

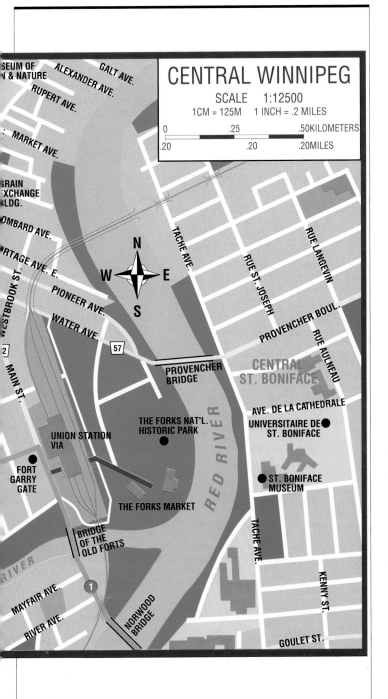

CENTRAL WINNIPEG

SCALE   1:12500
1CM = 125M   1 INCH = .2 MILES

0   .25   .50KILOMETERS
.20   .20   .20MILES

SEUM OF
N & NATURE
ALEXANDER AVE.
GALT AVE.
RUPERT AVE.
MARKET AVE.
GRAIN
XCHANGE
LDG.
OMBARD AVE.
RTAGE AVE. E.
ESTBROOK ST.
PIONEER AVE.
WATER AVE.
2
MAIN ST.
57
TACHE AVE.
RUE ST. JOSEPH
RUE LANGEVIN
PROVENCHER BOUL.
RUE AULNEAU
PROVENCHER
BRIDGE
CENTRAL
ST. BONIFACE
AVE. DE LA CATHEDRALE
THE FORKS NAT'L.
HISTORIC PARK
UNIVERSITAIRE DE
ST. BONIFACE
UNION STATION
VIA
FORT
GARRY
GATE
ST. BONIFACE
MUSEUM
THE FORKS MARKET
RED RIVER
BRIDGE
OF THE
OLD FORTS
TACHE AVE.
RIVER
MAYFAIR AVE.
1
KENNY ST.
RIVER AVE.
NORWOOD
BRIDGE
GOULET ST.

N
W   E
S

7

Welcome to this guide to Manitoba!

Whether you're a long-time resident of the province or visiting for the first time, here is a reliable, interesting, and entertaining guide to the best of what Manitoba has to offer.

To create this guide we sought out knowledgeable Manitobans and invited them to write about their part of the province, or on a topic of particular interest to visitors.

As you'd expect, there are several chapters describing Winnipeg and its key attractions — its historic Forks area, its parks, its famed North End district, its handsome Legislative Building, its architectural treasures. Other sections offer you guided tours of the best and most interesting attractions in every region of the province. We think many Manitobans will be surprised by the incredible array of places to visit and things to do in their province. So will visitors to Manitoba.

But there are other subjects travellers want information on. What about the history of this unique part of Canada? For two centuries the territory that is now Manitoba was at the heart of the encounters between native peoples, the British, and French Canadians. This history produced some of the most interesting places to visit in the province, and was the background for some of the most interesting events of Canadian history. You can read about Manitoba's history in the first part of this book in chapters written by knowledgeable contributors who offer an introduction to the most recent ideas and research of leading western historians.

Something else many travellers want is a reliable, independent overview of the best possibilities in a place, the most exciting opportunities for recreation, cultural activities, and entertainment. Whether it's one of the world's finest ballet companies, the spectacular polar bear migration at Churchill, unspoiled tall-grass prairie, or fine freshwater fishing, Manitoba has much to offer. We found local experts who share their knowledge with you. On topics like food, festivals, fishing, and culture our contributors give you background information to help you make the most of your travels in Manitoba.

And then there are special local topics that a curious traveller wants to know more about. We've selected just a few of those — for instance, those infamous Manitoba mosquitoes, or that 1919 General Strike that many of us heard about in history classes at school, or the romantic story of nature writer Grey Owl. You'll find special feature sections devoted to these topics in this guide.

A guidebook needs good maps. We've included key maps at the front of this book, and maps of each travel region of the province. On the regional maps, we've underlined the communities and places that our writers describe in the text. Details on accommodation, dining, and other practical information you need are grouped together in the listings section at the back of the book. The listings are based on the independent recommendations of our contributors, so you can rely on them for trustworthy advice on where to stay, where to eat, and other details. Remember, though, that things change quickly and no guidebook can be completely up to date. Be sure to phone ahead to check on details like hours of operation, prices, or other items of particular importance to you.

Like the other guidebooks we have published, this is an independent guide. We asked the contributors to write their chapters as if responding to a good friend who had asked them to recommend the best things to see and do while travelling in Manitoba. The contributors and editors decided what to include in this book solely on this basis. No one contributed to the cost of this publication, or even offered free rooms and meals to our writers. We wanted this to be a guidebook you can trust and rely on. We hope that you will enjoy this book, and that it will contribute to your appreciation of the rich and rewarding possibilities of travel in Manitoba.

— Carolyn MacGregor and James Lorimer, Publishers

MARILYN MORTON is a freelance editor living in Winnipeg. She was previously employed as managing editor of a literary publishing house and as a typesetter and graphic artist. She currently sits on the editorial boards of two Winnipeg publishing companies.

Most of the photographs in this guidebook have been contributed by the following photographers: John Bykerk, David Firman, Mike GrandMaison, Donna Henry, Henry Kalen, Dave Reede, Harv Sawatzky and Robert Taylor. For more details, see the photographic credits at the end of the book.

ROBERT ANDERSON (Mosquitoes) – Rob Anderson has done extensive research in mosquito biology and control since 1983. He has co-authored eight articles for scientific journals.

MARILYN C. BAKER (The Legislative Building) – A professor of art history at the University of Manitoba's School of Art, Marilyn Baker has written two books, including one on Manitoba's third Legislative Building.

JIM BLANCHARD (Wheat) – Jim Blanchard is a librarian at the University of Manitoba. He is the author of *The History of the Canadian Grain Commission* and numerous articles about the history of the grain business.

RUSSELL E. BRAYLEY (Recreation) – Head of recreation studies at the University of Manitoba's Faculty of Physical Education and Recreation, Russ Brayley has done research on recreational behaviour in Manitoba, has written about Manitoba's recreational opportunities, and has travelled extensively throughout the province.

JACK BUMSTED (The Great Flood of 1950) – Jack Bumsted is a member of the Department of History of the University of Manitoba, and has published extensively on both the history of Canada and of Manitoba.

LUCIEN CHAPUT (St. Boniface) – An author and former archivist, Lucien Chaput is currently writing the second volume of the French-language *Histoire de Saint–Boniface*. He has worked as a journalist at *La Liberté*, a St. Boniface newspaper.

CECILIA DANYSK (Homesteading and Wheat: 1870–1919) – A transplanted westerner, Cecilia Danysk teaches western Canadian history and agricultural development at Dalhousie University in Halifax. Her latest book is *Hired Hands: Labour and the Development of the Prairie Agriculture, 1880–1930*.

GERHARD ENS (Louis Riel) – Gerhard Ens is an associate professor of history at Brandon University. He has published numerous articles on Louis Riel and the Red River Métis, and is presently working on a history of Métis merchant families in the 19th century.

SANDRA FINDLAY (Parkland/Western Region) – Sandra Findlay is a freelance writer whose previous work has included stints as copy editor at the *Brandon Sun* and city editor at the *Portage la Prairie Daily Graphic*.

DONNA HENRY (North of 53°) – Currently regional director of Northern Manitoba Culture, Heritage and Citizenship, for the past 15 years Donna Henry has directed federal and provincial government programs that preserve, protect, interpret and celebrate the unique culture and heritage of northern Manitoba.

CATHERINE MACDONALD (Winnipeg Parks) – Catherine Macdonald is a historical research consultant who has researched a wide variety of subject matter including the history of hydroelectric development. Most recently she has written

Leisure: An Illustrated History of Parks and Recreation Services in Winnipeg 1893–1993.

JAKE MACDONALD (Fishing) – A professional fishing guide and freelance writer, Jake MacDonald is the author of *Lakes, Lures and Lodges: An Angler's Guide to Western Canada* and several books of fiction.

MELINDA MCCRACKEN (Culture; Ballet) – Melinda McCracken has worked on the staff of the *Toronto Globe and Mail*, has been published in *MacLean's*, *Chatelaine*, and *Rolling Stone*, and has been Manitoba correspondent for *Quill & Quire* and *NeWest Review*. She is the author of *Memories Are Made of This*, a memoir of the 1950s in Winnipeg.

RANDAL MCILROY (Summer Festivals; Winnipeg Folk Festival) – Randal McIlroy has worked as a Winnipeg freelance writer for more than 15 years. He is currently completing his first novel, *Floating*.

JOYCE MEYER (Eastern Manitoba) – Joyce Meyer has worked as a freelance writer for the *Winnipeg Tribune*, *The Financial Post* and the *Toronto Star* as well as an information officer for the Manitoba Department of Industry, Trade and Tourism. She has written two books, including one on the 1844 canoe voyage made by Grey Nuns from Montreal to the Red River Settlement.

ROGER NEWMAN (The Interlake) – Now editor of the *Interlake Spectator* in Gimli, Roger Newman previously worked for the *Toronto Globe and Mail*, the *Winnipeg Free Press* and the *Brandon Sun*.

KRYSTYL NICKARZ (The North End) – Krystyl Nickarz is a graduate of Red River Community College's Creative Communications program. She has written for various Winnipeg publications including the *Winnipeg Free Press*.

PETER NUNODA (Recession, Depression and War: 1920–1945; Heart of the Continent) – Peter Nunoda is a lecturer in Canadian history at the University of Manitoba. He is currently the holder of a Canadian Ethnic Studies Fellowship and is doing research on the Japanese–Canadian community.

LAURA PEERS (Contact: 1640–1870) – Laura Peers is the author of *The Ojibwa in Western Canada, 1780–1870* and numerous articles on Native history. Most recently, she has researched the Aboriginal community around Lower Fort Garry in historic Red River.

LEO PETTIPAS (Pre–Contact to 1640) – A heritage consultant for the City of Winnipeg, Leo Pettipas has published extensively on Canadian heritage, archaeology and history, including seven books, the most recent of which is *Other People's Heritage: A Cross–Cultural Approach to Museum Interpretation*.

ELLIE REIMER (Pembina Valley/Central Plains) – A Winkler-based freelance writer, Ellie Reimer has for several years been a regular contributor to the *Pembina Times*, a local weekly newspaper. She has been a Winkler resident most of her life.

RANDY ROSTECKI (The Forks and Upper Fort Garry; Old Downtown and Warehouse District; Architectural Treasures) – A Winnipeg-based historical consultant specializing in urban, architectural and development history, Randy Rostecki has published numerous articles and reports, as well as *Crescentwood —A History and St. Mary's Academy, Winnipeg*. He is a three-time recipient of the Margaret McWilliams Medal of the Manitoba Historical Society for historical writing.

DOUG SMITH (Winnipeg General Strike) – A Winnipeg writer and broadcaster, Doug Smith is the author of *Joe Zuken: Citizen and Socialist* and *Let Us Rise! An Illustrated History of the Manitoba Labour Movement*.

ROBERT TAYLOR (Polar Bear Migration) – A Winnipeg-based photographer and writer, Robert Taylor has done extensive research on Manitoba's north. He has published several books of his photographs and text, including *The Edge of the Arctic: Churchill and the Hudson Bay Lowlands*.

MARION WARHAFT (Food) – Marion Warhaft has been a restaurant critic and columnist for the *Winnipeg Free Press* for almost 20 years and has published articles in *Canadian Living*, *Chatelaine* and *Food Magazine*, as well as *Dining Out with Marion Warhaft*, a guide to Winnipeg restaurants.

TOM WATROUS (Grey Owl) – A cellist with the Winnipeg Symphony Orchestra, Tom Watrous has been interested in Grey Owl for many years. He has done extensive research on the conservationist and has given lectures in Ontario, Saskatchewan and the United States, as well as Manitoba.

ROBERT E. WRIGLEY (The Land) – Dr. Robert Wrigley is director of the Oak Hammock Marsh Interpretive Centre near Stonewall and previously acted as director and curator of birds at the Manitoba Museum of Man and Nature. He has published a dozen books in various fields of natural history, including *Manitoba's Big Cat — The Cougar in Manitoba*.

THE LAND

ROBERT E. WRIGLEY

Manitoba is a vast province encompassing six major ecosystems that support a remarkable diversity of plant and animal life. Its present-day landforms can be attributed to an intriguing geologic history that featured a huge glacial lake, immense mountains, and life dating back 570 million years.

LANDSCAPE

With a land and water area of 650,000 square kilometres (251,000 sq. mi.), Manitoba is big by any standard, approaching the size of Texas. For 1225 kilometres (761 mi.) north-south and 793 kilometres (493 mi.) east-west, it sprawls across the geographical centre of North America — a fact pointed out on a sign along the Trans-Canada Highway east of Winnipeg. Usually thought of as a prairie province, Manitoba is more accurately described as a patchwork of trees, rocks, and water.

Water covers 16 percent of the province. Of over 100,000 lakes, 38,000 surpass 33 hectares (80 acres) in size. At 23,900 square kilometres (9,230 sq. mi.), Lake Winnipeg

WHITESHELL PROVINCIAL PARK

PELICANS ON LAKE WINNIPEG OFF HECLA ISLAND

dominates south-central Manitoba, and lakes Winnipegosis and Manitoba account for another 10,100 square kilometres (3,900 sq. mi.). All of Manitoba's major rivers originate outside the province, as far away as Alberta, South Dakota, and Ontario. The Winnipeg, Red, Assiniboine, and Saskatchewan drain the south, while the Nelson, Churchill, God's, Hayes, and Seal collect the pure waters of the north. These and many smaller rivers finally empty into Hudson Bay at numerous points along its 644 kilometres (400 mi.) of marine coastline.

The populated, agricultural Red River Valley now appears relatively dry, but this was not formerly the case. This region was often marsh-like and difficult for settlers to traverse. An extensive system of ditches now draws off spring meltwater, allowing farmers to seed early, while enormous floodways around Winnipeg and several other towns carry away potentially devastating flood waters.

It may surprise you that Manitoba actually has mountains. Rising from the prairie is a series of uplands called the Manitoba Escarpment. Running to the northwest (and into Saskatchewan), these uplands are the Pembina

and Tiger hills, Riding Mountain, and the Duck and Porcupine mountains. The highest elevation in the province is the 831-metre (2,727-ft.) peak of Baldy in the Duck Mountains. Turtle Mountain straddles the United States border.

RED RIVER NEAR LOCKPORT

GEOLOGY

The pastoral plains and gently rolling hills of southern Manitoba belie a remarkable geologic history traceable back three billion years. Two periods of crustal upheaval, each involving both a submarine region of central Manitoba and rising volcanic islands, eventually built a mountain belt higher than the current Himalayas. Mountain building ended about 1.7 billion years ago, followed by a billion years of erosion that wore down this mighty range, leaving only its base as a flat plain known as the Canadian Shield. The Shield's pink and grey granitic bedrock lies exposed in many areas of eastern and northern Manitoba.

On either side of the elevated Shield are basins that have received enormous volumes of eroded sediment, both while submerged under seas and as dry land. To the

northeast lie the Hudson Bay Lowlands, a flat region marked by ancient beach ridges. Directly southwest of the Shield are the Manitoba Lowlands, and with a general relief of less than eight metres (26 ft.), this is one of the most level regions on the continent. This flatness is relieved by the Southwestern Uplands, whose eastern border is the Manitoba Escarpment. These layers of sediments were deposited during the Mesozoic Era, 225 to 65 million years ago, and included wind-blown, volcanic-ash clays originating from the Rocky Mountains. Within the last two million years, most of these regions became buried by glacial drift — a sorted mixture of gravel, sand, silt, and clay deposited by glaciers and meltwater.

Geologists have discovered the sites of at least six major meteorite impacts, with giant craters at West Hawk Lake, Lake St. Martin, and Poplar Bay.

From the evidence of fossils preserved in sedimentary rocks, scientists have learned that marine plants and animals existed in Manitoba as early as the Cambrian Period, 570 million years ago. Ordovician limestone, deposited under an equatorial sea some 450 million years ago, has yielded abundant, beautiful fossil corals, sponges, snails, brachiopods, and cephalopods (giant relatives of the nautilus) in quarries at Garson and Stony Mountain. You can see these at the Stonewall Quarry Park Museum. During the Mesozoic Era,

TUNDRA FLOWERS

early birds and immense fish and marine reptiles — mosasaurs, plesiosaurs, and turtles — swam in the warm sea that covered Manitoba. Their fossils have been excavated from quarries near Morden and Miami, and are on view at the Morden and District Museum and the Manitoba Museum of Man and Nature.

At the close of the Mesozoic Era 65 million years ago, the end of the Age of Dinosaurs, the continental sea finally retreated, allowing a fascinating sequence of plant and animal communities to evolve on dry land in this region. Unfortunately, erosion and Pleistocene glaciation during the past two million years have destroyed or deeply buried almost all fossil evidence of these times.

ICE AGE LEGACY

Everywhere in the province, glaciers and meltwaters have left their marks on the land. In our current glacial age, glaciers have crept down from the Arctic about 20 times. The Laurentide Glacier of the most recent Wisconsin glaciation reached its maximum southern advance (into the United States) 20,000 years ago. This mass of ice, three kilometres (1.9 mi.) high, crept southward across the land, its immense weight depressing the earth's crust as much as one kilometre (0.6 mi.). With irresistible erosive force, the mountain of ice levelled highlands, plucked bedrock and ground it into gravel, sand and clay, and obliterated or buried much evidence of earlier geological periods. It then piled up vast quantities of this rocky material (called glacial till) in characteristic patterns across the landscape.

Carried by the flowing glacier, gigantic boulders left long grooves and scratches in exposed bedrock surfaces. Some of these boulders (called glacial erratics) are strewn in unexpected places where they were dropped by the melting ice. In the southwest, countless "potholes" or ponds within rolling hills show where massive blocks of ice left depressions in the glacial debris.

LICHEN ON GREYWACKE ROCK

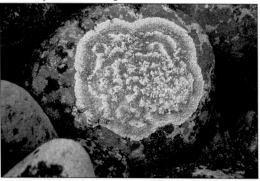

As the last glacier retreated during a period of rapid warming, several vast glacial lakes formed from the dammed-up meltwater, sometimes connecting to others as far away as eastern Ontario and the present Great Slave and Great Bear lakes in the Northwest Territories. In Manitoba, Glacial Lake Agassiz frequently altered its extent and direction of drainage. It dwarfed any of today's Great Lakes. The site of present-day Winnipeg lay under an estimated 83 metres (600 ft.) of ice-cold water. The lake received immense quantities of fine-grained sediment, which account for the rich soils of southern Manitoba. The nickname "Red River gumbo" was coined by settlers who frequently became mired in the sticky grey clay. Freed from the immense weight of glacial ice (12,000 years ago in the southwest, 6,000 years ago in the northeast), the land has rebounded, up to five metres (16.4 ft.) per century at first, slowing to a rate of 0.6 metres (2 ft.) per century at the present time in the northeast.

Moraines, eskers, and beach ridges are a few of the glacial deposits that contribute to a mainly flat topography. In some areas, these features are used as natural routes for highways and a source of road and building materials. Birds Hill Park northeast of Winnipeg is a delta deposit of sand and gravel that has yielded beautifully preserved mammoth tusks and teeth.

AFTER THE ICE AGE

Following the northeastward retreat of the most recent glacier and the draining of immense glacial lakes, zones of plant communities invaded from the south, west, and east. Tundra, forest-tundra woodland, boreal coniferous forest, mixed deciduous-coniferous forest, deciduous forest, aspen parkland, tall-grass prairie, and short-grass prairie crept back over the landscape. These bands of vegetation have shifted position over the last 12,000 years in response to fluctuations in temperature, precipitation, and winds. Surprisingly, during the peak of the warming trend, known as the "climatic optimum" (7,000 to 6,000 years ago in Manitoba), the northern treeline was 250 kilometres (155 mi.) north of its present position, and grassland extended north to The Pas.

Closely tied to these plant communities were wonderful assemblages of animals, as rich in numbers and diversity as those of present-day Africa. In tundra and boreal forest habitats roamed woolly mammoths, American mastodon, stag moose with enormous antlers, a beaver as large as a black bear, and giant species of bison, sloth, short-faced bear, and sabretooth cat. On the northern plains and woodlands lived the Columbian mammoth, yesterday's camel, large-headed llama, American lion (probably the same species as in

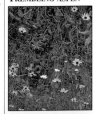

BELOW: BLACK-EYED SUSANS AND YARROW TALL-GRASS PRAIRIE

BOTTOM: TREMBLING ASPEN

the Old World), Scott's horse, Mexican wild ass, western bison, and a hyena-like dog. All of these creatures, along with dozens of other big species of mammals and carnivorous birds, died out by 8,000 to 10,000 years ago. Rapidly changing and segmented habitats, disrupted food chains, and the appearance of prehistoric peoples with

ANCIENT PRONGHORN

increasingly efficient hunting technologies are suspected in the demise of this "mega-fauna" within a relatively short period, but the exact circumstances remain a mystery. Only chance discoveries of these creatures' fossil teeth, tusks, and bones reveal that they roamed across southern Manitoba.

A WEALTH OF WILDLIFE

Fortunately, most small and medium-sized wildlife species survived the wave of post-glacial extinction. In recent times Manitoba has supported 90 species of mammals (several introduced) and over 360 species of birds, of which close to 300 occur here regularly. Many serious birders make special trips to "hot spots" such as Oak Hammock Marsh (see pp. 133-134) and Churchill to round out their "life lists" with rare species. There are also eight species of reptiles and 15 amphibians. Manitoba waters are rich in fishes, with 115 in fresh water (including 13 introduced species), two that frequent both fresh and salt water (but breed in fresh water), and at least 31 marine species in Hudson Bay. Fishing

GEESE AT OAK HAMMOCK MARSH

draws anglers to all corners of the province (see pp. 78-80). The list of insects, spiders, and other invertebrates grows with almost each new study. The number of native plants also continues to mount, with about 1,500 species recorded, along with hundreds of introduced species from Eurasia.

In surveying Manitoba's wildlife, it is helpful to consider plant and animal communities as natural units. These major ecosystems, termed "biomes," are based on the dominant vegetation and environment of the area.

ARCTIC MARINE BIOME

If most Manitobans lived and worked along the Hudson Bay coast, Manitoba would be known as a maritime province. The rocky coastline and cold salt waters of the

FISHING AT RAINBOW FALLS, WHITESHELL PROVINCIAL PARK

bay, with the exception of the site of Churchill, remain the wilderness first met by the Pre-Dorset Paleo-Inuit around 1700 B.C. and by the first European explorers and traders almost four centuries ago. Icebound for eight months of the year, the coast has open water from mid-June to late October. Even during this period, beautifully sculptured, house-sized icebergs are still carried in by the tides. These tides, powerful but slow-moving waves 4.3 metres (14 ft.) high, come and go twice daily, leaving an exposed inter-tidal zone of sand and mud flats of up to three kilometres (1.9 mi.). At low tide, you can find shrimp, scallops, blue mussels, and sea anemones stranded in the pools and hidden under beached bladder wrack — a seaweed with buoyant air bladders.

In deeper water, beyond the low-tide zone, you can see long blades of brown kelp, which reach gracefully up to the surface. These enormous algae are attached to the bay bottom by thick, branching fingers. Swimming here and there are a variety of bizarre-looking fishes with charming names — thorny skate, spiny lumpsucker, Arctic eelpout, moustache sculpin, and gelatinous seasnail — as well as the more ecologically important capelin, Arctic cod, and Arctic char. This is also the world of seals and whales. Although walrus are gone, and harp and bearded seals are rare, you can still see ringed and harbour seals. Thousands of beluga or white whales arrive in spring to feed, calve, and to moult their skins in the gravel shallows and river estuaries. Visitors who take tours in the Churchill estuary

BELUGA WHALES AT CHURCHILL

are thrilled by the sight of hundreds of belugas passing right under the boat. Even the gigantic, endangered bowhead whale has been spotted here.

TUNDRA BIOME

While the tundra was the first ecosystem to recolonize the glacial barrens of southern Manitoba, it has since migrated to the extreme north

(continued on page 22)

19

MANITOBA MOSQUITOES

ROBERT ANDERSON

Our fair province goes by the name of friendly Manitoba. This description might well apply to some of the 46 species of mosquito found here. These tiny insects will be more than happy to greet you and to help you leave a little of yourself behind in Manitoba. Some say mosquitoes get so big here that they ought to be accorded the status of provincial bird.

MOSQUITO CONTROL TRUCK

The scientific names of mosquito species often reflect the feelings of the people who are greeted by the little beasts. *Aedes vexans*, *Aedes excrucians*, and *Mansonia perturbans* are certainly vexing species with excruciating bites that cause considerable perturbation.

The immense populations of mosquitoes that make Manitoba legendary result largely from our abundance of well-protected standing water — in prairie potholes, freshwater marshes, bog, and temporary pools formed after rains. These provide excellent habitat for mosquito larvae.

The City of Winnipeg spends $1.1 million annually to combat mosquitoes, but many locals would tell you the bugs win the battle. The money is spent primarily on applying biological or chemical insecticides to bodies of water to stop mosquitoes in their tracks while they're still at the larval stage. If the mosquitoes score a resounding victory in this phase of the contest, the city brings out its heavy artillery — a fleet of 10 trucks that rumbles through residential neighbourhoods engaging in night-time chemical warfare with adult mosquitoes. But the positive effects of the adult-mosquito program can be quickly obliterated by winds that blow new mosquitoes into the area, and the city's larviciding efforts are only as successful as the next untreated pool of water.

Besides, mosquitoes are wily, resourceful creatures not easily done out of their dinner by mere human intervention. As a result, most Manitobans are tough, and we're proud of our ability to feed our share of mosquitoes and still enjoy summer. The town of Komarno (meaning "full of mosquitoes" in Ukrainian) even displays a huge mosquito statue and boasts that it's the home of the world's largest mosquito. Our Manitoban toughness doesn't usually extend to the family barbecue, however, and screened-in porches keep hungry mosquitoes at bay while hungry people consume burgers and hot dogs. Some enterprising individuals try to outsmart mosquitoes with citronella candles, electronic repellers, or bug-zappers, but these gadgets are completely useless for protection. If you visit rural areas in spring or summer, have a good repellent or perhaps a bug jacket on hand.

Mosquitoes feed on plant nectar and pollinate many plants while searching for it. Only the female feeds on blood, which is a source of protein for the eggs she lays. Although you may think every mosquito in Manitoba has found you and chosen you for fine dining, many females are in fact unable to find a source of blood during their short lives.

Some people have all the luck and are more attractive to mosquitoes than others. In fact, a good way to minimize your contribution to the next mosquito generation is to go for a walk with one of these lucky individuals and let him provide the smorgasbord.

Each mosquito species has a strategy for surviving from one summer to the next. Some make it through the winter as cold-resistant eggs in the soil. In other species, the adult female hibernates, perhaps in an animal burrow. One species spends the winter frozen as larvae in the fluid trapped in pitcher plants.

Some mosquito species have finicky appetites and feed on only one or two related groups of animals. For example, one feeds only on birds. Another feeds only on frogs, snakes, and turtles. Other species feed on virtually anything that moves, and these are the types that will likely tap into you for a donation.

One species of mosquito native to Manitoba is an interesting exception to the blood-sucking rule. It is found only in bogs that harbour the pitcher plant. Its larvae live in the water-filled pitchers and feed on decaying insects that have fallen into the cavity and drowned. Adults emerge from the pitchers with enough food reserves to produce a few eggs, and never blood-feed.

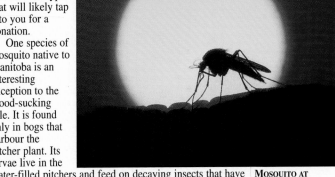

MOSQUITO AT SUNSET

So, the next time you hear the summer serenade of mosquito wings buzzing close at hand, remember that not all the mosquitoes in Manitoba are out to relieve you of a little blood, but all are rather fascinating creatures.

of Manitoba and along the coast of Hudson Bay. The modern town of Churchill, at the mouth of the Churchill River, has become well known in the international tourist trade for its easy access to an Arctic environment and biological riches. An excellent guidebook, *The Wildflowers of Churchill and the Hudson Bay Region*, describes many of the 400 species of vascular plants found here. In addition to the many diminutive but jewel-like wildflowers blooming from June to September, there are blazing red and yellow carpets of bearberry and snow willow, green moss hummocks punctuated with white puffs of cotton-grass, and white avenues of lichens. Even the beautifully glacier-polished, grey bedrock of Churchill quartzite is encrusted with patches of orange and red lichens.

The black spruce, white spruce, and tamarack trees that survive in sites sheltered from the winds are barely as high as a human, yet may have clung to a precarious existence for well over a century. The erosive power of wind-blown ice and sand particles has abraded all the windward upper branches of the trees — hence the local joke about having to tie two spruces together to make one Christmas tree. The lower branches of spruce may strike new roots where they touch the ground, so the plant seems to expand in a circle, all the while maintaining a low profile. Ancient, dwarfed species of willows may be only several centimetres (inches) high.

TUNDRA COLOURS

NESTING GOLDEN PLOVER

A major draw of the tundra is the rich variety of Arctic bird life, particularly nesting shorebirds such as the golden plover and northern phalarope. Over 210 species of birds have been reported near Churchill, including a breeding colony of the rare Ross' gull. Canada geese and tundra swans graze on the wet meadows of grass along the coast, common terns and parasitic jaegers swoop gracefully overhead, and long-tailed ducks, common eiders, and red-breasted mergansers dive in the bay for mussels and fish. Arctic terns nest colonially in tundra marshes and coastal beaches in late June, and by late August parents and young have left on their marathon migration, via the west coast of Africa, to wintering grounds in Antarctica.

The tundra is a magical place for a hike. On the wet muskeg and dry gravel ridges you can sometimes glimpse an arctic or red fox out prowling for a willow ptarmigan, arctic hare, collared lemming, or meadow vole. Along the northern coastal tundra, Arctic ground squirrels whistle to each other from distant boulders that mark their territories. Muskoxen, first seen here by European explorers, are gone from the region. However, the Kaminuriak herd of barren-ground

caribou, sometimes reaching a population of 150,000, still grazes and leaves its worn trails across these wind-swept barrens. Most of the caribou migrate from their breeding grounds in the Northwest Territories south into the forest-tundra zone of Manitoba and Saskatchewan for the winter.

Early winter brings a northward dispersal of polar bears along the coast, as they await the formation of new pack ice on the bay (see pp. 24-25).

CANADA GEESE

BOREAL CONIFEROUS FOREST BIOME

This is by far the most extensive ecosystem in Manitoba, and it continues east-west in a broad band across the continent. Over a vast transitional region, from the northern treeline south to around Southern Indian Lake, black spruce and tamarack form an open woodland of wet muskeg in flats and depressions, while lichen-moss and low shrubs grow on gravel ridges and sandy eskers. Trying to walk across a "quaking bog," surrounded by dwarf, lichen-shrouded spruce, is a strange experience. The deep, foam-like, and saturated sphagnum moss sucks at your unsteady feet, and your voice is quickly muffled by the sound-absorbing vegetation.

Further south, the soil layer is still thin and the

bedrock often exposed, but trees become increasingly dominant due to a warmer climate and longer growing season.

LEFT: ARCTIC FOXES

BELOW: BARREN-GROUND CARIBOU

BOTTOM: POLAR BEAR NEAR CHURCHILL

Black spruce-tamarack and eastern white cedar swamps occur in wet areas. Dense forests of white spruce, balsam fir, trembling aspen, balsam poplar, and paper birch cover well-drained slopes near lakes and in river valleys. Dry, sandy, or rocky uplands support jack-pine forest. With few plants present on the needle-carpeted floor, these pine forests have a dark, forsaken atmosphere, and the only sound is the wind swishing through the canopy high overhead. Another unusual

(continued on page 26)

THE POLAR BEAR MIGRATION

ROBERT TAYLOR

One of the great wildlife spectacles of the world is the annual congregation of polar bears along the shore of Hudson Bay. During October and early November, the bears move out to the coast from their summer resting areas inland. Here they will wait for the bay to freeze so they can head out onto the ice to hunt for seals.

From freeze-up until the following June or early July, they will roam the vast expanse of Hudson Bay in their quest for food. Pregnant females will go back to the denning area in December to have their cubs. In suitable places from about 16 to 55 kilometres (10 to 35 mi.) inland, they will dig dens in the snow and remain there with the young cubs until April. When the cubs are about three months old, the females will again go hunting seals on the bay, this time with their youngsters alongside them.

Spring is a good time for hunting, as the seals are having their pups on the ice, and catching them is relatively easy. The bears can feast until the "break-up" of the ice in late

POLAR BEAR AND CUB ON HUDSON BAY SHORE

June or early July. Then the fattened bears head for shore to find a place inland where they can rest for the summer.

Although it is possible to find a bear around Churchill during summer, the prime time for bear watching is when the bears are congregating along the shore in the fall. You may see upwards of 30 polar bears during a single day at peak time. Churchill lies directly on the bears' ancient migratory route and has become known as the "polar bear capital of the world."

If you come to see and photograph the polar bears, you will most likely be taken east of Churchill in a specially constructed vehicle, into the tundra region between Gordon Point and Watson's Point or to Cape Churchill. The vehicles range from a 4x4 van, to converted army trucks with "school bus" bodies, to the large custom-built Tundra Buggies®. All have wide, low-pressure tundra tires to facilitate travel over the uneven terrain. Most of the vehicles have on-board washrooms and are heated. Some have platforms on the back for observing the bears.

You'll find the people of Churchill helpful and friendly.

TUNDRA BUGGY NEAR CHURCHILL

25

**SPRUCE WOODS
PROVINCIAL PARK**

community is the salt marshes west of Lake Winnipegosis (e.g., Dawson Bay). Buried salt deposits, originating from ancient seas, have reached the surface through springs, and they support a variety of salt-loving plants such as the fleshy samphire and saltwort.

Enormous sections of Manitoba's coniferous forests burn each year. Two-thirds of the fires are started by careless people and one-third by lightning. Evidence in the soil reveals that fires have occurred here repeatedly for thousands of years. In fact, few stands of mature forest manage to escape fire for more than two centuries. Sophisticated methods of fire detection and suppression, practised by Manitoba Natural Resources staff, protect high-priority zones where towns, recreation sites, and tracts of valuable timber are located.

**HONEY-COLOURED
BLACK BEAR**

The boreal coniferous forest and its abundant lakes and rivers offer endless recreational opportunities, from camping and observing wildlife to hunting and fishing. Lake trout, northern pike, and pickerel are among the favourite catches of anglers. When you drive the great distances

between northern towns you are bound to see at least one black bear, since these lumbering, inquisitive scavengers roam this region in great numbers. Sometimes wolves and woodland caribou are observed as well, although the latter have declined seriously from habitat destruction and

GREAT GRAY OWL, THE PAS

disturbance. Moose are common, particularly along marshy edges of lakes and watercourses. Fairly recently, dozens of limestone caves were discovered throughout the Interlake region. Investigators are still mapping the caves and banding the colonies of little brown bats that winter in them. The caves are the bats' northernmost hibernating sites in Canada.

DECIDUOUS-CONIFEROUS FOREST TRANSITION

As the name implies, this transitional community incorporates species and environments representative of the Eastern Deciduous Forest and Boreal Coniferous Forest biomes. White spruce, jack pine, trembling aspen, and paper birch are typical of much of the area, while black spruce-tamarack and eastern white cedar swamps occupy poorly drained sites. Protected stands of the last remaining red pine, white pine, and largetooth aspen in the province are located in the extreme southeast.

Remarkably, packs of grey wolves and families of cougar and black bear roam these forests, relatively close to modern cities such as Winnipeg and Beausejour. Beaver and muskrat are found in almost every wetland and watercourse, and the region's tamarack swamps are the nesting grounds of the mysterious great gray owl, Manitoba's provincial bird. Huge sturgeon, reaching 2.4 metres (9 ft.) and living up to 150 years, have been caught in rivers such as the Winnipeg. However, this species has become scarce in most areas from habitat destruction and over-fishing. The mountainous regions in western Manitoba have served as refuges for many kinds of wildlife. White-tailed deer and a small population of mule deer occur here. In Riding Mountain National Park, majestic bison graze in meadows, moose and elk are frequently observed along trails, and, with luck, a lynx or grey wolf may make a brief appearance.

A 1.5-hour drive north of Winnipeg, near the towns of Inwood and Narcisse, are a series of limestone sinkholes that host famous congregations of the red-sided garter snake (see p. 134).

GIRL WITH RED-SIDED GARTER SNAKE

ASPEN PARKLAND TRANSITION

Aspen Parkland is a community characterized by groves of aspen trees interspersed in grassland. Since aspen is a widespread northern species, this community is actually a merging of the Boreal Coniferous Forest and the Grassland biomes, in spite of its current scarcity of spruce. Most of the area has been cleared for farms, although aspen are common because the control of fire has allowed them to spread widely. This attractive species

(continued on page 30)

GREY OWL

TOM WATROUS

If you visit Riding Mountain National Park, there's a good chance you'll hear about a man named Grey Owl or come across the trail leading to his cabin. Grey Owl spent only six months in the park, in 1931, but he was a colourful character whose reputation as one of Canada's first conservationists lives on.

GREY OWL'S CABIN

He was really an Englishman, Archibald Stansfeld Belaney, born in 1888. Assuming the identity of a North American Indian, he was able, through his books, films, and public appearances, to communicate the threat that civilization posed to Native peoples and to wildlife, with emphasis on the beaver.

Abandoned by both parents at an early age, Archie Belaney endured an unhappy childhood, being raised by two highly conservative aunts. An imaginative youth, he began to live in a fantasy world centred on Native Americans. He arrived in Canada in 1906 and began the slow transformation to a new identity, claiming that he was of mixed blood, his father being a Scotsman and his mother a Mexican Apache. Immersing himself in his beloved Northland, he served for years as mail carrier, guide, fire warden, and trapper, until a growing distaste for killing turned him to conservation.

ABOVE: GREY OWL AT RIDING MOUNTAIN NATIONAL PARK
RIGHT: GREY OWL'S BOTTLE-FEEDING BEAVER KIT

Adopting the name Grey Owl, he began to write and to live closely with beavers as a self-appointed protector. He joined the National Park Service in 1931 to help restore beaver populations. In mid-April of that year, he arrived in Neepawa, Manitoba, by train. He and his two semi-domesticated beavers, Jelly Roll and Rawhide, had survived a 3000-kilometre (1,860-mi.) rail journey from eastern Quebec, the animals comfortably housed in a specially designed metallic tank. Within days they were settled at Beaver Lodge Lake in the newly created Riding Mountain National Park.

Grey Owl's cabin, a magnificent two-room bungalow, was erected at the edge of the lake. Grey Owl suggested a number of design features that would enable him periodically to house his animals within the cabin. By far the most interesting of these is the beaver pen. Here you can easily observe a pair of rectangular apertures cut into the floor boards, likely intended as "trap doors," allowing the beavers to dig underground sleeping burrows. Also visible is a frame for a water tank, part of an indoor-outdoor beaver "toilet system" that was operated with a hand pump and funnel.

While in the park, Grey Owl had the opportunity to further test his personal and conservationist philosophies on an ever-increasing public. He collaborated with photographer W. J. Oliver on a film, *Beaver Family*, as well as a celebrated series of still photographs.

But he became alarmed as the water level of his small lake diminished to less than a metre (3 ft.) during that hot, dry summer. He feared the lake would freeze all the way to the bottom during the coming winter, endangering his

beaver family. As water levels were low throughout the park, he asked for a transfer, which was granted.

His new posting was in Saskatchewan's Prince Albert National Park. In late October, accompanied by his common-law wife, Anahareo, and an expanded family of six beavers, he left Riding Mountain forever.

His first book appeared that year, bringing him overnight fame. Three others followed. Two extensive speaking tours took him to locations in England, Canada, and the United States. Ever since he had crossed over to his new identity Grey Owl had lived in constant fear that his true origins would be exposed, and this fear increased as his fame grew.

Grey Owl died of pneumonia in a Prince Albert hospital in 1938. Just days after his death, a deceived public learned that he was the Englishman Belaney.

Now Grey Owl is in a state of re-evaluation. Today's readers are looking past the sensational aspects of his life to his ever-emerging status as one of Canada's most visionary outdoor writers.

The trail to his cabin is 17.5 kilometres (11 mi.) return, beginning on the north side of Highway 19 just one kilometre (0.6 mi.) east of Highway 10.

with trembling leaves often spreads by underground runners, so that a large aspen grove may be one enormous clone — all genetically identical trees. In spring and autumn, respectively, aspen splash the landscape with delicate lime green and brilliant yellow.

Along the banks of the many rivers in this region grows a deciduous forest of American elm, Manitoba maple, green ash, cottonwood, and peach-leaved willow. Many dozens of fish species inhabit the silt-laden waters, including 1.2-metre (4-ft.) channel catfish. Giant 15-kilogram (33-lb.) snapping turtles and 30-centimetre (12-in.) salamanders called mudpuppies are just a few of the strange creatures lurking below the slow-flowing rivers. Individual unionid clams packed in the bottom mud may be several centuries old. Colourful western painted turtles bask on logs, ready to dive when a predator threatens.

In historical times, the parkland was home to enormous herds of bison, elk, and mule deer. White-tailed deer, raccoon, sharp-tailed and ruffed grouse, great blue heron, and American woodcock are a few of the interesting species breeding here. In the Minnedosa area, hundreds of ponds or "potholes" provide quality breeding habitat for a number of species of ducks. Spring choruses of breeding frogs and songbirds are replaced on summer evenings by the howling of coyotes, in turn drowned out in autumn by the clamour of tens of thousands of migrating snow geese, resting during their passage from the Arctic to the Gulf of Mexico.

ASPEN TREES

PAINTED TURTLE

YELLOW-HEADED BLACKBIRD

GRASSLAND BIOME

As you drive west along the Trans-Canada Highway, down the former Glacial Lake Agassiz beach ridges, you'll notice that the forests of spruce and poplar disappear with surprising suddenness. You then look out over a completely flat terrain of farmland, which was formerly covered, from here to the foothills of the Rocky Mountains, by a sea of prairie. Grassland occurs where there is insufficient moisture (less than 50 centimetres or 20 inches of precipitation per year) to support forest. In prehistoric times the low precipitation was augmented by fire, which also contributed to checking the spread of trees. There are two grassland types represented in Manitoba. The tall-grass prairie formerly occupied 6000 square kilometres (2,317 sq. mi.) of the Red River Valley and extended all the way south to Texas. The deep, black, moist, and fertile prairie soil has been put to cultivation, leaving only a few remnants of tall-grass prairie at Oak Hammock Marsh, Winnipeg's Living Prairie Museum, and an area near Tolstoi.

Characterized by the two-metre-high (6.7-ft.) big bluestem grass, tall-grass prairie supports several hundred species of wildflowers and grasses. Many of these have developed various strategies of seed germination and have made remarkable adaptations to annual temperature ranges of 70 degrees C (158 degrees F) and to varying soil conditions from arid to saturated. Blazing star, ground plum, silverleaf psoralea, sunflowers, prairie clover, ragweed, and asters are some of the flowers transforming the spring and summer fields into a patchwork of colour, and maturing big and little bluestem grasses turn the autumn prairie to a purple haze. When the snow cover disappears, many people like to walk prairie sites to find the delicate blue blooms of the prairie crocus, floral emblem of Manitoba — a sign that spring has finally arrived.

TALL-GRASS AT LIVING PRAIRIE MUSEUM

The mixed-grass prairie of southwestern Manitoba consisted of a mixture of tall- and short-grass species, such as little bluestem, june grass, needle and thread grass, and purple prairie clover. These plants are capable of growing on soils that become parched under the hot summer sun. This community, too, has been replaced by

PURPLE SAXIFRAGE

cultivated fields and pasture. However, fascinating remnants of the original prairie persist in a number of extensive sandhill areas, such as Carberry, Lauder, and Oak Lake, as well as the crests and hillsides of the Assiniboine, Souris, and Qu'Appelle rivers. Many prairie plants maintain food stores in underground roots and stems, and have evolved to cope with frequent fires. In fact, this prairie ecosystem is rejuvenated by the nutrients released from the dead litter from fires, and a number of species appear to require the passage of fire to maintain their competitive edge within the thick prairie sod.

Typical grassland birds are the Swainson's hawk, marbled godwit, and western meadowlark, whose wonderful flute-like call can be heard even if you're speeding by in a car. Marshes of cattail, reed grass, bladderwort, and pondweed, as found at Oak Hammock

PURPLE CLOVER AT LIVING PRAIRIE MUSEUM

SUNFLOWER FIELDS

and Fort Whyte, attract the northern harrier and colonies of the yellow-headed blackbird, Franklin's gull, black tern and killdeer, and migrating flocks of over a million waterfowl, including Canada and snow geese, mallard, northern shoveller, northern pintail, and blue-winged teal. Formations of white pelicans or sandhill cranes gliding gracefully across the blue summer sky are breathtaking sights. In October, hundreds of tundra swans tip upside down to feed on submerged plants, while bald eagles patrol overhead in search of weakened birds. As winter arrives, snowy owls and rough-legged hawks from the far north appear as if by magic, perching fearlessly on roadside poles and hay bales. Several interesting large mammals of the prairie were exterminated in the late 1800s, such as bison, pronghorn, swift fox, and the plains races of the grey wolf and grizzly bear. However, there remain plenty of coyotes, badgers, white-tailed jack rabbits and white-tailed deer, and mule deer are still occasionally spotted. A number of isolated and rare species centred in the Carberry Sandhills and nearby areas of sandy soil are relicts of the

period when grassland was far more extensive. The plains spadefoot toad, northern prairie skink (a lizard), plains hognose snake, olive-backed pocket mouse, prairie vole, and northern grasshopper mouse are fascinating members of Manitoba's small fauna. Along the U.S. border around Emerson are large mounds of earth along the road — the work of the plains pocket gopher, which is found nowhere else in Canada. More common are the entertaining thirteen-lined and Richardson's ground squirrels, easily spotted along the roadside and adjacent pasture.

WHITE PELICAN, GRAND RAPIDS

HERITAGE

PRE-CONTACT TO 1640

LEO PETTIPAS

People have been living in the area we call Manitoba for some 11,500 years, and non-Indigenous peoples have been present for scarcely three percent of that time.

For many of those 11,500 years, only certain portions of the province were inhabitable.

THE ICE AGE

Eighteen thousand years ago, the entire land surface of Manitoba lay beneath an ice sheet several kilometres thick (see pp. 16-17). When the margins of the ice cap began to melt, the melting outpaced the southward flow of new ice, and the ice front began to "retreat" northward. For the most part, the glacier was replaced by lakes fed by huge volumes of meltwater that poured off the ice sheet. The largest of these was Glacial Lake Agassiz.

THE FIRST PEOPLES

The eventual drainage of the glacial lakes, along with the northward retreat of the ice, produced increasingly large

34

tracts of countryside suitable for human habitation. Archaeological evidence indicates that the original peoples of Manitoba entered from the south or west around 11,500 years ago. They were probably organized into small bands who lived by hunting and by gathering edible wild plants. Their food included big game animals — mammoths, mastodons, big-horned bison, and certain camels and horses.

By 10,000 years ago, a rich grassland west of Lake Agassiz provided a bountiful food supply for bison. The abundance of game induced people to locate in southern Manitoba. By 8,000 years ago, some of the early people had moved to the boreal forest of southeastern Manitoba, east of Lake Agassiz. Here, a favoured food source was *Cervalces*, a form of Ice Age moose.

AFTER THE ICE AGE

Lake Agassiz had finally disappeared by 7,500 years ago. The low country between the Manitoba Escarpment on the west and the Canadian Shield to the east now accommodated the remnants — lakes Winnipeg, Winnipegosis, Manitoba, and Dauphin — of the former inland sea. The grasslands expanded to the western shores of Lake Winnipeg and north almost to the Saskatchewan River. Boreal forest became established throughout the Canadian Shield, extending northward well into the District of Keewatin. These northerly regions were progressively inhabited by people from the south and west. By 7,000 years ago, small numbers of humans lived in all the major life zones of Manitoba as they existed at that time.

CLEAR LAKE, RIDING MOUNTAIN NATIONAL PARK

Archaeological findings in western Manitoba hint that local people may have used copper from around Lake Superior as early as 7,000 years ago, and the discovery of an ancient workshop east of Lake Winnipeg indicates that by 4,000 years ago people were importing copper nuggets and fashioning them into tools, probably using an early form of blacksmithing.

THE ALGONQUIANS

In Manitoba today, the two largest Aboriginal nations are the Ojibwa (Anishinabe) and the Cree (Nehayawuk). They speak languages that linguists refer to as "Algonquian."

It is believed that around 3,800 years ago a group of early Algonquians began to migrate east from present-day Utah and Idaho, birthplace of the Algonquian language family, toward country south of the Great Lakes. Their Proto-Algonquian language later diversified into several "daughter" languages, including Cree and Ojibwa. Many

MANITOBA POTTERY

MÉTIS BISON
HUNTER DIORAMA,
MANITOBA MUSEUM
OF MAN AND NATURE

nations indigenous to the east eventually abandoned their native languages in favour of Algonquian.

SOUTHERN CREE-SPEAKERS

By about 2,500 years ago, central North America's climate had begun to change. The boreal forest expanded southward, displacing the edge of the grassland to the south and west. Groups of Cree-speakers moved into southern Manitoba from the upper Great Lakes region. This was the first of several Algonquian migrations into Manitoba from the east.

Already at home in a forested environment, the newcomers took advantage of Manitoba's natural water resources. Their foods included wild animals, plants, birds and fish, and they were among the very first to use wild rice. They brought a new technology, the manufacture of clay pottery, and they introduced the custom of building burial mounds. The bow and arrow supplanted the throwing board and dart, or "atlatl," as the premier hunting implement.

ABORIGINAL AGRICULTURE

In the 11th and 12th centuries A.D., considerable population expansion in the area to the south of Manitoba and a period of severe drought prompted major population dispersion and out-migration. Some people migrated northward to the lower Red River Valley, bringing a new mode of food production. At Lockport, north of Winnipeg, archaeologists have discovered charred corn kernels, hoe blades made from the shoulder blades of bison, and underground storage bins, which are evidence of local cultivation, harvesting and consumption of domesticated plant foods during the early 1400s. Women were probably responsible for introducing farming to Manitoba. The practice did not persist, however, for when European explorers arrived in the early 1700s, the local Native residents were all hunters and gatherers.

CORN CULTIVATION

THE ASSINIBOINS

At least five Indigenous languages were spoken in Manitoba. One of these is Nakota, a Siouan dialect spoken by the "Assiniboins," whose ancestors lived in Minnesota. The Assiniboins broke away from their parent Dakota population early in the 17th century and came to southern Manitoba, where they established good relations with the resident Algonquian-speaking Cree. They traded regularly with the Mandan villages on the Missouri River. When the English established York Factory on Hudson Bay in 1682, the Assiniboins and Cree became middlemen in the trade with nations in the interior plains.

THE OJIBWA

Most historians believe the Saulteaux branch of the Ojibwa arrived in southern Manitoba during the late 1700s, as part of a long-term migration that began around 1300 A.D. somewhere near the Atlantic seaboard. The Ojibwa provide a good example of a people who moved from a forested to a prairie environment and enjoyed the best of both worlds. They were also key players in the fur trade.

With the acquisition of the horse in the early 1800s, the Ojibwa extended their territories westward into the grasslands. By the 1830s, many had become fully adapted to life on the plains, and the bison became vital to their economy and to the religious and ceremonial aspects of their culture. Certain traditional pursuits, such as hunting woodland animals, making maple sugar, and gathering and processing wild rice, continued.

Scattered throughout the Whiteshell district of southeastern Manitoba are sites containing effigies of snakes, turtles, humans, and geometric figures. These were formed by the placement of small boulders on surfaces of exposed bedrock. According to Ojibwa elders, they are places where novices received instruction in traditional medicine, where curative powers were obtained, and where healing ceremonies and practices were carried out.

WINTER TRAVEL
1,000 YEARS AGO

THE NORTHERN CREE

The northern Canadian Shield region of Manitoba has probably been inhabited since the disappearance of Lake Agassiz. The Cree, the main occupants of the boreal forest today, are descended from people who entered the boreal forest north of the Great Lakes many generations ago. With

PREHISTORIC PICTOGRAPHS

cultural diffusion and migration, the Cree language spread throughout much of the Canadian Shield, including the forested regions of Manitoba.

ROCK PAINTINGS, OR PICTOGRAPHS

One ancient cultural feature attributable to ancestral Algonquians and still visible in the Shield is the rock painting, or pictograph. Usually depicting humans, animals, and geometric shapes, the pictographs are generally found on cliff faces along lakeshores and rivers. The red paint used in making the images was a mixture of powdered hematite, or iron oxide, and a binder extracted from the insides of the sturgeon.

THE CHIPEWYAN

The Caribou Eater Chipewyan (Edthen-eldili-dené) of extreme northern Manitoba belong to the Athapascan language family. Early Athapascan language probably originated somewhere around eastern Alaska. Part of the population expanded from there into British Columbia about 2,500 years ago. Sometime after 500 A.D., an eastward Athapascan expansion reached the western precincts of Hudson Bay in northern Manitoba.

Traditionally, the movements and lifestyle of the Manitoba Dené were closely tied to annual cycles and movements of the barren-ground caribou. In winter the caribou herds occupied the semi-forested and forested country south of the treeline, and in spring they moved onto the tundra to their calving grounds.

BEFORE THE INUIT

About 4,000 years ago a people living in Alaska began an eastward journey via the frozen shores of the Arctic Ocean. They hunted seals, whales and walrus along the coast, and caribou on the tundra. Their culture is referred to as the "Arctic Small Tool Tradition" because of the minute, delicately fashioned implements they made from flint-like stone.

Only a few places in Manitoba have produced evidence of these people. The main sites, in the Churchill area, relate to a coast-oriented way of life where seals and other marine animals were the main food sources.

About 1,000 years ago another population of immigrants from the far northwest arrived in the central Arctic and replaced the people of the Arctic Small Tool Tradition. These newcomers, known as "Thule" (pronounced Too-lee), were the direct ancestors of the Inuit encountered by early European explorers.

ABORIGINAL, EUROPEAN AND MÉTIS: 1640-1870

LAURA PEERS

Manitoba has an extraordinary history. Here peoples from many nations — Cree, Ojibwa, English, Orcadians, Scots, Irish, Swiss, French Canadians and others — came face to face during the fur trade, exchanging furs, goods, and ways of living. Initially they bridged many differences to create friendships, marriages, and a new people: the Métis. By 1870, however, cultural differences had led to racial prejudice and the imposition of European law over Native and Métis people.

Manitoba's geography made it a historic crossroads. Both the Winnipeg River route from Lake Superior and the Hayes River route from Hudson Bay linked with Lake Winnipeg, the Red and Assiniboine rivers, and the

FORT PRINCE OF WALES, CHURCHILL

Saskatchewan River to the west. The Forks — the junction of the Red and Assiniboine rivers — thus became a crucial intersection in Canadian history. Located in what is now downtown Winnipeg, The Forks is a national park.

Europeans first entered this region searching for a route to the riches of Asia — or, failing that, to the continent's best fur-trapping grounds. By the mid-1600s, men such as French explorers Radisson and Groseillers realized that the best furs came from the west, and that the area could be entered by ship via Hudson Bay rather than by the slow canoe journey from Montreal. Unable to convince officials in New France that their plan would work, they went to London and persuaded their colonial rivals to finance an expedition. In 1668 a tiny ship, the *Nonsuch*, wintered on James Bay and

did a booming trade in prime furs. In 1670 Prince Rupert of England granted a royal charter to the Hudson's Bay Company (HBC), giving it rights to sole trade in the vast lands that drained into the bay — which were later known as Rupert's Land after their grantor. The Company quickly founded posts along the coast. York Fort (later called York Factory), built in 1682, became the HBC's key depot. Fort Churchill was founded in 1717, and in 1731 the British built Fort Prince of Wales of stone there, to guard routes inland. Several noted figures such as Samuel Hearne, Henry Kelsey and Anthony Henday set out with Native guides from Churchill and York Factory to explore the heart of Manitoba in the 1700s.

The bayside posts attracted Cree families from the interior who acted as middlemen, collecting furs from other peoples inland and then making the long canoe journey to the bay, where they traded the furs for such items as beads, cloth and knives, and then paddled home again. The following winter, they exchanged their used goods, at a markup, with the inland people for furs. The Cree jealously guarded their monopoly on trade routes and were shrewd traders who demanded higher-quality axes and guns. Other Cree, who lived closer to the bay, were hired to hunt and to make moccasins and snowshoes for the Company. English traders soon defied orders to have nothing to do with women while in Rupert's Land, and married into these bands.

At the same time, the French entered the western interior to trade directly with Native people. In 1738, French explorer La Vérendrye arrived at The Forks by canoe from Montreal. His men built several posts over the following years, including Fort Maurepas on Lake Winnipeg and Fort Rouge at The Forks. By 1780, both the HBC and its rival, the Montreal-based North West Company (NWC), were trading directly with Native people throughout Manitoba. The decades between 1780 and 1821 were the busiest of the fur trade, and hundreds of posts were built in the region.

With direct trade, the Cree lost their position as middlemen and, rather than becoming trappers, turned to the bison hunt, supplying posts with meat. By 1800, Native people in Manitoba included the bison-hunting Plains Cree and Assiniboin peoples; Ojibwa from the Great Lakes, who were excellent trappers; northern or "Swampy" Cree in the northernmost areas, who hunted, fished, and trapped; and mixed-blood people who were the children of fur traders and Native wives.

The trade was a meeting of peoples as well as an exchange of goods. Europeans learned Native hunting skills, while Native people learned to make bannock, a Scottish scone. Native people adopted muskets, while traders wore moccasins and collected Native artifacts. Many of these beautiful objects have recently been presented by the HBC to the Museum of Man and Nature.

Native women were the backbone of the fur trade: they tanned hides, made moccasins, laced snowshoe frames, and trapped small game for food. Lacking such skills, European men found it practical to marry into the band with which they traded. While some of these unions ended when the trader moved on, others were true marriages, recognized "according to the custom of the country," in the fur-trade phrase. The children of these marriages became the Métis (children of French Canadians and Natives) and "Country-born" (children of HBC fathers, often English, and Native women). Today, people come to the HBC Archives in Winnipeg to research their roots in fur-trade marriages. Many Métis people have maintained a special way of life in Manitoba, distinct from but drawing on both their Native and European heritages, and take great pride in their identity. The new languages they created, such as Mechif, part Cree and part French, are still spoken. Many Native families also bear the surnames of their fur-trade grandfathers. If you're driving along River Road from Winnipeg, compare the names in the Native graveyard at St. Peter's Church with those of the fur traders buried at St. Andrew's.

NATIVE WALL POCKET

Rival fur-trade companies, the rise of the Métis, and European ambitions came together in a violent struggle over The Forks when Lord Selkirk, a major shareholder of the HBC, determined around 1805 to establish a settlement there of disadvantaged Europeans who would be brought to North America. The HBC also thought such a community would provide a haven for retired employees and their Native families. The NWC, however, saw the proposed colony's location as a deliberate attempt to block its supply lines between the Great Lakes and its western posts.

HOME OF JOHN INKSTER, WINNIPEG, 1858

The first settlers arrived in 1812, Gaelic-speaking crofters from the Scottish Highlands who suffered terribly on the journey to Red River. More arrived in 1814. With no stores of food prepared for their arrival, and unaccustomed to hunting, they all would have starved had they not been taught to hunt bison by an Ojibwa band led by Chief Peguis. Their problems grew worse after the colony governor issued the "Pemmican Proclamation" of 1814. Intended to prevent the bison from being chased away from the starving settlers, it decreed that the Métis were not to hunt on horseback, as they were accustomed. Angry Métis and NWC employees intimidated some settlers into leaving in 1815, and burned the cabins of those who stayed. Peguis attempted to negotiate on behalf of the colonists, but was unsuccessful; his men provided a protective escort for the remaining settlers when they, too, were forced to leave. The refugees were persuaded to return by an HBC official, but faced further harassment that culminated in a gunfight between Métis and settlers in 1816, when the colony governor and 21 other men died at the Battle of Seven Oaks.

ST. ANDREW'S ANGLICAN CHURCH ON THE RED RIVER

The fur-trade rivalry ended in 1821 when the two companies merged. Red River became a remarkable community in which Scot, Métis, Country-born, Native, French-Canadian, and later groups of settlers — including a party of Swiss and some English — all contributed to the economy. The Europeans farmed, although without wheat adapted to the short growing season they were often unsuccessful. Natives sold game, hides, berries, and bark for canoes. The Métis organized legendary bison hunts. Twice a year, they took 1,000 two-wheeled "Red River carts" westward and southward to the herds' grazing areas. They elected police for the hunt, to ensure that the herd

PAUL KANE'S *HALF BREEDS RUNNING BUFFALO*

would not be frightened away by a lone hunter until the entire group was ready to give chase. The rules of the hunt also included "No buffalo to be run on the Sabbath-day." Once scouts found the herd, men on specially trained "bison-runners" spurred into full gallop, shooting and reloading on the move:

> Imagine four hundred horsemen entering at full speed a herd of some thousands of buffalo, all in rapid motion. Riders in clouds of dust and volumes of smoke, which darken the air, crossing and re-crossing each other in every direction; shots on the right, on the left, behind, before...Horses stumbling, riders falling, dead and wounded animals tumbling here and there, one over the other... (Alexander Ross, The Red River Settlement)

When the hunt ended, women dried the meat over fires and rendered tallow, and the carts creaked home with thousands of bales of dried meat and sacks of pemmican.

Red River's position made it a central point in the fur trade. Lower Fort Garry, built north of The Forks in the 1830s, was a transshipment point for furs coming eastward, which were sent north to York Factory and then to London (see pp. 126-128). Produce from local settlers was sent from here to other posts, and European goods arrived via York Factory and the lake on York boats, single-sailed sloops adapted from an Orkney design.

By the 1840s, Red River was a string of waterfront

YORK BOAT, 1910

ribbon lots running for miles on both banks of the rivers, with different peoples — Scots, Métis, Country-born, and Native — in distinct areas. You can still see something of the river lots along River Road. Churches, a cathedral, several trading posts, windmills, fenced gardens, and log cabins proclaimed that Red River was a social and economic centre. At the north end of the settlement, Ojibwa and Cree shared the parish of St. Peter's. Many of the Cree, who had come south for jobs, were Christian converts, lived in whitewashed cabins, and had livestock and gardens. Most Ojibwa still lived traditionally. St. Peter's is marked today by the old church on River Road, site of the graves of Chief Peguis and his family.

Crops failed regularly at Red River, and Swiss settlers left in disgust after a flood in 1826 that submerged the settlement; it flooded again in 1852. Other hazards were prairie fires and visiting Dakota, who nearly caused battles with the local Ojibwa in many years. And although neighbours traded milk for fish and hides for cloth, French Catholic Métis distrusted the English-speaking Protestants, and Europeans came to distrust Native people.

By the 1830s, company officers began to marry European women, and clergy began to speak of having to "raise" Native people to the level of European civilization. Gradually, racist attitudes took hold in Red River. The children of more than one prominent family expressed shame that their mothers were Indian. Although many mixed-blood men had been educated abroad, they could only find menial positions in fur-trade ranks. In frustration, some defied the Company's monopoly and sold furs privately in Minnesota. The Sayer trial of 1849, in which the HBC challenged two such traders, ended with a twist: although the court found the men guilty, it recommended mercy because it couldn't enforce a sentence in the face of the angry Métis outside the courtroom. When the verdict was announced, the crowd recognized that the Company was beaten, and roared jubilantly: "Le commerce est libre!" ("The trade is free!").

The following decades were filled with change. The first steamboat arrived from Minnesota and the settlement's first newspaper began in the late 1850s, bringing contact with new markets and ideas. Scientific expeditions came to determine the West's agricultural potential, and preparations began for the transfer to the Canadian government of the HBC's rights to Rupert's Land at Confederation in 1867.

Fearing the results of settlement from the east, Native and Métis people became uneasy. As early as the 1850s, Chief Peguis asserted his people's ownership of lands beyond those granted to the Selkirk settlement and wrote to Britain to express his concerns. Métis people also demanded that their rights be acknowledged, afraid that if a wave of Protestant farmers came from Ontario, they would be denied their language, their religion, and their way

ST. PETER'S ANGLICAN CHURCH, EAST SELKIRK, SITE OF CHIEF PEGUIS' GRAVE

(continued on page 48)   43

LOUIS RIEL (1844-1885)

GERHARD ENS

Officially recognized as a founder of Manitoba in 1992, Louis Riel has at different times been viewed as a traitor, martyr, madman, hero, messianic prophet, and most recently as a Métis Ché Guevara.

He was born on October 22, 1844, in a small log house in St. Boniface, which is now part of Winnipeg. Most of his ancestors were French Canadian. Only one of his eight great-grandparents was Aboriginal. His mother, Julie Lagimodière, was white, a member of the powerful French-Canadian Lagimodière family in the parish of St. Boniface. His father, Jean-Louis Riel, was born in the North West and was the son of a fur trader and a Chipewyan Métis. Jean-Louis became a farmer and miller.

PORTRAIT OF LOUIS RIEL

Educated first in St. Boniface, Louis Riel was chosen by a bishop to attend the College of Montreal (Seminary of St. Sulpice). Thus in 1858 at the age of 13 Louis left his family for Quebec. The expectation was that Riel would study for the priesthood and return to Red River as a missionary. Initially Riel's studies went well, but by 1864 his religious aspirations had begun to dissipate. His father's death that year had probably been a heavy blow. Additionally, he had fallen in love with a girl named Marie-Julie Guernon, and this development, among others, resulted in his expulsion from the college in 1865. He then turned to the study of law and made plans to marry Marie-Julie. When her parents forbade the marriage, Louis gave up his law studies and suddenly left Montreal in 1866. In 1868 he returned to Red River.

The Métis, whom Riel would eventually lead in resistance to the proposed annexation of Rupert's Land by Canada in 1869 and in rebellion against the Canadian state in 1885, were the descendants of European fur traders and Native women. Comprised of both English-speaking Protestant "Halfbreeds" and French-speaking Catholic *métis*, the Métis specialized in fur trade occupations such as provisioner, guide, interpreter, trader, and tripman (voyageur or freighter). Their sense of nationhood emerged in the 19th century through their political struggles with the Hudson's Bay Company (HBC) and their military clashes with Sioux on their communal buffalo hunts.

By the time Louis Riel was born, the Métis had settled on the long narrow river lots that lined the banks of the Red and Assiniboine rivers. In 1869, when the HBC sold its rights in Rupert's Land to Canada, no one bothered to consult the 12,000 inhabitants of the Red River Settlement. The Métis, who made up the vast majority of residents in Red River, became worried about their status and land rights in the new Dominion when the Canadian government began building roads and surveying around the settlement well before the date of transfer to Canadian jurisdiction (see also p. 48).

A number of Métis called a public meeting in July of 1869. This group included the traditional Métis leadership in the colony, and was led by William Dease, a prominent French Métis. Dease called on the Métis to defend their rights to land in the settlement, and disputed the validity of the Earl of Selkirk's purchase of that land from the Aboriginals. The Métis, he argued, should demand the £300,000 that Canada was about to pay to the HBC. They should form a new government in the colony to displace the HBC and make their case to the Canadian government. This initiative was opposed by Riel, who stated that it was the scheme of the anti-HBC Canadian faction in the settlement. Over the next three months a power struggle raged between the Dease and Riel factions. Riel was backed by the settlement's Catholic clergy, and together they stirred up fears that Confederation represented the annexation of Red River by Protestant Orange Ontario, threatening the religious rights of the Catholic Métis. By October Riel had won the power struggle, and he and his followers organized a "National Committee" and formed a provisional government to negotiate with Canada.

Riel was firmly in control of Red River by December of 1869, but his close partnership with the Catholic clergy prevented him from winning the allegiance of more than a small minority of the English-Protestant Métis. He did take steps to forge a consensus in the settlement by calling a number of representative conventions, but he suppressed those who continued to oppose him, imprisoning dozens of Métis and Canadians. His execution of Thomas Scott, an Orangeman from Ontario, would later come back to haunt him. Scott, who had arrived the previous year to help build a road to Red River, was tried and shot by a Métis tribunal for his attempts to overthrow the Riel government.

Riel and his provisional government drafted a List of Rights which became the basis of their negotiations with the Canadian government and the basis for the drafting of the Manitoba Act that brought Manitoba into Confederation. This List of Rights included demands for provincial status and self-government, protection of property rights, bilingual institutions, and denominational schools to protect the interests of the Catholic Church. The passage of the Manitoba Act in 1870 was a triumph for Riel and the Manitoba

RIEL'S COUNCIL, 1869

MONUMENT TO LOUIS RIEL AT ST. BONIFACE COLLEGE

Métis, but even as the negotiations were taking place between the Red River delegates and the Canadian government, Prime Minister John A. Macdonald was making plans to send a military expedition to Red River to secure Canadian authority in the new province. While this was described as a mission of peace, the volunteer militia from Ontario who made up a good portion of the expeditionary force were intent on avenging the execution of Thomas Scott. Warned at the last minute, Riel fled to the United States.

In succeeding years Riel was unable to take any official part in Manitoba and Canadian politics. In 1871 he was active in repelling a border raid into Manitoba by a group of Americans led by William O'Donoghue, but instead of receiving the amnesty he had been promised during the Manitoba Act negotiations, he was convinced to leave Canada by a payoff from John A. Macdonald. He was three times elected to represent Manitoba in the House of Commons, but was unable to take his seat because there was a warrant for his arrest in Ontario for the murder of Scott. He was eventually voted an amnesty in 1875, but only on the condition of his expulsion from the House of Commons and exile from Canada for five years. Shortly thereafter his friends and family became concerned for Riel's mental health and secretly committed him to an asylum in Montreal in 1876. From the first, Riel protested that he was not a madman but an inspired prophet. Despite these protestations he would remain in various asylums until 1878.

After his release from the Beauport asylum Riel gravitated to Montana, joining a band of Métis buffalo hunters. In addition to trying his hand at trading, Riel attempted to organize a military alliance of Métis and Natives to invade western Canada, and tried to secure a Métis reserve in Montana, but these efforts failed. In 1881 he married Marguerite Monet (dit Bellehumeur), the daughter of a Métis buffalo hunter. He became an American citizen in 1883. Métis delegates from Batoche found him in 1884 and convinced him to return to the North West to lead their political struggle against the Canadian government to secure their land rights in present-day Saskatchewan. The outcome was the North West Rebellion of 1885, in which the Métis were defeated at Batoche on May 15.

Following the defeat, Riel surrendered voluntarily and was taken to Regina to stand trial for treason. He had surrendered in the hope that his trial would highlight the injustices visited upon the Métis and explain his actions, but he was convicted by a jury, and, amid a controversy that has remained to this day, Riel was hanged on November 16, 1885. He was buried at the St. Boniface Cathedral.

When a statue of Riel was erected on the grounds of the Legislative Building in 1971, some Manitobans protested that it was wrong to honour a troublemaker and an opportunist. The Manitoba Métis Federation protested as well, claiming that the statue, which represented Riel as a tormented man with his face and naked body twisted in agony, was a horrible caricature and an insult to the Métis people. The controversial statue was removed in 1994 and has been set up on the grounds of St. Boniface College. A new statue, approved by the Manitoba Métis Federation and portraying Riel in a more conventional and idealized form, will be erected on the legislative grounds.

ST. BONIFACE CATHEDRAL

RIEL HOUSE

of life. Despite petitions to Ottawa, they were never seriously considered during the transfer process.

Resistance to annexation was finally provoked by surveyors who arrived from Ottawa in 1869. A Métis party stopped the survey, challenging Canada's right to acquire their territory, while another group prevented the new lieutenant-governor of Manitoba from entering the province. Louis Riel (see pp. 44-47) organized the capture of Upper Fort Garry at The Forks, complete with its cannon and ammunition, giving the Métis the power they needed for their campaign. Riel House in Winnipeg explores his family history.

Riel organized a provisional government, which gave notice that it was prepared to negotiate terms of union with Canada. Sir John A. Macdonald, Canada's first prime minister, belatedly began dealing with the people of Red River. Macdonald also organized troops to go to Red River to enforce the transfer, but other events weakened the resistance before the troops arrived. Métis forces executed Thomas Scott, an Ontario settler, arousing anger in Canada and creating divisions among Red River inhabitants. After some negotiation that won only limited concessions to Métis concerns, the Manitoba Act, which joined the new province to Canada, came into effect in July 1870. Macdonald's troops arrived in July as well, and marched the length of the settlement to proclaim Canada's control of Red River. The Métis people became exiles in their own lands.

Native people also found the transfer the beginning of a nightmare. Native leaders bargained hard for their future when Treaty Number One was signed at Lower Fort Garry in 1871, but they became subject to the federal government, which failed to fulfil its promises. Their reserves were opened to white settlement, farm equipment promised them never arrived, and they were plagued by racist laws that forbade their culture and religion. Since 1871, Native people have continued to lobby for their rights. On December 4, 1994, chiefs, elders, and government agents signed an agreement that will lead to Native self-government in Manitoba. Once again, very different peoples in Manitoba came face to face. Perhaps they will again achieve the level of cooperation that characterized the first encounters in the province.

HOMESTEADING AND WHEAT: 1870-1919

CECILIA DANYSK

In 1878, Manitoba stepped onto the stage of the international grain trade. A consignment of wheat travelled by riverboat, rail and steamship south to St. Paul, Minnesota, then by rail to the eastern seaboard, and by freighter to Scotland. The prairie economy began its metamorphosis from fur trading and self-sufficient farming to commercial agriculture for international markets, rapidly becoming a world leader in wheat production. In this transformation, Manitoba took the leading role.

First came settlement. Dominion surveyors carved the entire prairie region into uniform parcels, and millions of acres were thrown open for homesteading. The Dominion Lands Act of 1872 offered 160 acres (65 hectares) to any man who would pay a $10 filing fee, construct a habitable building, live on the land for three years, and bring a specified area of new land under cultivation each year.

But for 25 years after the act, migration to the prairies was slow and uneven. To speed settlement, the federal government offered incentives to colonization companies and to some European groups. Manitoba's rural population spread out gingerly beyond the initial settlement on the banks of the Red and Assiniboine rivers, following the railways. As the 19th century drew to a close, the trickle of settlers became a flood, and in less than 20 years Manitoba's population swelled to more than half a million. By 1911 most agricultural land was settled.

WHEAT FIELD NEAR HOLLAND

IMMIGRANTS ARRIVING ON THE CPR, 1927

YOUNG ICELANDIC IMMIGRANT, 1911

When Manitoba became a province in 1870, its population was predominantly French-speaking Métis, but other groups were also well represented: Cree, English-speaking Métis, Scots, English, Irish, French, Ontarioan, and American. In the next two decades, migration to Manitoba was overwhelmingly Anglo-Canadian, particularly from Ontario. In 1890 the provincial government rescinded French rights in language and religious education. Manitoba at the close of the century had a strong Ontarioan flavour.

But other groups had begun moving into Manitoba as well. In 1874, Mennonites from Russia settled near present-day Steinbach. Another reserve was established in the Winkler and Altona area. In 1875, a small group of Icelanders formed the community of Gimli on the west shore of Lake Winnipeg. Since this was outside Manitoba's boundary at the time, they were granted the right to establish the Republic of New Iceland, a political structure for local self-government that is unique in Canadian history.

A trickle of other peoples moved in during the 1880s and early 1890s. Jews began to arrive under sponsorship of Jewish organizations. Most joined Jewish communities in Winnipeg and in towns and villages throughout the province. Other private sponsorship schemes helped Highland crofters move to the west of the province and Hungarian colonists move to the valley of Stony Creek, northwest of Neepawa. More Icelanders came to Gimli, and to the east shore of Lake Manitoba and the area around Glenboro. Small numbers of Swedes, Danes and Norwegians went to a reserve of land named New Scandinavia, north of Minnedosa. Belgians moved to south-central Manitoba near St. Alphonse, and Germans settled west of Russell. Expatriate French-Canadian families arrived from the United States to join the French-speaking population along the Red and Assiniboine rivers. But the vast majority of newcomers were Anglo-Canadian and British. Along with English-speaking arrivals from the United States, they settled throughout urban and rural Manitoba.

ALL PEOPLE'S MISSION, 1904

After large-scale immigration began at the end of the 19th century, most newcomers were still Anglo-Canadian and British, but federal immigration policy encouraged agriculturalists from throughout Europe. More than a million immigrants flooded into the West in only 15 years. By 1910, most of southern Manitoba and the Interlake area was settled, and pockets of distinct cultures existed. Ukrainian and Polish sites were established in the Dauphin and Interlake regions. Icelandic settlements grew along the southwest shore of Lake Winnipeg at Gimli and Argyle. Hungarian settlement expanded around Minnedosa and Neepawa. Belgian communities emerged at Bruxelles, Swan Lake, Mariapolis, Somerset, Deloraine, and Ste. Rose du Lac. Finnish settlement grew in the area of Rorketon and Meadow Portage, and in the Lac du Bonnet and Elma region.

Pioneers on Manitoba's agricultural lands faced remarkable challenges. Settlers in wooded areas could build log houses, but those who moved onto the open prairie constructed dwellings from sod. Cultivating the hard-packed virgin soil usually required a team of oxen. Grain growing on the prairies was still at an experimental stage in the late 19th century. In response to the inhospitable climate and landscape, newcomers developed and adopted new technologies and techniques to create a method of dry-land farming.

In the 1870s Manitoba farmers began growing Red Fife wheat, which had already ensured a place for Canadian wheat in international markets. There was continuous experimentation with gang-ploughs, self-binding reapers, steam threshers, and mammoth tractors. The completion of the Canadian Pacific Railway (CPR) in 1885 allowed an all-Canadian transportation route to the Great Lakes, and thence to Europe. The rush of settlement that began around 1897 ushered in a period of unprecedented prosperity.

During the boom years, millions more acres of prairie land were cultivated, and wheat exports soared to place Canada in the forefront of world wheat production. Two new transcontinental railways were chartered, countless branch lines were built, and grain elevators were erected every 48 kilometres (30 mi.) and soon were surrounded by villages and towns.

Manitoba's grain growers resented strictures imposed on them by the federal government, the international grain trade, and the CPR. Western agrarian protest had begun in the 1870s, with grievances against tariffs, grain-handling procedures, railway and elevator monopolies, marketing and transportation practices, and freight rates. It expanded over the decades to include demands for lower interest and mortgage rates, public ownership of elevators, better schools, political reform, and votes for women.

PRAIRIE GRAIN ELEVATORS

The Manitoba Grain Growers' Association was established in 1903, and in 1906 its members formed the Grain Growers' Grain Company, a farmer-owned grain marketing organization. In 1909, Manitoba grain growers joined farmers across the country in pressing for tariff reduction, control of grain marketing, political reform, and the nationalization of railways.

Winnipeg soon became the hub of the West. Its first spurt of growth came hard upon the creation of the province. Ontarioans flocked to the site, land prices rose, businesses were established, and in 1873 Winnipeg became an incorporated city. Within two years the population stood at 5,000, and commercial and financial activity geared to settlement and agriculture displaced the fur trade as the main economic enterprise.

The city's leaders launched a vigorous campaign to induce the CPR to run its line through Winnipeg. It paid

(continued on page 55)

WHEAT

JIM BLANCHARD

ALTONA FARMLAND

The development and growth of the export wheat economy in the Canadian West is a remarkable success story. Settlers transformed the prairie into one of the world's great breadbaskets, converting the rolling grassland into a patchwork of family farms. The tiny trickle of wheat that began to flow out of the West in 1876 swelled to a mighty river of millions of bushels by the late 1920s. A deadly combination of drought, low prices, grasshoppers and rust slowed things down in the 1930s, but by 1939 the growth resumed, and new records for wheat exports have been set approximately every 10 years.

Wheat has occupied from one-third to one-half of the cropland in Manitoba since before 1900, and it continues today to far outstrip any other crop in terms of hectares (acres) planted. Agriculture, including the grain trade, employs close to 20,000 people in Winnipeg. In the rest of Manitoba agriculture provides another 45,000 jobs.

TRADING FLOOR, WINNIPEG GRAIN EXCHANGE

The industry had its humble beginnings in 1812 when the first Selkirk Settlers arrived in the Red River district. Their first crops were a total failure, but, as the years went by, wheat and other grain crops gained a foothold at the Red River Settlement. A small milling industry grew up in the colony.

But wheat was grown only on a fairly modest scale in the Red River Settlement. Yet by 1885 it had surpassed furs in importance as an export from Manitoba, and by 1912 it was the major export of Canada. This dramatic change was the result of a combination of factors.

First, the prairie climate was ideal for growing hard red spring wheat, a type that was in high demand in Britain and continental Europe. Red Fife, a variety of red spring wheat, fuelled the first wheat boom in the 1880s.

In 1892 scientists at the Brandon Experimental Farm began using plant breeding in an attempt to produce a wheat that would mature early enough to avoid the frost. The process ended in 1906 with the introduction of Marquis. It is still the standard by which new varieties are judged.

Another essential element in the wheat economy was

the railroad that linked the wheat lands with markets in the outside world. The single thread of Canadian Pacific Railway (CPR) track that connected Manitoba with eastern Canada in 1881 was only the beginning of a massive rail infrastructure that went on expanding until the 1930s.

The foundations of the business of handling grain — buying it from the farmer and forwarding it for sale in the export market — were laid in the 1880s when the Winnipeg Grain Exchange was established. In 1906 the Grain Exchange moved into the vast new building at the corner of Rorie and Lombard that continues to stand as a monument to the prosperity and confidence of those times.

In some respects, the wheat industry in western Canada evolved in a uniquely Canadian way. It developed a bulk handling system that moves grain in carloads and shiploads instead of in bags. Individual lots of grain belonging to many producers are mixed together and classified with grades that are defined in terms of the physical characteristics of the grain. The grading system is, therefore, very significant in Canada.

A by-product of the bulk shipping method is the enormous infrastructure of bulk handling elevators. The clean, well-built Canadian elevators provide protection from the weather and pests.

The bulk handling system, with its endless possibilities for disagreements over such things as weight and grades, and the immense profits that the private grain traders were making inevitably led to conflicts between the wheat producers and the rest of the industry. There was widespread belief among grain growers that the CPR and

the grain companies that operated the country elevators where farmers sold their grain were in cahoots to cheat the honest farmer. There were charges, not altogether unfounded, of price fixing and of cheating on weights and grades.

HOPPER CARS TRANSPORT GRAIN BY RAILWAY

WINNIPEG GRAIN EXCHANGE

Since 1900, western Canadian grain farmers have probably lobbied harder and achieved a larger share of the power in their industry than their counterparts in any other grain-producing country. In the first decade of this century, the Grain Growers' organizations on the prairies won legislated safeguards to protect them from unfair treatment from the grain companies. Fair weights and grades at the country elevator and government control over the grading system were achieved after hard political battles.

The Grain Growers' movement invaded the previously closed sanctum of the Winnipeg Grain Exchange with the formation of the Grain Growers' Grain Company in 1906. This farmer-owned concern has grown into the giant United Grain Growers company of today. In the mid-1920s three farmer-organized provincial wheat pools came onto the scene in Manitoba, Saskatchewan, and Alberta. Almost immediately, they gained control of close to 50 percent of the prairie wheat crop. With the success of the wheat pools and the beginning of the Canadian Wheat Board monopoly of the wheat trade in 1940, the Winnipeg Grain Exchange and the private grain firms lost their dominant position.

CPR YARDS, WINNIPEG

During the last half century the wheat industry has continued a slow but steady growth in production and exports, but the number of farms has shrunk by more than 50 percent. Most wheat farms are now large, super-efficient enterprises, although they are still family operations. The local market towns that once stood every 16 kilometres (10 mi.) along the railway lines have, for the most part, shrunk or disappeared.

Today's farmers often have a different world-view from the farmers of 50 years ago. Their attitude toward agencies like the wheat pools and the Canadian Wheat Board is frequently one of indifference or active hostility. They see

GRAIN ELEVATOR WEST OF WINNIPEG

VINTAGE GRAIN ELEVATOR

themselves as entrepreneurs, capable of competing in a free market without the protection of marketing boards and regulations. Although the board and the pools continue to have significant numbers of supporters, their once-dominant position in the industry is being seriously challenged.

The markets for western wheat have also changed. Britain and other European countries grow their own wheat, and western grain now finds its way into dumplings and noodles in China, bread in Russia and Brazil, and other products all over the world.

off: in 1881, the CPR decided to cross the Red River at Winnipeg, and the city became the "gateway of the West."

WINNIPEG MAIN STREET, 1904

Boom followed immediately. Real-estate offices sprang up, property auctions took place day and night, and prices soared to $2,000 a front foot (0.3 metre), outstripping the price of prime land in Chicago.

By late 1882 the boom collapsed. But the city continued to grow, boosted by a civic government and commercial establishment whose membership overlapped and whose goal was to make Winnipeg the "Chicago of the North." The city geared its policy decisions toward ensuring that businesses and entrepreneurs would find a favourable economic climate. Winnipeg became the focal point for three transcontinental railways. It was the wholesale and financial centre of the West, controlling a hinterland from British Columbia to northern Ontario. It was the major service and supply centre for the growing grain trade of western Canada. By 1914 the Winnipeg Grain Exchange was the largest grain centre in North America.

Winnipeg was a sprawling, thriving metropolis whose cultural and educational amenities rivalled those of central Canadian cities. At the height of the boom it more than tripled its size in only a decade. By 1911 it ranked as the fourth largest manufacturing centre and the third largest city in Canada.

PEASANT WOMAN AND CHILDREN, 1907

But the rapid growth and the civic government's commercial agenda had serious social consequences. As the railway centre of the West, and the site of Dominion Land offices and a Federal Immigration Building, Winnipeg was the first stopping place for immigrants seeking land and jobs. Many stayed in the city, crowding into the already overpopulated working-class area. The city could not keep up with the burgeoning demands for housing, water, sewage disposal, educational facilities, and health services.

In 1870, French-speaking Métis had made up 81 percent of Winnipeg's population. By 1881, 84 percent of the population was of Anglo-Saxon origin. During the boom the proportions shifted again, and by 1921 only 67 percent was of Anglo-Saxon origin, with most of the remainder a mixture of European populations. The shrinking majority saw the newcomers as a threat to Canadian society, to be assimilated or excluded.

Winnipeg was the central clearing-house for labour in western

MAIN STREET, 1910

Canada, housing a large supply of skilled and unskilled workers, both immigrant and Canadian. Unions were formed early in Winnipeg's history. By the 1890s a Trades and Labour Council had been established, and a labour newspaper advocated wide social reform, including restriction of immigration. Labour-capital relations in Winnipeg were marked by open hostility and frequent conflict. With the economic boom, the number of strikes increased, especially among railway workers. In 1906 motormen and coachmen at the Winnipeg Electric Railway Company walked off the job, and the company brought in strikebreakers from eastern Canada.

AUTOMOBILE, 1916

After two days of violence, the mayor called on the Canadian Mounted Rifles to restore order. Machine guns were mounted at the corner of Main and Henry streets to subdue the crowds. The conflict increased the tension between workers and employers in a city sharply divided by class and ethnicity, where poverty existed in the midst of unprecedented economic growth.

But the heady boom was short-lived. By 1913 the limits of economic expansion had been reached, and the western economy faltered.

MINNEDOSA FAIR, 1912

Ironically, World War I rescued the prairies from the brink of depression. With grain production knocked out in Europe, prairie farmers could sell all the wheat they could produce, at soaring prices. Grain growers expanded their holdings and went into debt to reap the benefits of seemingly unlimited markets.

War put a brake on immigration, but exacerbated already-strained ethnic relations. In 1916, Manitoba made English the only language of instruction. As a direct consequence, one-third of its Mennonite community emigrated to Mexico and Paraguay. Immigrants from "enemy" countries faced restrictions on their organizations, press, and personal liberties. Many spent time in internment camps. Even their countrymen who had been naturalized were disenfranchised and subject to official strictures, and often faced public animosity and even violence.

DECORATION DAY PARADE, 1916

As part of a larger reform movement that had been building, Manitobans in 1916 voted for a reform government. They also voted for prohibition. Education was made compulsory. That year, Manitoba women were the first in Canada to win the right to vote and to hold provincial office.

As the war progressed, labour shortages gave new strength to unions and increased worker determination to share wartime economic gains. In the latter years of the war — in the wake of the Russian Revolution, as conscription was enacted, and as inflation outstripped wages — union membership grew, strike activity reached new heights, and a near-general strike took place in Winnipeg in 1918.

After the war, the return of veterans added to ethnic and labour tensions in Winnipeg. Most returning soldiers looked for jobs in towns and cities rather than on farms. As unemployment soared, some voices demanded that immigrant workers be fired to make room for veterans. Support grew for organized labour's increasingly militant stance. Early in 1919 a successful strike was held by civic workers in Brandon.

In Winnipeg on May 15, a strike in the building and metal trades quickly grew into a general strike (see pp. 58-59). Civic and provincial authorities refused to negotiate with the strikers. The federal government enacted legislation to quash the strike. By the time it ended in June, Winnipeg's working men and women had been given the clear message that governments at all levels sided with employers. In the long term, the strike subdued Winnipeg's workers and further embittered class and ethnic relations. It was a harsh legacy.

RANCHING
DAIRYING
GRAIN RAISING
FRUIT RAISING
MIXED FARMING

ISSUED BY DIRECTION OF HON. SYDNEY FISHER
MINISTER OF AGRICULTURE, OTTAWA, CANADA.

THE WINNIPEG GENERAL STRIKE

DOUG SMITH

WINNIPEG GENERAL STRIKE, 1919

On May 15, 1919, half of Winnipeg's labour force — over 35,000 workers — walked off the job at the start of the country's most famous general strike, which would paralyze the city for six weeks. It was both a local labour dispute over the right to strike and the high-water mark of a decade of turmoil in Canada and around the world.

Two years earlier, radical workers and disaffected soldiers had brought down the Russian tsar, replacing a feudal monarchy with a Bolshevik-led government. The notion of proletarian revolution inspired and haunted workers and employers worldwide. Industrialization, urbanization, and war had created social pressures and antagonism. In Winnipeg a radicalized working class and a proud business community forced those pressures to the bursting point.

Winnipeg metal-shop and building-trade workers had created a Metal Trades Council and a Building Trades Council, comprising all the unions in each sector. The owners of Winnipeg's metal shops were prepared to deal with individual plant committees — as long as they could pick half the committee members. The builders conducted talks with the Building Trades Council for a while, and then announced they would not deal with it. In early May, strikes were called in both industries.

For labour the issue was fundamental: could employers refuse to bargain with duly selected worker representatives? The Labour Council held a referendum on whether to hold a general strike. The vote was 8,667 to 645 in favour.

On the first day of the strike, veterans passed a resolution backing the strikers. They later staged parades supporting strikers' demands for compulsory collective bargaining.

GENERAL KETCHEN, J.A.M. AIKINS AND GROUP AT ST. JOHN'S COLLEGE

Arrayed against the strikers was the Citizens' Committee of One Thousand, created by leading business figures. It attempted to blame the strike on immigrant workers, whom it labelled "bolshevik agitators." In many ways the committee operated as an unelected civic government.

The General Strike Committee asked dairy workers not to strike, but the dairies were afraid strike supporters might attack their delivery wagons. Signs were issued at their request, reading, "Permitted by Authority of the Strike Committee." The Citizens' Committee claimed these signs proved the strike was a revolution.

Allowing the delivery of milk and bread was probably the strikers' most revolutionary undertaking. Instead of stirring people to overthrow the city government, strike leaders urged them to stay home. The strikers' newspaper advised, "Do not say an angry word. Walk away from the fellow who tries to draw you."

Striking civic, provincial and federal employees were told to return to work or lose their jobs. When city police officers refused to disavow their support for the strike, they were dismissed. With the help of the Citizens' Committee, 2,000 untrained "special" police officers were recruited.

Early on June 17, the Royal North West Mounted Police raided union offices and scooped up strike leaders, who were taken to Stony Mountain Penitentiary where they faced charges of sedition. Bail was granted after they promised not to play any further role in the strike.

Veterans organized a protest march for June 21, and men marshalled on Main Street in front of the city hall. Before the parade began, some strikers attacked a streetcar that was being run by strikebreakers, setting it on fire. The mayor called for the Mounted Police, who charged down Main Street right through the protesters, firing their revolvers. One man was shot in the chest and another in the head.

MOUNTED POLICE ON MAIN STREET, JUNE 21, 1919

By day's end, soldiers with machine guns stood on the main streets. On June 25 the Strike Committee announced the strike would end the following day.

Thousands of workers were dismissed from their jobs and blacklisted from new ones. Many strikers were deported or imprisoned. But the strike leaders never lost public support. The following year several strike leaders were elected to the legislature, and in 1921 J. S. Woodsworth, who edited the strike paper during its dying days, was elected to the House of Commons.

The strike widened divisions between affluent South-End and working-class North-End Winnipeg. The city's rulers eventually eliminated all the strike landmarks and meeting places. It was not until 1994 that a plaque commemorating the strike was placed at the Manitoba Legislative Building.

RECESSION, DEPRESSION AND WAR: 1920-1945

PETER NUNODA

CONSTRUCTION OF SEVEN SISTERS FALLS HYDRO-ELECTRIC PLANT, 1929

For Manitoba, the years 1919 to 1921 were turbulent, as working-class, agricultural and First-Nations protest combined to create a distinct provincial and regional identity. With the abortive end of the Winnipeg General Strike and the election in 1921 of a Liberal government to Ottawa, the province entered its "modern" period.

The combined British and French portions of Manitoba's population had declined from a high of 75 percent in 1881 to 64 percent in 1921. However, acceptance of newcomers like the Ukrainians, Mennonites, and other European immigrants by the dominant culture would take considerably longer. As a result of wartime nativism, many of these new Manitobans felt compelled to deny their ethnic identities by changing their names or engaging in other forms of "passing."

The 1920s marked the beginning of the end of wheat's economic domination in Manitoba. The years 1920 to 1924 saw a post-war depression in agricultural prices with the spin-off effect of a lagging commercial economy in the province's urban centres. The second half of the decade was marked by steady growth of large capital industries,

especially in the northern frontier. Central and Northern Manitoba, which had been ignored since the end of the fur trade because they lacked agricultural potential, suddenly became the focus for economic development.

The mining, pulp and paper, and hydroelectric industries grew, with new towns like Flin Flon, Pine Falls and The Pas becoming the hubs of such activity.

SWATHED BARLEY CROP, PEMBINA VALLEY

It would be wrong to imply that agriculture declined in this decade, but farming certainly changed. For the first time, Manitoban farmers made a concerted effort to diversify by growing barley and raising livestock. However, the primary crop was still wheat. In the five years following the war, the Canadian wheat economy faced increasing competition. With the fields of Europe once again producing, as well as increased production from the southern hemisphere, world wheat prices declined.

This signalled potential disaster for prairie farmers. Many had expanded their holdings at high interest rates to meet the

MAKING BOMB SHELLS, 1941

production demands of the wartime economy. Pricing and marketing had been stabilized by the federal government's Canadian Wheat Board during the war, so farmers had been relatively prosperous and secure. With the end of the war, the government terminated the Wheat Board, allowing grain marketing to revert to the private sector. In conjunction with a general economic depression, the wheat economy was thrown into turmoil by its peculiar problems.

The first response in western Canada was the election of 65 Progressive candidates to Ottawa in 1921. The National Progressive Party of Canada was essentially a western Canadian farmers' party. It forced the minority Liberal government to reinstate the 1918 Crow's Nest Pass rates on the shipment of grain and flour in favour of farmers. But when the Liberals refused to re-establish the Wheat Board, prairie farmers organized province-wide voluntary pools and in 1924 established the Canadian Co-operative Wheat Producers Limited in Winnipeg as a central marketing agency to handle all pool grain.

In this province, the general feeling of agrarian alienation resulted in the election in 1923 of a United

CANADIAN WHEAT BOARD BUILDING, WINNIPEG

PLOUGHING WHEAT

Farmers of Manitoba government. However, the turnaround in the agricultural economy that occurred between 1925 and 1928 had little to do with government policies. International circumstances, technological advances, and more efficient marketing strategies led to higher prices and bigger harvests in western Canada. The practice of offering farmers advances on crops in the spring, established by the pools, stabilized farmers' costs. Mechanization reduced manpower costs and increased productivity.

In the early 1920s the First Nations of the West began the long journey to political activism. The stimulus was World War I. The Canadian government had actively recruited from the First Nations, believing that their culture made Aboriginals particularly suited to combat. Because of the poor economic conditions on reserves, many Natives had volunteered for military service. At the end of the war these veterans returned to a country that continued to treat them as second-class citizens, denying them even the franchise. Canada's First Nations began to organize for political action on issues like better education, ownership of property, and improvement in health programs. First Nations peoples of the prairies played a leading role by broadening the base of protest to include recognition of treaty and Aboriginal rights, revision of the Indian Act, and the need for economic development.

The fortunes of Winnipeg and other urban centres like Brandon and Portage la Prairie were still tied to the agricultural economy, so the depression of 1920-24 brought development in Winnipeg to a standstill. The wholesaling and warehousing businesses, two of the pillars of Winnipeg's economic supremacy in western Canada, experienced permanent declines. One reason was the generally poor economy. Another factor was the opening of the Panama Canal in 1914, which diverted some of Winnipeg's grain business to Vancouver, especially after World War I when shipping space became more readily available. Finally, the growth of Regina, Saskatoon, Calgary and Edmonton led to the establishment of distributing centres in those cities.

Unlike other prairie cities, Winnipeg was a cosmopolitan centre where many ethnic cultures flourished. But it was divided by class and ethnicity. Working-class immigrants of central and eastern European backgrounds resided in the North End, north of Portage Avenue on either side of Main Street. The British middle class gravitated to the West End, along both sides of Portage Avenue. The

Franco-Manitoban community was located in St. Boniface. And the British-Ontario elite were spread out south of Broadway in the Wolseley area, and to a growing extent south of the Assiniboine River along Wellington Crescent. There was little contact among these neighbourhoods. While this had been true before 1919, these divisions had crystallized as a result of the general strike.

To some extent, Winnipeg's losses in warehousing and wholesaling were offset by manufacturing expansion. Despite the post-war depression, demand for construction materials in the West grew throughout the twenties. As well, the newly organized Canadian National Railway announced a massive branch line construction program. Much of the construction would occur in Manitoba, benefiting the local steel and manufacturing industries. Finally, provincial government hydro and highway projects provided impetus both to manufacturing and to construction contractors in Winnipeg.

But Winnipeg's boom came with the recovery of the agricultural economy and the opening of the northern resource frontier after 1924. The economic recovery produced tremendous local and national demand for everything Winnipeg could offer, and this increased employment in the city. In turn, Winnipeg's growth fuelled the province's economy as demand for hydro and water increased.

But the next decade would bring Canada's "Great Depression," an economic crisis unlike any other. The 1930s were especially difficult for western Canadians. The decade was characterized by agricultural collapse, but urban poverty was equally prevalent. Prairie farmlands were ravaged by drought, grasshoppers, and rust. While the poor yields were disheartening, the low world price for wheat was devastating.

CORN FIELD IN DROUGHT, 1934

Despite some positive changes such as new ploughing techniques, soil reclamation and water conservation projects, and the development of an effective poison bait to combat the grasshopper plague, many farmers simply left. The 1936

DROUGHT, 1934

census showed about 800 abandoned farms in Manitoba. But in comparison to Saskatchewan and Alberta, the number of farm failures in the province was relatively small. Since 1921 more than half of Manitoba's seeded acreage had been devoted to crops other than wheat, and this diversification stabilized the agricultural economy to a degree. Also, even during the worst drought years, rain did fall in some areas of the province.

Winnipeg's economy slowed considerably between 1930 and 1933 as agriculture continued its downhill slide. Contributing to its problems was the fact that Vancouver made further inroads into the western grain trade. But the local grain trade received a boost from the long-awaited opening of the port at Churchill on Hudson Bay in 1931. Between 1930 and 1933, employment in Winnipeg shrank by 22 percent. Unemployment was especially severe in the construction and transportation sectors, which were integral parts of the city's economy. There was an average of over 2,000 relief cases in the city between 1929 and 1933.

Social welfare was within provincial and municipal jurisdiction, but the junior levels of government were ill-equipped to deal with the demand for services during the economic crisis. For many people, relief became the only option. But before a family could apply for relief it had to prove total destitution. Indeed, the entire system discouraged initiative. As the Depression dragged on it was increasingly difficult for white-collar workers even to apply for jobs, as their relief clothes became a stigma. Despite all the deprivations, there was little significant revolutionary activity or violence in Manitoba.

The watershed in the Depression for Winnipeg came around 1934. From that point to the beginning of World War II, the city's economy showed a steady if unspectacular recovery. Part of the growth was attributable to demand for Winnipeg's services from both the old agricultural sector and the new resource frontier. The greatest success story was the massive expansion of the city's garment and needle trades to a position that rivalled Montreal by 1939. Winnipeg's historical role as a major transportation centre was enhanced in 1937 when the city was designated as the main base of the newly created Trans-Canada Airlines. This decision created immediate employment. But there were over 4,000 families on relief in the city in 1938 and 1939. Full employment would not return until 1941.

Manitoba's economy benefited in all areas from the demands for production during World War II. Winnipeg firms were given contracts for various military supplies from munitions to clothing to aircraft. While it was clear with the resumption of full employment that the provincial economy had recovered, the general mood of Manitobans was guarded as the war neared its end. Another post-war recession was expected, and the people and politicians braced themselves for the worst. The mentality of the Great Depression was not easily shaken.

HEART OF THE CONTINENT: MANITOBA AFTER 1945

PETER NUNODA

Following World War II, the expected post-war recession never materialized, to the surprise of many. In fact, after 1945 Manitoba entered a period of sustained though not spectacular economic growth. Perhaps the most significant development that took place during and after the war years was totally unconnected to the general economic recovery. The rural population steadily declined in absolute and relative terms from 408,000 (56 percent) in 1941 to 296,000 (29 percent) by 1981. There were three main reasons for this trend. First, smaller land holdings were consolidated into larger farm units as technology permitted farmers to cultivate more land. Second, there was an exodus from the more marginal lands along the northern frontier because of poor soils, low profitability, and short growing seasons. Finally, employment in larger cities like Winnipeg and Brandon attracted many rural residents.

The result of this rural depopulation was the shrinking or disappearance of many hamlets and small towns across the province. What hastened the population shift was highway construction and improvement programs of

CANOLA FIELDS NEAR BALDUR, PEMBINA VALLEY

successive Manitoba governments, beginning in the 1920s. With the evolution from gravel to asphalt and finally to concrete, roads in the province could be maintained on a year-round basis. According to W. L. Morton, the dean of western Canadian historians, this fact, combined with the increasing reliability of vehicles, ended rural isolation that since the 19th century had characterized the prairie farming experience. Due to their increased mobility, farmers and their families more frequently patronized the larger service centres in the province like Brandon, Winnipeg, and Portage la Prairie. This change in consumption trends spelled the end to the small local general store. As well, rural students were increasingly bussed to schools in bigger towns.

TRACTOR OPERATOR

At the same time, the business of farming had been altered forever by the Depression. The new technologies introduced during the 1930s were widely adopted only after the Second World War. The Manitoba Power Commission began a rural electrification program in 1946, and by 1950 some 20,000 farms had received electrical service. Advanced machinery, combined with better tillage techniques, new hybrids, crop rotation, chemical fertilizers, and pesticides, produced higher yields. To increase profitability, crops other than wheat, such as potatoes, vegetables, sugar beets, sunflowers, corn, and canola, were increasingly grown. Finally, cattle became an important component of agricultural production in Manitoba. The days of endless fields of wheat had come to an end. Despite all these changes, there has been no significant growth in the agricultural sector in Manitoba since 1945.

If the balance between rural and urban population permanently shifted in the forties, another demographic trend remained the same. As in most of the provinces in Canada, the population of Manitoba was disproportionately distributed between the north and south. If a line were

PORT OF CHURCHILL

drawn across the province just north of The Pas, 95 percent

of the population would live to the south of it. Settlement of the north was confined to isolated fishing villages, resource towns, First Nations reserves, and the port of Churchill, a transshipment centre on Hudson Bay.

This is not to say that the northern frontier was unimportant to Manitoba. In fact, the development of northern resources had begun in the 1920s, and resource development was an important factor in the province's post-war economic prosperity. The beginning of the post-war boom came with the discovery of a major copper/nickel ore body at Lynn Lake in 1946. That was followed by the discovery of another huge nickel/copper deposit in the Moak Lake - Mystery Lake region in the 1950s, which led to the founding of the town of Thompson. The paper mill at Pine Falls was expanded by a forestry complex that also opened a paper plant at The Pas. The other major area of resource development in Manitoba was hydro. Provincial demand for power increased with industrial development and rural electrification. The existing Winnipeg River system could no longer meet Manitoba's requirements, so three further projects were undertaken. One was located at Seven Sisters Falls; the others were on the Nelson and Churchill rivers. In addition, in 1960 the federal government announced that its second nuclear generator would be located at Pinawa.

WINNIPEG SKYLINE ON RED RIVER FROM ST. BONIFACE

As the rural population declined, the provincial focus naturally shifted to Manitoba's cities, especially Winnipeg.

OLD MARKET SQUARE, EXCHANGE DISTRICT

(continued on page 70)

THE GREAT FLOOD OF 1950

J. M. BUMSTED

In the spring of 1950, southern Manitoba's Red River Valley, including the city of Winnipeg, experienced a flood that was described by the national director of the Red Cross for the United States as "the worst disaster of its kind in the history of North America." It necessitated the largest mass evacuation of people in Canada's history. The ordeal extended over many weeks and was observed with

ABOVE: FLOODED STREETS IN EMERSON

RIGHT: EATON'S FLOOD RELIEF

concern around the world. Damages were assessed, in 1950 values, at $50 million. But the event also had a positive side: it united Manitoba's diverse population.

SPRUCE WOODS PROVINCIAL PARK, ASSINIBOINE RIVER VALLEY

Thousands of individuals, driven by courage and round-the-clock determination, pulled together in a massive effort to save their communities.

The Red River Valley serves as the drainage basin for an area of 287,475 square kilometres (111,000 sq. mi.). Part of that area is drained by the Red River and part by the Assiniboine, which in turn drains into the Red. The drainage flows north, thus presenting the possibility that spring meltwater from the south will meet ice blockages at any point up to and including its ultimate destination in Hudson Bay.

By March 1950, all the elements for a

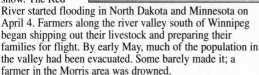

devastating flood were present in the Red River Valley. The drainage basin had been saturated by several years of heavy rain, and the winter of 1949-50 had been severe, with thick ice and heavy snow. The Red River started flooding in North Dakota and Minnesota on April 4. Farmers along the river valley south of Winnipeg began shipping out their livestock and preparing their families for flight. By early May, much of the population in the valley had been evacuated. Some barely made it; a farmer in the Morris area was drowned.

EVACUATING LIVESTOCK FROM FLOODED AREA

Residents of low-lying areas of Winnipeg had begun to move out by late April. By mid-May, when the flood crested in the city, more than 80,000 had left Winnipeg, and others were still expected to go. Thousands had pitched in to build and repair dikes. For many fathers and "flood bachelors," cut off from their families outside the city and their homes within it, the soup kitchens of the volunteer organizations were the only source of nourishment. Only 13 city schools remained open, and the Department of Education ruled that 135 days would constitute a full school year. Hospitals were closed, and the elderly and sick were moved to destinations hundreds of miles away. Radio stations were on 24-hour alert to report the collapse of dikes and further flooding. An estimated 10,500 houses in Winnipeg were affected by the flood. The dramatic struggle to save the city made headlines around the world. Relief assistance poured in: sandbags, pumps, blankets, medical supplies, and money.

The 1950 disaster resulted in the eventual construction of the Red River Floodway, which now protects Winnipeg from a similar event by diverting flood water around the city. The floodway was a giant engineering project that involved the excavation of 76 million cubic metres (100 million cu. yd.) of earth over a length of 47.3 kilometres (29.4 mi.), more than had been moved for the St. Lawrence Seaway Project or the Panama Canal.

EMERSON RESIDENTS ENTERING A LOCAL STORE BY BOAT

Not surprisingly, Winnipeg was the chief beneficiary of the population drift from the farms as well as new immigration to the province. Between 1941 and 1981, Winnipeg's population increased from 302,000 to 585,000, while in the same period the province's population only increased from 730,000 to 1,026,000. The most significant growth in the city's manufacturing sector was in the aerospace industry, agricultural implements, garment making, and other light industries. By far the most important development in Winnipeg during this period was the consolidation of seven cities and five suburban municipalities into Metropolitan Winnipeg in 1960, giving the regional authority control over matters such as planning, zoning, building, flood control, and transportation. The regional government plan was subsequently replaced in 1972 by the Unicity format, in which Winnipeg came under the control of a single city council.

By the early 1980s Winnipeg dominated Manitoba's economy. The city contained half the province's population and 68 percent of its employees, produced 83 percent of its manufactured goods, and accounted for 62 percent of its retail sales. The city's most important function continued to be its role as a transportation centre, and a considerable proportion of its industry was devoted to the manufacturing and servicing of transportation systems. In the recent past, the service sector, both public and private, has provided significant employment in the city.

To a degree, the provincial governments since 1945 have facilitated Manitoba's development with their generally progressive policies. Beginning with the Conservative administration of Duff Roblin elected in 1958, the Manitoba government embarked on almost three decades of expansion in government services and spending. Roblin increased spending on health, education, and public works. He also initiated plans for consolidated schools, the Winnipeg Floodway, and new sports and cultural facilities. Roblin's successor, Walter Weir, was a more typical Tory who attempted to reduce government spending in the late 1960s when the mood of Canadians and Manitobans was very positive. Weir's style of government seemed out of tune with the times, and as a result the majority of Manitobans opted for the young leader of the New Democratic Party, Ed Schreyer, the next time they went to the polls.

The election of the New Democrats in 1969 represented a significant shift in Manitoba politics. The NDP advocated positive government, including the extension of social welfare programs and experiments in economic development. These were clearly policies that appealed to the NDP's traditional

THE ROYAL WINNIPEG BALLET IN *ALLEGRO BRILLIANTE*

supporters (the working class and non-British Canadians) as well as new forces in Canadian politics (First Nations peoples, recent immigrants, and working women). In a sense, the election of the NDP was an outright rejection of the traditional pattern of Manitoba politics, which had been characterized by its British, elitist, pro-business nature. But the essential difference between the political revolution of the 1970s and the discord of the early 20th century was that the disagreements were now settled peacefully at the ballot box rather than in the streets of Winnipeg.

With the tremendous increase in Winnipeg's size and the advent of multicultural awareness, the arts, sports, and the cultural life of the city have received more and more attention. One of the earliest expressions of this interest was the establishment of the Royal Winnipeg Ballet, a world-class company. Winnipeg's international status was enhanced further when the city hosted the 1967 Pan-American Games. The legacy of sports facilities left by this

JAPANESE DANCERS AT FOLKLORAMA

event was influential in Winnipeg's successful bid to host the Games again in 1999. For the present at least, Winnipeg possesses two major professional sports franchises, the NHL's Jets and the CFL's Blue Bombers, but each is plagued with the problems of so-called small-market teams.

Since 1970, an annual two-week festival called Folklorama has celebrated the ethnic heritage of Manitoba. That Folklorama has become such an integral part of the community's life is not surprising. During the hearings of the Royal Commission on Bilingualism and Biculturalism in the mid-sixties, delegations from Manitoba's ethnic groups were instrumental in convincing the government of the need for a federal multicultural policy, which was established in 1972. Like the rest of Canada since the end of the Second World War, Manitoba has welcomed immigrants from all parts of the globe. The cultural transformation of the province is clearly demonstrated by its changing ethnic composition. Between 1921 and 1961, the combined British and French portions of the population declined from almost 64 percent to 52 percent, while other ethnic communities increased their representation from 36 percent to 48 percent. The province can now boast significant and active Filipino, Vietnamese and West Indian

ICELANDIC FESTIVAL, GIMLI

communities, among others, along with the Mennonite, Jewish and Ukrainian communities that were founded in the early 20th century as parts of its cultural mainstream. The Festival du Voyageur, an annual winter event, highlights the cultures of the Franco-Manitoban, Métis, and First Nations communities. Folklorama and the Festival du Voyageur, along with other festivals held in rural communities, have come to define the multicultural fabric of Manitoban society (see pp. 87-92).

While ethnic groups now openly share their cultural backgrounds, one important component of Manitoba's society continues to struggle to have its position in that society recognized. The First Nations of Manitoba, which include the Cree and Ojibwa people, have had a significant impact on local, provincial, and national politics. Perhaps the most notable contribution by an Aboriginal leader was Elijah Harper's single-handed defeat of the Meech Lake constitutional amending formula in the Manitoba legislature in 1990. This action was symbolic of the First Nations' dissatisfaction with the Canadian Constitution. Harper was ably advised by Phil Fontaine, grand chief of the Assembly of Manitoba Chiefs, and Ovide Mercredi, a Cree leader from Grand Rapids who was to become the grand chief of the Assembly of First Nations. Along with the Métis community, the First Nations of Manitoba have worked tirelessly to bring their concerns to the attention of the province's non-Aboriginal population and have lobbied the provincial and federal governments to make substantive changes that would recognize their rights as Indigenous people.

DOME OF THE MANITOBA LEGISLATIVE BUILDING

As Manitoba prepares to enter the 21st century, its prospects seem guardedly optimistic. While government funding to essential services such as education, health care and social welfare appears to decrease on an almost daily basis, the systems continue to struggle on. On the positive side, much of the provincial government's focus is on the introduction of new hi-tech industries to bolster Manitoba's economy. What is likely, given Manitoba's history since 1920 and, indeed, since 1870, is that Manitobans will continue to adapt to rapid global changes and, above all, survive.

RECREATION, CULTURE AND ENTERTAINMENT

RECREATION

RUSSELL E. BRAYLEY

SHOOTING RAPIDS ON THE GRASS RIVER

For more information about the following activities, please refer to the Travel Tips section of this guidebook.

GOLF

Manitoba offers a wide range of golf experiences, with numerous short (nine-hole, par-three) courses and several highly rated, very challenging courses such as "The Links at Quarry Oaks" in Steinbach. Seven of Winnipeg's 20 courses are open to the public. The picturesque holiday areas anchored by Elkhorn Resort in Riding Mountain National Park, Gull Harbour Resort at Hecla Provincial Park, and Falcon Beach Resort in Whiteshell Provincial Park provide some of the most enjoyable golfing environments you could imagine.

FALCON BEACH GOLF COURSE IN WHITESHELL PROVINCIAL PARK

CANOEING, KAYAKING, AND SAILING

If recreational canoeing is your style, you may enjoy one of the two routes that connect Petersfield and Netley Creek Recreation Park. The novice route winds through scenic parkland with many historical points of interest, while the expert route follows the Red River to a network of channels leading onto Lake Winnipeg.

A longer, historical route winds 128 kilometres (80 mi.) along the Red River from Winnipeg to the lake.

The picturesque Chain Lakes canoe route in Duck Mountain Provincial Park is an easy eight-kilometre (5-mi.) loop that is highly recommended for novices. In the same area, but not recommended for novices, is the Beaver Lake canoe route. This six-kilometre (3.7-mi.) course encompasses five small lakes.

Further north is the Waterhen. This 486-kilometre (302-mi.) route takes you through six lakes and six rivers from Ste. Rose du Lac to Anama Bay on Lake Winnipeg.

CANOEING

Wilderness canoeists and kayakers will prefer the fast, exciting rivers in eastern Manitoba. Popular routes include the Bloodvein, Berens, Hayes, Grass, or Manigotagan rivers. Portages are often necessary.

Canoes and kayaks can be rented at many equipment-rental establishments and at some sporting-goods stores. Water conditions vary during the season; check water levels and forest-fire conditions before setting out.

Major international sailing events are hosted here each year. With its new resort and extensive harbour facilities, Gimli is a hub for sailing. It is also home to some of the finest sailboarding anywhere. Victoria Beach on the other side of Lake Winnipeg is the training site of a world-champion sailboarder.

WINDSAILING AT LAKE AUDY

WATER-SKIING

The three lakes on Manitoba's recreational pro tour are excellent places to ski. The best site is in Portage la Prairie, although access is limited. The other two sites, which are sometimes a little windier but nonetheless offer good water, are Lac du Bonnet and White Lake (on Hwy. 307 in Whiteshell Provincial Park). Ski clubs at each lake can supply a full range of equipment and, for a minimal fee, towing. To make arrangements, contact Penny at Lac du Bonnet (345-2252) or Roger at White Lake (253-8372).

DOWNHILL SKIING, SPRINGHILL

Of course, dozens of other lakes and even some of the rivers provide good skiing if you have the equipment. To ski the Red River from Winnipeg, it is recommended that you put in at Maple Grove Park and go south (upstream).

ALPINE SKIING

The full range of alpine skiing opportunities, from easy to difficult, can be found at most ski hills. A great place for families is Holiday Mountain in La Rivière, which has numerous runs with varying levels of challenge. It is the only ski hill with on-site lodging and limited night skiing (two evenings per week). Springhill, just north of Winnipeg near Birds Hill Park, is a popular area that has skiing every night. The biggest ski area in Manitoba is Mount Agassiz

Ski Resort near McCreary. It has 10 runs, the longest being 1.6 kilometres (1 mi.), and it operates throughout the week. Another good hill is Ski Valley near Minnedosa.

All these ski areas provide rental equipment, ski patrols, ski schools, and individual instruction.

CROSS-COUNTRY SKIING

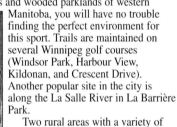

CROSS-COUNTRY SKIING IN ST. VITAL PARK, WINNIPEG

From the mountain-like trails of Whiteshell Provincial Park to the open prairies and wooded parklands of western Manitoba, you will have no trouble finding the perfect environment for this sport. Trails are maintained on several Winnipeg golf courses (Windsor Park, Harbour View, Kildonan, and Crescent Drive). Another popular site in the city is along the La Salle River in La Barrière Park.

Two rural areas with a variety of short, intermediate, and long groomed trails are Grand Beach and Beaudry provincial parks. Other provincial parks also maintain ski-trail systems.

Birch Ski Area, a commercially operated cross-country ski park, is located in Roseisle and offers miles of scenic and challenging trails.

HORSEBACK RIDING

More than 20 riding stables rent horses for short trail rides, and several opportunities exist for overnight horseback trips. The best wilderness and natural areas that offer real back-country trail-riding experiences are in Riding Mountain National Park, and Duck Mountain and Whiteshell provincial parks. Just north of Winnipeg is Birds Hill Provincial Park with its network of riding trails for all levels of skill. The park's riding academy stages guided breakfast and steak-roast trail rides.

HORSEBACK RIDING, BIRDS HILL PROVINCIAL PARK

SWIMMING

A long stretch of sandy beach on the east side of Lake Winnipeg, appropriately named Grand Beach, is fantastic for swimming. Victoria Beach is nearby. On the other side of the lake, Winnipeg Beach offers a similarly grand experience. Other popular swimming beaches include St.

Malo Recreation Area, Falcon Lake, West Hawk Lake, Spruce Woods Provincial Park, Delta Beach, and Clear Lake in Riding Mountain National Park.

DELTA BEACH, LAKE MANITOBA

BICYCLING

For road touring, a very popular and interesting route begins at Winnipeg's Henderson Highway and follows the Red River north to Lockport and then to Selkirk. The first 17.5 kilometres (11 mi.) are on a scenic bike path, and the remaining nine kilometres (5.6 mi.) are on the paved shoulder of a provincial highway.

Trails for mountain bikes can be found in most provincial parks. Though few have been designated as bike trails, cycling is permitted on cross-country ski trails. Ask for a cross-country ski trail map at the park office. The best areas for mountain biking are Falcon Lake, Sandilands, Spruce Woods, Riding Mountain National Park, Turtle Mountain, and most other provincial parks and recreation areas. A commercial property that accommodates mountain biking is Birch Ski Area near Roseisle.

CAMPING

The range of camping options extends from back-country primitive campsites to fully serviced trailer sites in campgrounds with extended amenities. The *Manitoba Accommodation and Campground Guide* lists 234 campgrounds and provides descriptions of their services.

HIKING

Trails in the Whiteshell Provincial Park area wind their way around rocky outcrops and along swift, clear rivers and streams from one beautiful wilderness lake to another. This is the setting for the strenuous 60-kilometre (37-mi.) Mantario Hiking Trail that connects Caddy and Big Whiteshell lakes.

MANITOBA'S "DESERT," SPRUCE WOODS PROVINCIAL PARK

On this one, prepare for mosquitoes (July and August), wildlife (including black bears), and breathtaking vistas.

Interpretive trails of varying distance are found in most provincial parks. Two that are particularly interesting are the Cedar Bog Self-guiding Trail in Birds Hill Park and the Ancient Beach Self-guiding Trail at Grand Beach.

For a truly unique and unexpected hiking experience, wander around the Spirit Sands in Spruce Woods Provincial Park. This sandy desert seems terribly out of place in the middle of the fertile prairie.

Riding Mountain National Park's 35 trails include short courses for day use as well as a variety of overnight hikes.

FISHING VACATIONS

JAKE MACDONALD

THE WINNIPEG RIVER NEAR PINE FALLS

With dozens of rivers and 100,000 lakes, Manitoba has an abundance of pristine habitat for pike, walleye, trout, and other prized gamefish. The government publication *Manitoba Fishing and Hunting Adventures* provides an extensive summary of opportunities in the province and suggests where you might catch "the big one." There are numerous outfitters to guide you and supply equipment, if needed. Non-residents do require a fishing license and should become familiar with the catch-and-release program and other limits and regulations.

Generally, Manitoba fishing gets better as you travel north. If you're looking for the ultimate experience, think about flying into a remote resort. There are about a hundred remote fly-in fishing lodges in northern Manitoba, and most offer excellent, professional service. You can connect with your flight into the lodge at the Winnipeg International Airport. It's extremely expensive to operate a

CATCH OF NORTHERN PIKE, WRONG LAKE

fly-in lodge, so first-class fishing trips tend to come with first-class price tags. But these lodges give you the deluxe treatment, with smooth airplane journeys, comfortable cabins, and an experienced guide who can cook a shore lunch equal to any expensive restaurant fare.

Most fly-in lodge operators in the north have adopted catch-and-release fishing, so most lodges have a no-kill policy on all fish except those you keep for shore lunch. (Fish grow slowly in northern lakes, and catch-and-release policies guarantee a future resource for our kids. But aside from that, catch-and-release lakes have the best fish populations, and some smart anglers insist on booking their visits at lodges with catch-and-release policies.)

FLOAT PLANES AT BURNTWOOD RIVER NEAR THOMPSON

If your pocketbook limits you to something less extravagant than a $2,000-$3,000 fly-in fishing trip to Manitoba's remote north, you might consider an intermediate option and travel by car to a drive-in fishing lodge. Every year more roads are pushed into the Manitoba mid-north, and you can drive to resorts in the wilderness areas around Flin Flon, Cranberry Portage, Thompson, or The Pas.

These drive-in lodges offer two types of packages. "American plan" resorts provide all the amenities of a fly-in lodge (meals, the boat, the guide, and the shore lunch). "Light housekeeping" resorts provide accommodation only, and guests supply their own groceries and boats. Each type has its own benefits. Fishermen who aren't pressed for time may prefer driving to a lodge that gives them all the amenities of a fly-in resort, for about $1,500 per week. And anglers who like cooking their own meals and using their own boats may prefer the independence (and lower cost) of a light housekeeping lodge.

If you're an adventurous sort with some time on your hands, you may want to camp. The provincial government maintains a variety of good, clean campgrounds. There are dozens of serviced

campsites in remote locations throughout northern Manitoba, and these usually have basic amenities such as showers, boat-launching ramps, and barbecue pits. Unserviced campsites are simpler yet, but they normally offer better fishing. If you bring a canoe, look for a campground with no boat-launching ramp. Lakes that have no ramps experience little or no fishing pressure.

RAINBOW FALLS, WHITESHELL PROVINCIAL PARK

In northern Manitoba, camping out means staying in country that pretty much resembles the stereotypical Northland: evergreen forests, blue lakes, and rolling ridges of bare granite and birch woods. In southern Manitoba the landscape looks more like everyone's image of the lonesome prairie. On the prairie, anglers focus on rivers rather than lakes. But that doesn't mean the fishing is less spectacular. The Red River regularly produces some of the largest walleyes in North America. The October migration of so-called "greenback" walleyes attracts serious anglers from across the continent. Ten-pound (4.5-kilogram) walleyes are fairly standard, and every year specimens in the 15-pound (6.8-kilogram) class are weighed and released. The Red also produces more whopper channel catfish than any other river in North America, and some excellent local guides provide full-service fishing trips for both species.

HECLA PROVINCIAL PARK

CULTURAL LIFE IN WINNIPEG

MELINDA McCRACKEN

MAINSTAGE AT THE WINNIPEG FOLK FESTIVAL

For a regional prairie city, Winnipeg has an exceptionally rich cultural life. Festival follows festival all summer; in fall, the activity moves indoors and continues non-stop until spring. The winter season comprises literally hundreds of events that lure audiences out of their homes on dark snowy nights.

This whirlwind of activity is the result of years of hard work and strong traditions in classical music, theatre, and dance. Geography, history, and politics combine to create this vibrancy in Winnipeg.

Geographically, Winnipeg is in the middle of nowhere, isolated from other centres by miles of trackless wasteland. It's an incubator for ideas. We know if we want things to happen, we have to make them happen ourselves.

Historically, in the early 20th century, Winnipeg was the main Canadian centre between Toronto and Vancouver. The city had 21 millionaires in 1919. These merchant millionaires had gone to concerts in the east and had contact with art and music. People had expectations; they aspired to cosmopolitanism. If culture was not available here, they would force-feed it into existence.

Politically, there are two traditions in Winnipeg. The conservative tradition is rooted in the Ontario Orange business elite that defeated Louis Riel. The socialist tradition rose out of the waves of British, Irish and Scottish immigrants, working-class and labourist, who sailed from Great Britain in the early part of the century and came to Winnipeg. These socialists, together with the left-wing

MANITOBA THEATRE CENTRE

Jewish immigrants who settled in Winnipeg's North End, established their own tradition.

As the conservative and socialist traditions in Winnipeg are reflected geographically in the South End and the North End, so they are reflected culturally in the Royal Winnipeg Ballet and the Contemporary Dancers, in the Winnipeg Symphony Orchestra and the Winnipeg Folk Festival, in

the Manitoba Theatre Centre and the activist Popular Theatre Alliance of Manitoba.

But these once sharply defined traditions are now blurred by other factors. In the past decade, thousands of Native people have moved from northern reserves into Winnipeg, giving it the largest Aboriginal population of any city in Canada. Winnipeg has many other ethnic groups — French, Poles, Ukrainians, Italians, Filipinos, Germans, and West Indians. The latest immigrants are from El Salvador, Guatemala, Somalia, Ethiopia, and Eritrea. Struggling Native people and immigrants often start and support their own cultural organizations.

And there's also a tradition of excellence. The Royal Winnipeg Ballet (see p. 84) set a precedent for this. The first professional ballet company in Canada, it was founded in 1939 and achieved international status in the 1950s. The Contemporary Dancers, one of Canada's first modern dance companies, built on the ready-made dance audience when it was founded in 1964. You can attend its performances from September through early June.

LATINORAMA FESTIVAL IN WINNIPEG'S OLD MARKET SQUARE

Winnipeg's tradition of excellence is apparent in its music. Groups such as the Manitoba Chamber Orchestra, Winnipeg Chamber Music Society, Virtuosi, and MusikBarock offer concert series. The Winnipeg Symphony Orchestra performs from September until May. In 1990, WSO conductor Bramwell Tovey and composer Glenn Buhr established the du Maurier Arts Ltd. New Music Festival, held annually in January. New-music composers work within the institutions of classical music. They include minimalists, serialists who are adherents of Viennese composer Arnold Schoenberg's 12-tone system, neo-romantics, and composer/performers such as Alexina Louie who have incorporated world music into their compositions. The New Music Festival has tapped into a young audience that makes the connection between new music and experimental rock.

GroundSwell, an avant-garde new-music group whose season runs from October until May, has featured solo performances such as "The Stein Way," in which pianist/composer Diana McIntosh plays a Steinway grand while uttering snippets from the poems of Gertrude Stein.

Performances of folk music take place from September through May at the West End Cultural Centre, a Portuguese church converted into a hall with a labour flavour.

The Manitoba Opera offers fully staged opera productions, and concerts by artists such as American bass star Samuel Ramey. Performances are held from November until April at Winnipeg's two newly furbished historic theatres, the Walker and the Playhouse, and at the Centennial Concert Hall.

Winnipeg is a strong theatre town, and has a number of first-rate companies. The Manitoba Theatre Centre was the first regional theatre in North America. It offers six plays on its Mainstage from October through April, ranging in 1994-95 from *Hamlet* to David Mamet's *Oleanna*. Its alternative theatre, the Warehouse, produces four riskier plays, which in 1995 included gay playwright Brad Fraser's *Poor Superman*. The Warehouse season runs from October through February. Prairie Theatre Exchange offers plays with a Manitoba focus, often dealing with historical themes and often written by local playwrights, such as *Thirteen Hands* by Pulitzer Prize winner Carol Shields. You can see PTE productions between September and March.

THE PRAIRIE THEATRE EXCHANGE

Since 1992, First Nations people have started three theatre companies. The Red Roots Theatre stages plays of trials and treaty signings. Heritage Proud offers dancing, drumming and singing in traditional costumes, while the Prairie Buffalo Theatre, whose director is Métis, produced a play based on the Highland Clearances whose Scottish peasants emigrated to Canada and became the Selkirk Settlers.

Theatre Projects offers three original one-act plays by local playwrights between September and March. The Popular Theatre Alliance of Manitoba produces issue-oriented plays. Its season runs from September until June. Primus Theatre, a theatre of movement, is based on the work of Denmark's Odin Teatret. Its six actors rehearse five hours a day and are totally committed to this avant-garde theatre of physical expression.

The Winnipeg Jewish Theatre presents plays with

(continued on page 85)   83

THE ROYAL WINNIPEG BALLET

MELINDA McCRACKEN

Founded in 1939 by two British ballet mistresses, Gwyneth Lloyd and Betty Farrally, the Royal Winnipeg Ballet (RWB) was the first professional dance company in Canada, and is the longest continually operating ballet company in North America.

The RWB embodies the regal and most glittering traditions of classical ballet. It has developed a reputation for versatility, excellence, and a captivating style. In 1953, Queen Elizabeth II granted the company royal status. It established an international reputation in the 1950s under artistic director Arnold Spohr. Now, under the direction of William Whitener, its 32 dancers and 16 musicians tour the world with full-length classics and one-act ballets.

The RWB presents four to five programs from September through May at Winnipeg's Centennial Concert Hall,

ELIZABETH OLDS AND ALEXEI RATMANSKY IN *DEUCE COUPE IV*

ranging from classics such as *Swan Lake*, *Sleeping Beauty* and *The Nutcracker* to fresh contemporary masterworks. Recent productions include Balanchine's *Pas de Dix*, Mark Godden's *La Princesse et le Soldat*, Robert Joffrey's *Pas des Déesses*, Sir Frederick Ashton's *Les Patineurs* and *Five Brahms Waltzes in the Manner of Isadora Duncan*, and Antony Tudor's *The Lilac Garden* and *Dark Elegies*.

Artistic director since 1993, Whitener was formerly a leading dancer with the Twyla Tharp Dance Company in New York. He has worked with both Mikhail Baryshnikov and Margie Gillis, and has choreographed dance, opera, and musicals. In 1995, the RWB became the first company to mount a work by Tharp, presenting her *Deuce Coupe IV*, which expressed the flavour of the beat generation.

EVELYN HART IN *ESMERALDA PAS DE DEUX*

In 1983, ballerina Evelyn Hart, partnered by the late David Peregrine in the modern pas de deux *Belong*, became the first Canadian to win a gold medal at the International Ballet Competition in Varna, Bulgaria, as well as the rarely awarded Certificate of Exceptional Artistic Achievement. Hart has been hailed for her interpretations of the classic ballerina roles, especially in *Swan Lake*, *Giselle*, *Romeo and Juliet*, and *Onegin*. In addition, she has received world acclaim for her performances of contemporary ballets, notably in Jiri Kylian's *Nuages*, in Norbert Vesak's *Belong*, and in Jerome Robbins' *Other Dances*, with Manuel Legris. Her charming presence has been captured in the National Film Board documentary *Moment of Light* by filmmaker Gordon Reeves, and she has been awarded the Companion of the Order of Canada and several honorary doctorates.

Jewish content from September until May, and the francophone company Le Cercle Molière presents plays in French in St. Boniface between October and April.

The St. Norbert Arts and Cultural Centre is located on the site of an old Trappist monastery. SNACC's young artists are experimental multi-media people interested in collaborative art. The group has programmed many delightful outdoor events — even belly dancing — on the aesthetically stunning site, and hosts avant-garde performances, installations by visual artists, and readings year-round. Its concerts in the monastery ruins have the atmosphere of European *son et lumière* productions. In summer 1994, SNACC produced the outdoor community play *Travois*, based on events during Louis Riel's time. Hundreds of volunteers acted and sang outdoors in the dew and scent of smudges on August evenings.

Winnipeg is known for its filmmakers. The Winnipeg Film Group has won international acclaim for the animations and quirky films produced by members such as Guy Maddin, who directed the bizarre part-talkie *Tales from the Gimli Hospital*. Its Cinematheque theatre, located in the Artspace building at the corner of King and Bannatyne, programs the latest independent art films year-round. This is where you'd go to see films by Atom Egoyan or Krzysztof Kieslowski.

TALES FROM THE GIMLI HOSPITAL

Artspace also houses Video Pool, where a whole crew of young artists makes videos. Their work is first-rate and lots of fun. Call Video Pool to find out about events.

A good place to see visual art is the Winnipeg Art Gallery, a modernist building made from Tyndall stone. The building is shaped like a boat; you can run your hand down the sharp "prow," where the two exterior walls of the building's triangle meet. The gallery has good permanent exhibits, particularly of Inuit carvings and traditional silver, and exciting travelling exhibits. It sometimes shows work by local painters such as Ivan Eyre, Eleanor Bond, and Kevin Mutch.

THE WINNIPEG ART GALLERY

Musicians give jazz performances on the penthouse level. There's an open-air sculpture garden and an excellent restaurant.

On exhibit in another sculpture garden, in Assiniboine Park, are sculptures by the late Ukrainian sculptor Leo Mol. The figures of animals, children and young women are dark, simple and lovingly made.

The Brian Melnychenko Gallery on McDermot is a magnificent warehouse space where works by Wanda Koop and Esther Warkov are shown, along with major paintings by other top artists. Plug-In and Ace Art are two good independent galleries that display local artists' video and experimental electronic and computer installations. Artspace houses the Floating Gallery, a photography gallery with regular exhibits. Artspace's Main/Access Gallery displays work by local artists and craftspeople.

The work of craftspeople and potters can be purchased at Craftspace in the basement of Artspace, in the gift shop at the Winnipeg Art Gallery, and at the Leonard Marcoe Gallery. Jordan van Sewell makes cunning ceramic newts who drive chubby little cars or sit in shiny puce-coloured chairs while seemingly pondering metaphysical questions. There's the celebrated lacy pottery of Barbara Balfour, and the exquisite jewellery of David Rice, available in his shop at River and Osborne. Native crafts are available at Northern Traditions in Polo Park Shopping Centre, and Inuit crafts at Northern Images in Portage Place.

WINNIPEG CRAFTS: CERAMIC BOWL BY VALERIE METCALFE (TOP), AND *LAST STAGES III*, CERAMIC SCULPTURE BY DOUG SMITH

There are many writers in Winnipeg. The Underground Cafe and the Heaven Art and Book Cafe frequently host readings by poets such as Patrick Friesen, Patrick O'Connell, Di Brandt, or the Native poet Annharte. Check with the Manitoba Writers' Guild for information. Winnipeg is the home of several small presses, among them Turnstone (literary), Moonprint (women), Blizzard (plays) and Pemmican (Métis and Native books). Good places to find books by Manitoba writers and publishers are McNally Robinson Booksellers, Mary Scorer Books, and the Heaven Art and Book Cafe.

Winnipeg's francophone community lives in St. Boniface. In February St. Boniface erupts in the sounds of fiddling and clogging when it celebrates the annual Festival du Voyageur. Residents dress up in raccoon hats, traditional red shirts and moccasins, tie braided *ceintures fléchées* around their middles, and go forth to drink, dance, build ice sculptures, and run dog teams on the river.

In winter, there's a rich smorgasbord of concerts and exhibitions in winter. When Winnipeggers get going, not all

of them go shopping. Instead, they get up and play, sing, dance, act, paint, write, or pick up a Hi-8 camcorder and whir away. For, on 30-below evenings, with the windchill factor at 2,000, what else is there to do?

SUMMER FESTIVALS

RANDAL MCILROY

The civic and provincial tourist boards offer a number of guides listing the many events that take place throughout and beyond Winnipeg during the summer festival season, and there is always a wave of festival coverage in the Winnipeg media.

CHILDREN'S ENTERTAINMENT

Festival season in Winnipeg kicks off in June with the Winnipeg International Children's Festival, featuring an eye-opening variety of music, dance, theatre, and hands-on entertainment for children, from native son Fred Penner to vaudeville. The event is held at The Forks National Historic Site, and you'll find plenty to see and do on the grounds and in the

SCENES FROM WINNIPEG'S LATINORAMA FESTIVAL

THE WINNIPEG
INTERNATIONAL
CHILDREN'S
FESTIVAL

nearby Forks Market. This festival offers some of the best in international entertainment, and you don't have to be a parent to appreciate what you'll see here.

MUSIC AND THEATRE

Winnipeg's first adult attraction of the season is the Jazz Winnipeg Festival, held later in June in a variety of locations. Since its founding in 1990, the festival hasn't always followed through on its trumpeted themes. However, it has been successful in drawing people out not only to the formal evening shows — where the roster has included Branford Marsalis, Sonny Rollins and Shirley Horn — but also to such free outdoor events as the daily noon-hour show downtown and an all-day, open-air show Saturday in historic Old Market Square. If you want a picture of the local jazz scene, try going to clubs, where the local representation is stronger. Check out such weekly events as Mardi Jazz, held Tuesday nights at the Franco-Manitoban Cultural Centre, for a showcase of the city's best homegrown jazz players.

Music plays a part in the annual Red River Exhibition, which begins at the end of June and offers free concerts daily in Winnipeg Stadium, adjacent to the midway. The emphasis is on the rides and the games, however, and if you're looking for local colour you won't find it here.

Live entertainment as the glue binding a wider experience is the theme of the Winnipeg Folk Festival (see pp. 90-91), and this also applies to the Winnipeg Fringe Festival in July. What began in 1988 as a weekend of brave new theatre has become a 10-day carnival with up to 100

FRINGE FESTIVAL
PARADE

productions mounted across more than half a dozen downtown venues. With a roster that spans professional companies and absolute beginners alike, the quality curve is extreme, and media hyperbole tends to err on the side of advertising. However, patience, planning, and an open mind can pay off. If your tastes are more traditional, save your ticket money for Rainbow Stage, a roofed but otherwise open venue in Kildonan Park offering two family-palatable musicals per summer. Gimli is one of Manitoba's most popular resort towns. It hosts two major music festivals, Sun Country Jamboree for country fans in July, and Sun Fest for the rock audience in

August (with the latter, beware exuberant recreational drinking). Both attract major acts from Canada and the U.S., and both are held at Gimli Motorsport Park.

FOOD

July in Winnipeg is the time for A Taste of Manitoba, a kind of giant al fresco buffet that features samples from more than 30 restaurants. The setting is downtown in Memorial Park, and the samples are temptingly priced.

HERITAGE FESTIVALS

Summer is when Manitoba's ethnocultural diversity becomes more than a catch phrase. Various summer events across the province offer their own insights into the social fabric, from Italian to Mennonite.

TRADITIONAL ICELANDIC DRESS AT GIMLI

The province's Scottish lineage is one cause for celebrations. In late June, The Forks is host to the Scottish Heritage Festival. In addition to tests of might, there are piping, drumming, and highland dancing. Selkirk hosts the Manitoba Highland Gathering in July, reflecting the town's Scottish origins. Events include everything from strong games (such as caber tossing) to sheep shearing.

Blackorama Reggae Festival kicks off Winnipeg's heritage celebrations late in July, with three days of local and visiting acts. This is an event that draws its audience from the city's entire spectrum of citizens (as compared, say, to the predominantly young, white crowds at rock concerts). Early August sees the Caripeg Caribbean Carnival Festival, notable for the annual street parade with the most exotic — and often erotic — costumes this side of Mardi Gras.

During the August long weekend, the town of Gimli hosts the Icelandic Festival of Manitoba, otherwise known (albeit with difficulty) as *Islendingadagurinn*. The Icelandic heritage is strong in this province, and Gimli is the largest Icelandic community beyond Iceland itself. Look past the plastic Viking helmets so popular here at this time of year, and you'll find much to enjoy.

The biggest heritage festival is Folklorama, a two-week August celebration numbering more than 40 national pavilions throughout Winnipeg, all offering indigenous food, entertainment, and displays. Some people argue that

YORK BOAT RACES AT GIMLI'S ICELANDIC FESTIVAL

Folklorama has become too big (the pavilions now operate on staggered schedules, each pavilion running only one week, to forestall overkill), and increasingly there are complaints that the resolutely apolitical event promotes a shallow concept of

(continued on page 92)   89

THE WINNIPEG FOLK FESTIVAL

RANDAL MCILROY

INTERNATIONAL FOOD VILLAGE AT FOLKFEST '93

The Winnipeg Folk Festival began modestly in 1974 as a one-time event marking Winnipeg's centennial. Now the early-July gathering at Birds Hill Provincial Park, just northeast of Winnipeg, is an integral part of Manitoba's summer. From Thursday night's opening concert to the farewell singalong on Sunday, the fields are alive with music, spectacle, and people, with 38,000 attending the 1994 event. As fans will tell you, this is a community — during festival weekend the site is the fifth-largest population centre in the province — and music is only the biggest part.

The music is as varied as the people, and neither is as conveniently rooted in sandals and protest songs as media coverage suggests. Long gone are the days when electric instruments were banned; folk music is not always one singer and one guitar. In any given year you're as likely to hear American gospel, African jazz, or Jewish klezmer. The festival deliberately plays lightly on stars, following an egalitarian approach, but such stars-to-be as Bruce Cockburn played here before the greater public caught on. One main stage is reserved for night-time variety-concert bills. During the daytime, smaller stages set in open fields or nestled in wooded pockets of the park hold single-artist concerts, jam sessions, and workshops.

While experienced fans — and some have been regulars since festival one — rush to mark their ground early for the evening shows, a little time with the official program guide will enable you to develop a personal schedule that's both energizing and humane. The first thing to keep in mind is that with more than 100 acts and 150 hours of concert programming, you can't hear it all. The second is to beware the elements. Shade and shelter are at a premium, an important consideration when the sun is high, when the evening winds blow chilly or, as has been known to happen, when the rain slashes. Be sure to bring extra layers of clothing and a hat, and for goodness' sake don't let small children run naked when the sun is hottest. A medical team is on site.

There are good reasons to stay mobile. A crafts village on the site offers a range of goods from local and visiting artisans, and its quality is increasing yearly. A music store run in a tent by Home Made Music (a division of the Folk Festival) is enormously popular and a great place to pick up recordings of favourite stage acts. One area of the site is set aside for performances and activities for children. The International Food Village caters to almost every taste, and the park itself offers a beach and plenty of room to wander if you want to get away from the festival crowds.

In recent years, festival organizers have endeavoured to make the event as pleasant as possible for all listeners. The camping zones, for example, are subdivided into loud and quiet areas. (The loud zone tends to be the scene for all-night parties.)

PARACHUTE TOSS AT THE FOLK FESTIVAL

multiculturalism. Yet the best productions are enchanting, and if you enjoy tasting an array of exotic dishes drawn from many of the world's cultures, you'll be delighted with the offerings at Folklorama pavilions.

There are a number of summer events mounted by, and honouring, Manitoba's First Nations and Métis populations. The many traditional pow-wows offer a chance to learn more about a hitherto ill-covered aspect of Manitoba life, without the carnival hoopla. Moreover, the growing success of a North American touring circuit for professional dancers and musicians ensures strong performances. Program guides

SCOTTISH HERITAGE FESTIVAL AT THE FORKS

available from the tourist boards are essential for the whole story, but gatherings to keep in mind are the Roseau River Pow-wow (late June in Roseau River), Peguis Treaty Days and Pow-wow (Peguis Reserve, mid-July), Sioux Valley Pow-wow (Sioux Valley, mid-July), Long Plain First Nation Pow-wow (Manitoba's largest, held in late July in Portage la Prairie), and Opasquiak Indian Days (late August, The Pas). Activities vary, but generally include traditional drumming, singing, dancing, and moccasin games. In late July, St. Laurent is the site for Métis Days, featuring fiddling, jigging, square dancing, and traditional costumes.

The last Winnipeg festival of the season is Oktoberfest, held for a week in September at the Winnipeg Convention Centre. Bavarian music and entertainment are the draw. Drinking is rather popular as well, and you can expect some raucous high spirits.

STAMPEDES AND AGRICULTURAL FAIRS

A perennial strong draw is the Manitoba Stampede and Exhibition, held in late July in Morris. One of the major stops on the rodeo circuit, the Morris stampede attracts top cowboys and chuckwagon racers. As well, the event features a midway and agricultural exhibitions. Agricultural fairs abound in Manitoba in the warm weather, attracting visitors with country cooking and history. Two to watch for are the Winkler Harvest Festival and Exhibition (entertainment ranges from horse shows to tours of local Mennonite-colony villages) and the Morden Corn and Apple Festival (a free stage, gospel entertainment, midway and more), both in August.

FOOD

MARION WARHAFT

THE FORKS MARKET

While there are restaurants in many Manitoba towns and cities, Winnipeg offers the most, and most varied, dining experiences. These range from savoury ethnic specialties in simple surroundings to sophisticated cuisines in elegant establishments (see Listings section).

Goldeye, probably the most famous local product featured on menus, is a rich, delicately flavoured fish that is always smoked and served either simply filleted with a lemon wedge, in vinaigrette sauce, or as a hot entrée. Somewhat similar, but coarser (and less expensive), is tullibee, a lake herring that is also invariably smoked. Pickerel (also known as walleye pike) is a superb fish. Lean and sweet-fleshed, it is usually simply sautéed and, to best preserve its subtle flavour, served

THE KELEKIS RESTAURANT IN WINNIPEG'S NORTH END

sauceless. Local char is another fine product that is baked, grilled, or smoked. Probably the most abundant product of our lakes is whitefish, also important for its "golden caviar." Processed with no colouring or preservatives other than salt, this fine luxury caviar is exported all over the world.

Manitoba's fabled winters produce lean lamb with a protective layer of outside fat. The meat is tender and mild-flavoured.

The bison is Manitoba's emblem. Pasture-raised bison (which resembles ultra-lean beef) frequently turns up on menus, most often as burgers. A growing number of game farms supply pheasant, grouse, and wild boar to fine restaurants, where they are cooked in both classic and modern fashions. They may be accompanied by Manitoba's genuinely "wild" wild rice, most of which is naturally grown in clear lakes instead of paddies.

Much Manitoba food is a reflection of the province's many immigrant groups, and ethnicity is the hallmark of many small restaurants. Chinese restaurants abound all over the city. They offer everything from anglicized dishes to authentic provincial cuisines and an infinity of dim sum. From Asia there are also Vietnamese, East Indian, Japanese, Korean, Thai, and Philippine restaurants. Italian restaurants run the gamut from small family trattorias to fine dining establishments.

There are particularly high concentrations of restaurants in Corydon Avenue's Little Italy, Osborne Village, St. Boniface (the French quarter), and the Exchange District, where many are housed in restored historic buildings.

THE FORKS MARKET

At The Forks Public Market, a number of self-service booths feature Caribbean, Greek, Italian, Ukrainian, and Vietnamese cooking, as well as English fish and chips and standard Canadian fare. Fresh produce is also sold from stalls there, much of it local in season. A cheese specialty store stocks a rare Oka-like cheese, which is made by Trappist monks in Holland, Manitoba. You can also buy the superb Dairyworld natural cream cheese, an essential ingredient in the best of the city's renowned cheesecakes.

Festivals such as Folklorama, A Taste of Manitoba, and the Festival du Voyageur offer an informal atmosphere in which to sample different foods (see pp. 87-92). Also, ethnic

foods are featured at festivals elsewhere in the province, most prominent among them Dauphin (Ukrainian), Gimli (Icelandic), and Steinbach (Mennonite). The International Food Village at the Winnipeg Folk Festival offers dishes from many nations.

Many towns have farmers' markets on weekends, and market gardeners' stalls dot certain roads. The most comprehensive and picturesque market is in St. Norbert (almost a suburb of Winnipeg), where you can buy products from all over the province, such as buckwheat or sunflower honey, boar meat, farmers' sausages, perogies, homemade breads, jams, and raspberry juice.

THE FORKS AND UPPER FORT GARRY

RANDY R. ROSTECKI

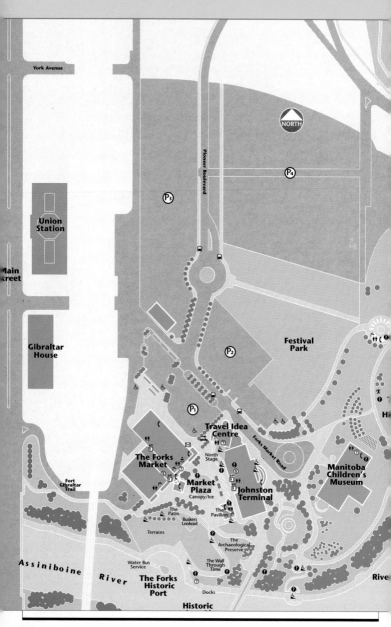

The area east of Main Street and south of Water Avenue, at the junction of the Red and Assiniboine rivers, is Winnipeg's birthplace. The land is now divided between The Forks National Historic Site, which is Manitoba's newest

THE ASSINIBOINE RIVER AT THE FORKS

national historic park, and The Forks Renewal Corporation. The latter area is a bustling place that has become one of Winnipeg's most popular attractions for locals and visitors alike. Among the things you'll find inside the refurbished historic buildings are specialty boutiques, restaurants, a market where you can buy fresh produce and meats, the Manitoba Children's Museum, and the Manitoba Sports Hall of Fame. The Forks National Historic Site is primarily those sections of land to the north of these buildings, a vacant area under which lies a rich archaeological past.

Winnipeg's origins can be largely attributed to Aboriginal trade and social activities at this site. Abundant archaeological evidence has demonstrated that the area was a gathering spot in pre-contact times for both local inhabitants and outsiders. With the arrival of Europeans, the Native gathering places and trails were used by traders wishing to exploit the fur resources of the region. The construction of Fort Rouge by explorer La Vérendrye during the 1730s pointed to a possible future for the Forks area.

This potential was not recognized for another 70 years. In the early 1800s Thomas Douglas, the Scottish Earl of Selkirk, established a colony that was centred around the forks of the Red and the Assiniboine. Though initially met with indifference by the Hudson's Bay Company (HBC)

UPPER FORT GARRY GATE

and violent hostility by the HBC's fur-trade rivals, the North West Company (NWC), the Red River Settlement eventually prospered in a small way, despite being destroyed by the NWC in 1815-16. To counter Fort Douglas, which was built at the foot of present-day George Avenue by the settlers, the NWC built Fort Gibraltar. Both forts were dismantled by their opponents between 1815 and 1817. Once peace was restored after 1817, the Fort Gibraltar site remained a trade centre. It became Fort Garry after the HBC and NWC united in 1821.

Fort Garry was badly damaged by the great flood of 1826, which inundated the low-lying Forks area. In 1835, construction of a new Fort Garry began on higher ground

UNION STATION

to the southwest of the old site. The new fort, called Upper Fort Garry to distinguish it from the Lower Fort Garry that was built north of present-day Winnipeg during the same decade, became the paramount trading facility of the Hudson's Bay Company. Indeed, because the fort was at the centre of settlement for Rupert's Land (the name by which western Canada was then known), it also served as the legislative and judicial capital. After the HBC bought back the land grant from the Selkirk interests at the Red River Settlement in 1835, the company assumed the mantle of government, ruling via the Council of Assiniboia and the governor of Rupert's Land, who was housed at Fort Garry.

Upper Fort Garry was doubled in size in 1852-54. After Manitoba became a Canadian province in 1870, the fort was the seat of government for the District of Assiniboia. Today, all that remains of it is the Upper Fort Garry Gate, located south of Broadway off Fort Street. This gate was built during the 1852-54 expansion as a rear entrance to the fort, for the fort's front portal faced the Assiniboine River.

The rise of Winnipeg doomed the fort as a commercial centre. A land boom during 1881-82 increased realty values in this area, and the walls of Upper Fort Garry were taken down and used for foundation stone. The fort's property was divided into two streets and 60 building lots at that time, but the remainder of the complex was not razed until 1888. What became Winnipeg's first heritage battle began that year for the retention of the gate, by then a derelict structure. In 1897 the Hudson's Bay Company donated the gate and six lots to the City of Winnipeg for use as a park. The gate has been restored several times since then.

And what of the Red River Settlement itself? For the first two decades of the colony's existence, the settlers quietly farmed the generous tracts of land that had been allotted to them by Selkirk. A new generation after 1835 began to question the HBC's governance of the colony, largely because of the HBC's proprietorship of the land and because of restrictions that reinforced the HBC's trade monopoly. The former factor served to keep the size of the colony's population in check, as tracts were either granted to retiring HBC employees or sold to existing farmers. The presence in the settlement of retired employees possessing trade know-how led initially to much illicit trade and smuggling as these individuals sought to operate outside HBC law. The prize was a growing trade with St. Paul, Minnesota, after the 1830s. The HBC sought to forbid these operations, sometimes in a forceful and high-handed manner.

HOTEL FORT GARRY

The end of the HBC's monopoly came in 1849 with the Sayer Affair, which saw a Métis trader on trial at the HBC courthouse outside the walls of Upper Fort Garry. A show of force by his brethren caused the collapse of the case against Sayer. After this, "free traders" at The Forks prospered on a small scale. To some degree, the free traders offered better terms than the HBC and thereby stole its business. By engaging in the St. Paul trade, they could bring cheaper goods to the settlement than the HBC could supply from its English sources. Cart traffic between Red River and St. Paul was gradually replaced by small steamboats that were used on the rivers after 1859. These steamboats led to increased business for the free traders. By 1862 the first land boom was under way at Red River, with at least one trader advertising lands for sale instead of goods.

In the 1860s and 1870s, gradual development north of The Forks marked the beginning of downtown Winnipeg. After 1872, the Forks area was partially subdivided into building lots. However, flooding of this low property and

MANITOBA CHILDREN'S MUSEUM

nearby industries to the north created an area of urban poverty and vice on what became known as the Flats. Few people ventured onto the Flats, largely because of the presence of houses of prostitution.

This area changed substantially after the arrival of the railway lines in Winnipeg. A station and luxury hotel, now demolished, were built at the southwest corner of Water Avenue and Main Street. Later, a group of railways expanded the "East Yard" into a terminal that took in much of the Flats. Between 1907 and 1911 a large railway depot,

JOHNSTON TERMINAL

the Union Station, was built on Main Street, and between 1911 and 1914 the elegant Fort Garry Hotel was erected nearby on Broadway.

The decline of the East Yard began with the construction of new Canadian National Railway shops elsewhere. After the mid-1960s it was relegated to the status of a storage yard, with only the CNR's Union Station to keep the area nominally

alive. Most buildings at the yard were allowed to deteriorate, and many were demolished by the railway. The recent rehabilitation of the area began in the late 1980s and continues to the present time.

Today, The Forks Market occupies two brick stables that were built by the railway companies during 1909 and 1910. Later they were converted to garages. Now you can dine here, or shop for fresh foods, clothing, and hand-crafted merchandise.

The nearby Johnston Terminal presents more shopping opportunities. This four-storey warehouse building was constructed by the CNR between 1928 and 1930. There is a Tourism Winnipeg office on the third floor. Another excellent place to obtain travel information is the Explore Manitoba! Travel Idea Centre attached to the northwest end of this building. Travel counsellors are available to help you.

The Manitoba Children's Museum occupies a renovated building with a blue roof. This structure, built in 1888, was originally the shops of the Northern Pacific and Manitoba Railway. The museum features three galleries, a "real" television studio, and interactive video exhibits.

Outdoors at The Forks, the Wall Through Time presents a linear display of events that took place here over the centuries. You can take a water-taxi tour along the Red and Assiniboine on the Splash Dash Water Bus or stroll along the Riverwalk to the Manitoba Legislative Building.

From July to October the Public Archaeology Program enables you to work alongside professionals in the recovery, cleaning, and cataloguing of artifacts. Advance registration is required for hands-on participation.

THE FORKS

THE WALL OF TIME AT THE FORKS

THE OLD DOWNTOWN AND WAREHOUSE DISTRICT

RANDY R. ROSTECKI

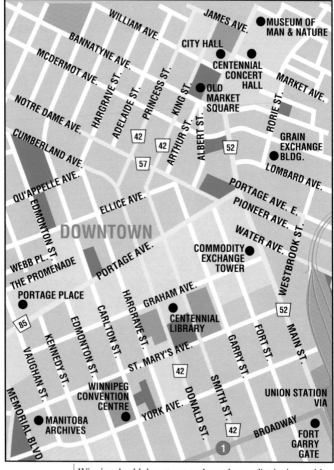

Winnipeg's old downtown and warehouse district is roughly the area that extends east and west from Main Street, north of Portage Avenue. Today, it is an eclectic mixture of the old and the new. Rows of terra-cotta and cut-stone commercial and warehouse buildings line many streets, their exteriors virtually unaltered since the late 1800s and early 1900s. They

stand in marked contrast to modern structures such as City Hall and the Centennial Concert Hall. Although much of the city's commercial activity has moved to newer parts of downtown and to the suburbs, this district remains the heart of Winnipeg's cultural life. Numerous restaurants and specialty shops contribute to the area's flavour.

The origins of Main Street as a thoroughfare go back as far as the 1820s, when it was the King's Road or King's Highway. It connected river-lot farms that made up the Red River Settlement. The long, narrow, waterfront lots began at the Red or Assiniboine rivers, which were the early transportation corridors for the settlement, and usually extended about 3.2 kilometres (2 mi.) inland. The names of many owners of these early lots — Bannatyne, McDermot, Ross, and others — are perpetuated as street names in this area. Many of these streets served to demarcate property boundaries.

WAREHOUSE AND
EXCHANGE DISTRICT

**FORMER ASHDOWN
WAREHOUSE**

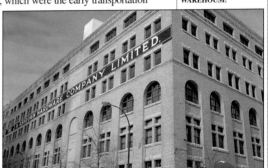

After the 1830s, when the two Fort Garrys were built (Lower Fort Garry north of present-day Winnipeg and Upper Fort Garry south of Broadway), the King's Road became increasingly known as the Garry Road, because it connected the two places. This name persisted until the mid-1870s, when Main Street was formalized in usage.

In 1862, a trader built a store at what is now the northwest corner of Portage and Main. He was seeking to exploit the east-west Portage (la Prairie) Trail that extended westward across the prairies to the trading posts of the Hudson's Bay Company. A second entrepreneur built a house and store at the same intersection in 1863. The men's buildings established the corner, and this marked the beginning of downtown Winnipeg.

**NORTHWEST
TRAVELLERS'
BUILDING**

The area along Main Street north of the Portage Trail grew slowly through the 1860s, and by the time of the Riel Resistance of 1869-70 (see pp. 44-47), a compact village of about 200 people lived and did business there. Through the 1870s, the area

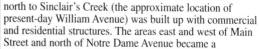

TOAD HALL TOYS

north to Sinclair's Creek (the approximate location of present-day William Avenue) was built up with commercial and residential structures. The areas east and west of Main Street and north of Notre Dame Avenue became a residential district that housed both operators and employees of the Main Street businesses.

The positioning of the Dominion Post Office at the northeast corner of McDermot and Main in 1874 and the construction of the City Hall and Market buildings at William and Main during 1875-77 served to anchor Winnipeg's business district.

A western Canadian land boom was one result of the building of the Canadian Pacific Railway during the early 1880s. This led to the erection of many western towns such as Brandon, Regina, and Calgary, and also led to the beginning of wholesaling efforts by Winnipeggers who had formerly been retailers but who now smelled greater profits over larger areas. Some of the earliest Winnipeg warehouses were constructed during this building boom. Main Street between Graham Avenue and the City Hall evolved into a central business district containing no dwellings. To the west and east of Main was the beginning of a warehouse area.

The ensuing recession halted the growth of the warehouse district. A few buildings went up between 1882 and 1895, but the area was mainly one of aging housing. Here and there, large brick warehouses loomed over their smaller neighbours.

ROYAL ALBERT ARMS

During a huge immigration and wheat boom from 1896 to 1912, Winnipeg began to emerge as a manufacturing centre. Its population quadrupled between 1901 and 1911. Along Main Street, the aging buildings of the first boom — and their predecessors — were replaced by many of the fine bank buildings that still exist today.

At the same time, however, high realty values along Main Street prompted retailers to begin moving to Portage Avenue, where land was cheaper. This happened primarily after 1905, although some large commercial buildings had existed along Portage as early as 1882.

The city developed as a wholesaling concern during the boom. Wholesalers stayed on the streets around Main, and the residential portion of the warehouse district was largely eliminated.

The boom collapsed after 1912, and a period of war and retrenchment followed. The increased importance of other cities with their own wholesaling and retailing functions, such as Regina, Saskatoon, Calgary and Edmonton, curbed the rise of Winnipeg's fortunes. While Winnipeg firms continued to operate branches in those cities, Winnipeg's control gradually lessened during the 1920s. In addition, many local companies were bought up by eastern Canadian businesses that either shut them down or made them into branch operations, diminishing their importance. Bankruptcies felled other firms.

The result was vacant warehouses. A solution to the problem came with the rise of the garment industry during the 1920s. By the 1940s, the garment trade dominated the old warehouse district. But in the 1960s these structures began to face another crisis. The rise of industrial parks in the suburbs, with modern plants and convenient transportation access, made many of the inner-city garment facilities obsolete. The old warehouse district began to experience vacancy rates that equalled those of half a century before. By the mid-1970s,

CENTENNIAL CONCERT HALL

demolitions and negligence had taken their toll on the once-proud warehouses.

Meanwhile, a series of bank failures and mergers from the 1920s to the early 1960s resulted in a reduced need for elegant premises, and many structures passed from the ownership of banks. The virtual abandonment of many Main Street buildings by the early 1970s attracted the attention of developers, and redevelopment brought the destruction of many potential heritage sites.

The area was ultimately saved through the intervention of the local heritage movement. The Historic Winnipeg Restoration Area was created by a city by-law in 1978 and subsequently renamed the Exchange District. Since then the area has been streetscaped, and many premises have been rehabilitated.

Today, much activity takes place in the Exchange District, in both historic and modern buildings. The current City Hall, erected in 1963-65, is a landmark at the corner of Main and William. Across Main Street is the Centennial Concert Hall. This is where you would attend performances by the Winnipeg Symphony Orchestra, the Manitoba Opera, or the Royal Winnipeg Ballet.

Directly north of the concert hall is the Manitoba Museum of Man and Nature, at 190 Rupert Avenue. The Boreal Forest Gallery and the Urban Gallery are two of its seven display areas that explore man's relationship with the world. You can board a full-size replica of the *Nonsuch*, a

MANITOBA MUSEUM OF MAN AND NATURE

ketch that sailed from England to Hudson Bay in 1668 in search of furs. The museum also houses the Planetarium and the hands-on Touch the Universe Science Gallery. In July and August, the museum is the starting-point for one-hour walking tours of the Exchange District.

Two blocks north of the museum, at 184 Alexander Avenue East, is Oseredok, North America's largest repository of Ukrainian cultural and historical artifacts. It contains a museum, art gallery, library, and archives.

PANTAGES PLAYHOUSE THEATRE

Pantages Playhouse Theatre is south of the Centennial Concert Hall, at 180 Market Avenue. The original structure was built in 1913, when Winnipeg was prominent on the touring circuits of many theatrical chains such as the Pantages and the Orpheum. It was expanded in 1991-92. The 1,475-seat theatre is now a "rental house" that offers a variety of entertainment.

East of the Pantages Theatre is the Manitoba Theatre Centre, at 174 Market Avenue. The MTC is regarded as one of

GRAIN EXCHANGE BUILDING

the leading regional theatres in North America. Six plays are performed here each year. The MTC's alternative Warehouse Theatre is situated further north, at 140 Rupert Avenue.

South of the MTC, at the northeast corner of Lombard Avenue and Rorie Street, is the Grain Exchange building. It was constructed in stages between 1906 and 1928 and was once the largest office building in Canada. The Winnipeg Grain Exchange — particularly its trading floor — was the heart of western Canada's wheat economy, and this building was the scene of intense activity for almost 75 years. It is still occupied by some offices of the grain industry.

ARTSPACE BUILDING

West of Main Street at the corner of Arthur and Bannatyne is Artspace, Canada's largest artist-run centre. It houses three galleries, the Cinematheque theatre, and a variety of arts groups. The building was constructed in 1900 and 1903, renovated in the mid-1980s, and reopened as Artspace in 1987.

St. Boniface

Lucien Chaput

St. Boniface, Winnipeg's francophone neighbourhood, is the geographical focal point of French-language culture in Manitoba. A Roman Catholic mission founded in 1818, St. Boniface was incorporated as a town in 1883 and as a city in 1908, and was amalgamated to the City of Winnipeg in 1971.

The best way to experience its early history is in February at the Festival du Voyageur, western Canada's largest winter festival, because the origins of St. Boniface lie in the fur trade of the late 18th and early 19th centuries, when numerous French Canadians settled in the Northwest with their Aboriginal wives. Their children would form a distinct people, the Métis. Led by Louis Riel (see pp. 44-47), they would be instrumental in the creation of Manitoba in 1870.

A nucleus of institutional buildings took root along Taché Avenue after the arrival, in 1818, of two French-Canadian Roman Catholic priests. On land given to them by Lord Selkirk, they built a modest chapel and residence. From this would

FESTIVAL DU VOYAGEUR, ST. BONIFACE

107

ST. BONIFACE BASILICA

rise a parish, an archdiocese, and a city all called St. Boniface. Between 1818 and the early 1870s, St. Boniface was essentially an agricultural and rural parish. Historical panels along the Taché Promenade, on the east bank of the Red River across from The Forks, explain the early history of St. Boniface and the Red River Colony.

The St. Boniface Cathedral (190 avenue de la Cathédrale) and its cemetery still occupy the original 1818 site. The present cathedral is the fourth, built in 1972 inside the ruins of the third.

The western wing of the Archbishop's Palace (151 avenue de la Cathédrale), just across the street from the cathedral, dates back to 1864. The eastern wing was constructed in 1899. This is one of the oldest surviving stone buildings in western Canada.

South of the cathedral is the former Grey Nuns convent, whose construction dates back to 1846. A fine example of Red River (post on sill) construction, it is the largest squared oak log building in North America. Since 1968 it has housed the St. Boniface Museum (494 avenue Taché).

To the east, behind the cathedral, is the Collège universitaire de Saint-Boniface (200 avenue de la Cathédrale), a former Jesuit college and now the francophone campus of the University of Manitoba. The former Collège building was destroyed by fire in 1922. All that is left of it is the kitchen (607 Langevin). With the arrival of

ST. BONIFACE COLLEGE

French-Canadian settlers to the new province after 1870, a small village took root north of Provencher Boulevard. The Royal House (147 Provencher) was built in 1875. It was owned by the founder of western Canada's first French-

language newspaper, *Le Métis*, whose first issue appeared in 1871. The Bernier House (265 Provencher) was built in 1882. Its grandeur underlines the fact that Provencher Boulevard was then the address of choice for the St. Boniface elite.

The early 1900s were a period of urban boom in Manitoba. The population of St. Boniface grew from 2,019 residents in 1901 to 11,021 just 15 years later. At the turn of the century, French-speaking European immigrants began arriving in St. Boniface. The Belgian Club was founded in 1905, and moved into its building (407 Provencher) in 1908.

Across from the Belgian Club, at the southwest corner of Provencher and DesMeurons, is the Centre culturel franco-manitobain (340 Provencher). It is the home of many cultural associations, including Le Cercle Molière, Canada's oldest theatre company, and l'Ensemble folklorique de la Rivière-Rouge, a traditional dance troupe that hosts the French-Canadian pavilion of Folklorama each August. It has a boutique where you can buy works by Franco-Manitoban artists and artisans.

The building at 321 avenue de la Cathédrale is the former site of the St. Joseph Academy. Built in 1912 and run by nuns, the academy was the feminine equivalent of St. Boniface College. Across from this building is Provencher School (320 avenue de la Cathédrale), whose origins date to

1818. It started teaching young boys in the present building in 1908.

Gabrielle Roy, author of *The Tin Flute*, was educated at St. Joseph Academy. Her parents' home still stands at 375 rue Deschambault. Built in 1905, it was the setting for her novel *Street of Riches*.

THE NORTH END

KRYSTYL NICKARZ

**GUNN'S BAKERY,
SELKIRK AVENUE**

A vast area, the traditional North End of Winnipeg is bordered by Enniskillen and Logan avenues from north to south, and the Red River and Arlington Street from east to west. Walking down North End streets nowadays, it is hard to imagine what they must have been like when the area was first settled back in the late 1870s, when Winnipeg was still a prairie town eager to become a big city. Simple wooden buildings lined the mud roads. The horse and buggy were the main means of transportation, and the majority of the settlers who resided here were of Anglo-Saxon origin.

As the years passed, individuals prospered and a middle-class neighbourhood developed. Then, almost as soon as the area had begun to establish itself in this particular direction, the progression changed course. The coming of the Canadian Pacific Railway to Winnipeg in the 1880s and the arrival of a huge wave of eastern- and central-European immigrants during the early part of the 1900s altered the North End drastically. Thousands of Slavic (Ukrainian, Polish, and Russian), Jewish, German, and Scandinavian people

CP RAILWAY TRACKS
SURROUND THE
NORTH END

immigrated to Manitoba from 1896 to 1914, many of them settling in the North End. This section of the city went from a newly prominent neighbourhood to an over-populated, over-developed, culturally diverse working-class area in a short time span. It was almost as if the North End became a city unto itself.

The routing of the CPR main line through Winnipeg resulted in a huge economic boom for the city. Now a railway city, Winnipeg became a prosperous, energetic place. But the new railway, located in the North End, eventually overwhelmed this area by its very presence. The size of the railway yards made many people neighbours of the CPR. And CPR employees flooded the district, causing a large population increase that resulted in a lack of adequate housing. Because of an absence of bridges, which would have allowed traffic over or under railway lines, North Enders were virtually confined to their own area. This also meant, of course, that residents from other parts of the city had difficulty reaching the North End.

Many different ethnic groups, including the British, combined to create the North End of yesterday and today. They created their own bustling commercial district, which was, to a large extent, on Selkirk Avenue. This would eventually become one of Winnipeg's legendary streets. Everything from department stores (Oretzki's) to bakeries (Gunn's) to movie theatres (The Palace Theatre) could be found on Selkirk.

Eventually bridges and railway crossings were built, but the North End remained, for the most part, its own unique neighbourhood. Although its progression has slowed somewhat in the past few years, its residents maintain a strong sense of community that, when combined with the North End's culture, will continue to make this one of Canada's notable neighbourhoods well into the 21st century. An integral part of the North End's future is its recent group of settlers, the Natives, who are the new life of the area. An example of this is the Indian Family Centre (470 Selkirk Avenue). Murals designed by the late Jackson Beardy decorate the walls of the

JACKSON BEARDY MURAL ON THE INDIAN FAMILY CENTRE

centre and symbolize hope for universal peace and harmony. Unfortunately, Beardy died prior to painting these murals. The project was completed by the students of R. B. Russell

**HOLY TRINITY
CATHEDRAL**

**ST. JOHN'S
CATHEDRAL**

**ASHKENAZI
SYNAGOGUE**

Vocational School.

Much of the North End's cultural landscape can be observed through its various churches, cathedrals, and synagogues. The Holy Trinity Cathedral (1175 Main Street) is Greek Orthodox and features art by famed Winnipeg artist Leo Mol. The Manitoba branch of the Ukrainian Museum of Canada is housed here as well. Byzantine domed, this is a Winnipeg landmark. Further down Main Street is St. John's Cathedral (135 Anderson Avenue just off Main). An Anglican cathedral, it is the burial site of many notable Winnipeg pioneers. The St. Nicholas Ukrainian Catholic Church (737 Bannerman Avenue) is worth seeing for its brilliant stained-glass window and large mosaic of Christ. The St. Vladimir and Olga Cathedral (94 McGregor Street) holds over 1,000 people, and

more of Leo Mol's art adorns the walls here. Another notable place of worship is the Ashkenazi Synagogue (297 Burrows Avenue). A historical site synagogue is now used mainly for holiday periods. It is worth a visit because of its beautiful interior. A newer structure, the B'Nay Abraham Synagogue (235 Enniskillen Avenue) offers more Jewish history in the form of a Holocaust memorial.

To gain more insight into the history of the North End, browse through some of the museums. Ross House (140 Meade Street) was built in 1854 and was the first post office on the Canadian prairies. It is also one of the oldest examples of Red River log frame construction in Manitoba. Seven Oaks House (Rupertsland Avenue) goes back to 1851 and is furnished in accordance with the period.

To completely immerse yourself in the past and present of the North End, participate in a guided walking tour of Selkirk Avenue. The popular tours are conducted during July and August, and are organized by the Selkirk Avenue Business

Association. For more information contact Sylvia Todaschuk at 586-3445 or 586-2720. Whether you choose to join a tour or explore on your own, there is a multitude of sights to observe. Some Selkirk Avenue businesses go back many years. The Wonderful World

of Sheepskin (579 Selkirk) is a good example of the tradition on this street. For over 40 years, this family business has specialized in high-quality, custom-made sheepskin and accessories. It manufactures and exports inter-nationally, and is one of four manufacturers worldwide producing sheepskin dust-wands. Oretzki's Family Shoes Ltd. (493 Selkirk) is another old tradition. Originally Oretzki's Department Store, this was the place to find every type of item imaginable, particularly durable, inexpensive underwear. This North End institution opened in 1911. Another long-standing Selkirk Avenue store is the Original Fashion Shop (509 Selkirk). This well-kept establishment has been selling quality women's fashions for over 40 years. If your tastes lean more towards food than fashion, enjoy a treat from one or all of Selkirk Avenue's five bakeries. The famous Gunn's Bakery (247 Selkirk) is the oldest on the street, and is also kosher. Doughnut fans can feast at the Donut House (500 Selkirk), and Polish specialties are available at the Honey Bee Bakery (284 Selkirk). Buns World Bakery (600 Selkirk) offers Italian goodies, and Dilit's Pan-De Buns Bakery and Grocery (735 Selkirk) features Filipino breakfast bread.

When all your food is eaten, stroll around Kildonan Park (2021 Main Street). One of Winnipeg's most beautiful spots, Kildonan Park offers several leisure activities year-round. During colder months (December through March), enjoy cross-country skiing, ice skating, and tobogganing. Warmer months bring fragrant formal gardens, the refreshing feeling of the outdoor swimming pool, and leisurely walks along riverside trails lined with some of the oldest and largest trees in Winnipeg. As well, summer in Kildonan Park is synonymous with Rainbow Stage, Canada's longest-running outdoor theatre. It has presented professional musical productions for over 40 years. The theatre presents two musicals a season, one in July, the other in August. Ticket prices are reasonable.

If you prefer the music of a slot machine to the strains of Broadway musicals, enjoy games of chance at the McPhillips Street Station (484 McPhillips Street). Try your luck at traditional bingo, various types of slot machines, or state-of-the-art video games such as poker, blackjack, or keno.

113

Manitoba's Legislative Building

Marilyn Baker

The Manitoba Legislative Building

Stairway at the Manitoba Legislature

Manitoba's Legislative Building, at the corner of Broadway and Osborne in downtown Winnipeg, is an unusual and surprising public structure. The murals inside the building, the statuary both inside and out, and the opulent architecture are the creations of artists from all over Europe, the United States, and Canada.

It is actually Manitoba's third legislative building. Around 1908, local politicians and businessmen began to push for a new structure to house Manitoba's expanding government. The Manitoba Association of Architects declared that it would be "the most magnificent in Canada." An Empire-wide design competition was held, and the president of the Royal Institute of British Architects came to Winnipeg to select the winners — architects Frank W. Simon and Henry Boddington of Liverpool, England.

Construction began in 1913. The building's first contractor worked on the job until 1915 but was then jailed for improprieties associated with the contracts. The premier, Sir Rodmund Roblin, and his ministers were forced to resign and put on trial, but they weren't convicted. Now seriously behind schedule, the building was finally finished in 1919 and dedicated on July 15, 1920. Originally estimated to be affordable at $2 million, its price had skyrocketed by 1920 to around $9 million. (Sir Rodmund's son Duff would later enter politics and return to the site of his father's shame. He became premier in 1958.)

You can stroll through the Legislative Building every day of the year except Christmas. In July and August, free tours are offered Monday through Friday between 9 a.m. and 6:30 p.m. Other months, tours are by reservation only (call 945-5813). Visitor parking is at the north of the building off Broadway.

As you approach the main entrance, which faces Broadway, notice the six ionic columns supporting a pediment filled with emblematic sculpture. Created by British sculptor Albert Hodge, the sculpture is an allegory of Dominion. A full explanation of its meaning, along with details of other highlights in the building, is provided in a booklet available from the Travel Manitoba office just inside the entrance, on the left. This office is an excellent source of other tourist information as well.

The building's exterior and part of its interior are indigenous Tyndall stone, dotted with fossils. Note the interior trim, made from Marsano marble, and the Tennessee marble floors. At the base of the main staircase are wonderful life-size statues of bison by sculptor Georges Gardet of Paris. Climb the staircase and gaze at the mural by Frank Brangwyn, an English artist, over the entrance to the legislative chamber. It is a memorial marking Canada's participation in World War I. Inside the chamber you will see paintings of Virtues and Vices in classical robing, by American artist Augustus Vincent Tack. The paintings of naked figures flanking the central apse memorialize Canada's courageous soldiers. Lemoine Fitzgerald, a local

MANITOBA LEGISLATIVE ASSEMBLY CHAMBER

TOP AND LEFT: CARYATIDS AND BISON SKULL MOTIF IN THE MANITOBA LEGISLATURE'S GRAND STAIRHALL

GOLDEN BOY STATUE BY GEORGES GARDET ATOP THE LEGISLATURE DOME

artist who became principal of the Winnipeg School of Art and who replaced one of the original members in the Group of Seven, is rumoured to have worked as an assistant on the Tack murals. After leaving the legislative chamber, notice the caryatids (sculptured female figures used as columnar supports) that look down on the entranceway hall from the second landing.

When you've finished exploring the building's interior, take some time to look at the statuary outside the east and west entrances, and elsewhere on the grounds. On the east portico are Lord Selkirk and French-Canadian explorer La Vérendrye; on the west are General Wolfe and the Marquis of Dufferin, third governor-general of Canada. Other

LEGISLATURE AT CHRISTMAS

statuary includes Ukrainian hero Taras Shevchenko, poet Robert Burns, and the Next-of-Kin Memorial, a work by female sculptor

THE ROTUNDA

Marguerite Taylor in honour of those who fell in World War I. Note the

statue of Queen Victoria facing Broadway. It was created by English sculptor George Frampton and placed in front of the previous legislative building in 1904. Its cost was $15,000.

Finally, cross Broadway and look back at the Golden Boy on top of the building's dome. This is another work by French sculptor Georges Gardet. A youthful figure striding through space, it more than any other part of the building has become Manitoba's symbol.

ARCHITECTURAL TREASURES

RANDY R. ROSTECKI

BANK OF MONTREAL BUILDING, PORTAGE AVENUE AT MAIN STREET

One legacy of Winnipeg's former economic prominence is a number of architectural treasures. Many buildings constructed in the early 1900s reflected Winnipeg's role as an important commercial centre. You can find some of Winnipeg's finest early-20th-century architecture within easy walking distance of the corner of Portage Avenue and Main Street.

The Bank of Montreal at the southeast corner of Portage and Main is an outstanding example. Constructed during 1910-13, it is the sole surviving historic structure at western Canada's most famous intersection. With its Corinthian-capped columns and temple styling, it marked the southern end of Winnipeg's bankers' row, which began near City Hall. Its architects were McKim, Mead and White of New York; associate architect was John Semmens. By setting the building back from the street and positioning it at an angle, they created a plaza in front of this bank that wasn't present in its rivals north of Portage Avenue. The styling of this structure and its imaginative use of the corner site made it an instant landmark. Its spectacular interior and exterior have been sensitively renovated since 1976.

North of Portage Avenue at 395 Main Street (on the east side of Main) is the Bank of Hamilton building, constructed during 1916-18. American-born architect John D. Atchison

FORMER BANK OF HAMILTON AND FORMER BANK OF COMMERCE BUILDINGS

executed this edifice in a stretched Italian palazzo style, with bronze grille-work on the main entrance. This building has a handsome banking hall. Like its neighbour at 389 Main Street, which was the Canadian Bank of Commerce, it symbolized the importance of banking to economic society. This section of Main Street had been part of the central business district since the 1860s and had evolved into the banking row. Atchison was also the architect of the National Bank building at northeast Main and Lombard.

NATIONAL BANK BUILDING

Farther north, at 441 Main Street, is The Bank cabaret. This structure was built during 1906-07 as the western headquarters of the Imperial Bank. It has been said that architects Darling and Pearson modelled this building on the Bank of England in London. A merger of the Imperial Bank with the Canadian Bank of Commerce in 1961 turned this into a branch of the Canadian Imperial Bank of Commerce. This small neoclassical building later sat vacant for many years.

The Confederation Building, once occupied by the Confederation Life Association, is at 457 Main Street. With its curved façade and cornice, this 1912 steel-framed office structure makes a dramatic impression. Architect J. Wilson Gray gave the skyscraper a Renaissance treatment with the white terra-cotta façade. Confederation Life moved to a less prominent building in 1960, and eventually this structure was abandoned and sold for the value of its site. New owners and tenants renovated it and made it viable. The selling of life insurance was a highly profitable economic enterprise in 1912, as this building indicates.

Across Main Street, at the southwest corner of Main and William, is the Royal Bank building. Constructed during 1903-05, this is western Canada's oldest surviving skyscraper. Its architects were Darling and Pearson. Demonstrating its faith in the future of western Canada, the Quebec-based Union Bank transferred its national headquarters to Winnipeg in 1912. This building functioned as the head office of the Union Bank until its merger with the Royal Bank in 1925. Until 1966 this was the Royal Bank's western headquarters. Now abandoned, this building has a doubtful future.

Toward the south is the Ukrainian-Canadian Committee building, at 456 Main Street. Architect Howard C. Stone's Corinthian-capped colonnade and the cast-iron façade behind it have been a visual landmark since this building was erected during 1905-07. The Bank of Toronto occupied the building until merging with the Dominion Bank in 1955. This structure was then sold to the UCC, which has

CONFEDERATION LIFE BUILDING

ROYAL BANK BUILDING

ROYAL BANK BUILDING

maintained it in its original state.

The Leon Brown Building at 460 Main Street was formerly occupied by the Royal Bank of Canada. Built using the side walls of the 1900 Imperial Dry Goods Building, this Renaissance-inspired façade building with its heavy bronze grille-work was one of the smaller, though prominent, banks in the area. Sold after the Royal Bank moved to the Union Bank building at Main and William in 1925, this structure has been generally well kept by its private owners.

LEON BROWN BUILDING

WINNIPEG PARKS

CATHERINE MACDONALD

By the early 1890s, Winnipeg's city fathers wanted to transform the sprawling, unattractive railway town into a commercial metropolis rivalling Chicago. To be like Chicago, Winnipeg needed green spaces. The Winnipeg Parks Board, created in 1893, set about providing a system of neighbourhood parks and planting American elms on the wide grassed boulevards of every street.

Winnipeg's boom, lasting from 1900 to 1913, enabled the Parks Board to add significantly to the tally of neighbourhood parks and to secure two large suburban parks, Assiniboine Park in the south end and Kildonan Park in the north.

SHAKESPEARE AT THE ASSINIBOINE PARK PAVILION

Both are designed in the English Landscape style popular in 19th-century North America. Kildonan Park is a particularly pleasing example, showing how this style was adapted to the prairie. Taking advantage of the slightly undulating Selkirk Creek bed, it is more heavily treed than Assiniboine Park. In 1954 Kildonan Park became home to Rainbow Stage, an open-air summer theatre that offers musical classics.

A DRIVE THROUGH ASSINIBOINE PARK

Assiniboine Park, which opened in 1909, was the first and largest of the two early suburban parks.

From downtown, drive west on Portage Avenue to Maryland Street, turn left, and cross the Maryland Bridge. Take an immediate right from the bridge onto Wellington Crescent, where wheat barons and real-estate magnates built their stately houses. Wellington Crescent ends at the east gate of Assiniboine Park.

Inside the park, on Centre Drive, enjoy the combination of curving driveways and broad tailored lawns with trees in the distance. Without anything remotely resembling a hill to add visual interest, Frederick Todd, the park's designer, had to rely on the lawns to lead the eye across a vista where he would provide trees, shrubs, or a garden as a focal point. Before you reach the pavilion, turn right onto Perimeter Drive. Just after the footbridge is a small parking lot. Park opposite the duck pond and take a moment to enjoy the swans and ducks.

On the parking-lot side of the road is the entrance to the English Garden where the "boy with the boot" fountain stands guard. This was called the Informal Garden when it was created in 1927, to distinguish it from the Formal Gardens. It is informal in the sense that its drifts of flowers are planted asymmetrically and are allowed to run together in a way that

BOY WITH BOOT SCULPTURE IN ASSINIBOINE PARK

LEO MOL SCULPTURE GARDEN

looks more natural than the Formal Gardens' geometrically-laid-out beds.

Just west of the English Garden is the Leo Mol Sculpture Garden. Bronze and stone sculptures by artist Leo Mol are arranged along red gravel pathways with comfortable oak benches. A pool with goldfish and water lilies stands in front of the chrome-and-green-glass Leo Mol Gallery. Inside are smaller-scale sculptures and paintings.

Return to your car, continue around Perimeter Drive heading west, and make a left turn towards the zoo parking lot. Since it deserves a full morning or afternoon, you may want to visit the zoo another day. A professional zoological facility with a wide range of native and exotic animals, it is especially appreciated by children. The Tropical House and the Kinsmen Discovery Centre are highlights.

From the zoo parking lot, continue around the park on South Drive past the miniature train track and the junction with Conservatory Drive. The conservatory, with its permanent exhibition of tropical plants and other floral displays, will be on your left and is well worth a visit. (The conservatory parking lot entrance is on Centre Drive just east of the pavilion.) Stay on South Drive heading east and pass the Formal Gardens at the main gates of the park. Remain on South Drive and continue around to the junction with Centre Drive. Turn left there and approach the pavilion.

The pavilion was built in 1930. With its Tudor half-timbering and roof line reminiscent of thatching, it evokes the ambiance of an English village. Inside are concession stands and a wonderful but under-used large hall space. The pavilion has become a beloved landmark.

ENGLISH GARDEN AT ASSINIBOINE PARK

To exit the park, take Conservatory Drive south to Corydon Avenue or take Centre Drive back to the east gate.

MANITOBA'S REGIONS

THE INTERLAKE

ROGER NEWMAN

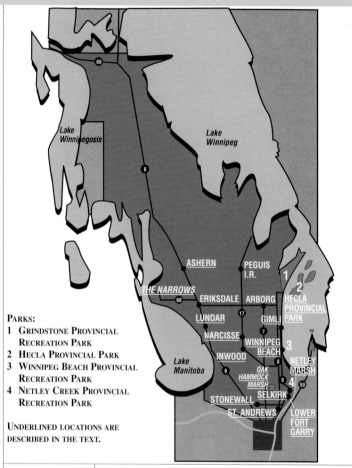

Lake Winnipegosis

Lake Winnipeg

ASHERN

PEGUIS I.R.

THE NARROWS

ERIKSDALE **ARBORG**

HECLA PROVINCIAL PARK

LUNDAR

GIMLI

NARCISSE

WINNIPEG BEACH

INWOOD

Lake Manitoba

OAK HAMMOCK MARSH

NETLEY MARSH

STONEWALL **SELKIRK**

ST. ANDREWS

LOWER FORT GARRY

PARKS:

1 **GRINDSTONE PROVINCIAL RECREATION PARK**
2 **HECLA PROVINCIAL PARK**
3 **WINNIPEG BEACH PROVINCIAL RECREATION PARK**
4 **NETLEY CREEK PROVINCIAL RECREATION PARK**

UNDERLINED LOCATIONS ARE DESCRIBED IN THE TEXT.

ST. ANDREW'S ANGLICAN CHURCH

The Interlake region, which begins just north of Winnipeg, is nestled between two large bodies of fresh water, Lake Winnipeg on the east and Lake Manitoba on the west. Lake Winnipeg is the 11th largest lake in the world. Lake Manitoba is only one-third the size of Lake Winnipeg, but still has 190 kilometres (120 mi.) of beaches along its coastline. These two lakes make the Interlake a haven for summer cottagers, owners of pleasure boats, and tourists.

ST. ANDREWS

Drive north on Winnipeg's Main Street and remain on this artery after it becomes Highway 9 at the city limits. After entering the Rural Municipality of St. Andrews, continue a few miles on Highway 9 and turn right at PR 238, also known as the River Road. It will take you back in time to

the early days of Manitoba.

Your first stop should be St. Andrew's Anglican Church, which has been used continuously for public worship since it was built in 1849. The oldest stone church in western Canada, St. Andrew's still has the buffalo-hide kneeling benches that were used in the days when parishioners arrived by York boat.

Next door is the St. Andrew's Rectory, which was built in the 1850s as a school to teach trades to Métis bison hunters. Now the restored rectory contains exhibits describing the role of the Anglican Church in the settlement of the West.

Farther down River Road is the Captain Kennedy Museum and Tea House. Completed in 1879, it was originally the home of Captain William Kennedy, a fur trader and Arctic explorer. His study and living room have been redone in period furnishings. You can watch an audio-visual presentation of the district's history and stroll in the terraced English gardens by the water.

Scott House, featuring hand-hewn wood beams and one-metre-thick (3-ft.) walls of local limestone, was built in 1855-56 for Hudson's Bay Company crewman William Scott and his 12-year-old bride. Twin Oaks, now a private residence, was also built in the 1850s as a girls' school for

CAPTAIN KENNEDY HOUSE, RIVER ROAD

THE LOCKS AT LOCKPORT

the daughters of Hudson's Bay Company officers.

The river road eventually winds its way to Lockport, site of the St. Andrews Lock and Dam. The lock, still in use today, was built in 1910. Lockport has developed into a popular recreation area. Fishing is the biggest attraction in both summer and winter. Lockport is also a gem for professional and amateur archaeologists. Digs are frequent,

HORSE-DRAWN BUGGY RIDES AT LOWER FORT GARRY

and artifacts from community and agricultural life dating back 3,000 years are housed in the Kenosewun Interpretive Centre on the east bank of the river.

LOWER FORT GARRY

At Lockport, return to Highway 9 and drive a couple of miles north to the Lower Fort Garry National Historic Park. The lower fort was the walled settlement where the Hudson's Bay Company (HBC) administered the northern Manitoba fur trade in the 19th century.

HUDSON'S BAY COMPANY CAIRN

THE BIG HOUSE, LOWER FORT GARRY

The fort was the creation of Sir George Simpson, governor of the vast fur-trading territory that stretched from the Great Lakes to the Pacific Ocean. He established Lower Fort Garry in the 1830s because he was tired of the flooding and economic problems that the HBC was experiencing at Fort Garry, situated at the forks of the Red and Assiniboine rivers.

The new post became the HBC's most impressive fort in the West. While wood was the material of choice at the other posts, the lower fort consisted entirely of imposing stone buildings inside a stone wall one metre (3 ft.) thick. Masons took five years to build the walls, which feature round bastions at each corner.

Today Lower Fort Garry is North America's oldest still-intact stone fur-trade post. Parks Canada has restored the fort's buildings, gates, and walls. The fort's employees wear period costumes

LOWER FORT GARRY BLACKSMITH

SOUTHWEST BASTION

and impersonate the Red River settlers so that the atmosphere of the 1850s is re-created. When you stroll the grounds, you will meet the governor and his wife, the blacksmith, and the clerks and labourers going about their daily chores.

The governor's mansion is one of the centrepieces at the lower fort. You will also see the chief factor's cottage, the fur loft and sales shop, a blacksmith's shop, a farm that fed the HBC employees and their families, and the Native encampment on the nearby river bank.

Also a must-see are the York boats that were built by the HBC to carry heavy freight on the navigable waters of the West. Each spring, brigades of York boat sailors would set out from the lower fort to carry provisions to the HBC's fur-trading posts throughout the territory. They would return in the fall with their boats laden with furs. There were an incredible number of portages where the heavy boats had to be carried around river rapids.

RED RIVER CART

MARINE MUSEUM, SELKIRK

Concessions to modernity at the fort include the visitor reception centre where you will receive orientation information from parks staff and have the opportunity to take in an audio-visual presentation about the history of the fur trade. The centre has a gift shop and a restaurant.

SELKIRK

Selkirk is the largest community in the region. It is on Highway 9A just beyond Lower Fort Garry. Its early economy was tied to the commercial freight traffic on the Red River and Lake Winnipeg, and it has one of only two lift bridges still operating in North America.

WORLD'S LARGEST OXCART, SELKIRK PARK

Selkirk's maritime heritage is commemorated in the Marine Museum of Manitoba, a collection of half a dozen former lake vessels that stand at the entrance to Selkirk Park. The museum includes such ships as the S.S. *Keenora*, Manitoba's oldest and most beloved steamship, and C.G.S. *Bradbury*, a former federal government patrol vessel.

Selkirk Park covers 115 hectares (284 acres) and includes a wildlife sanctuary, campsites, and a boat ramp. It is the display site for the world's largest Red River oxcart, measuring 13.7 metres (45 ft.) long and 6.5 metres (22 ft.) high.

The Manitoba Highland Gathering, a Scottish festival in early July, draws bands, dancers, and caber tossers from across western Canada.

NETLEY MARSH

After sampling Selkirk's attractions, you can either take Highway 9 straight to the Lake Winnipeg beaches or follow a more scenic route, PR 320, along the Red River to the Netley Marsh.

Netley Marsh is one of the major waterfowl nesting areas in North America. It is at the end of the river road at the point where the Red River enters the lake. Among

RUDDY TURNSTONES ON MIGRATION AT NETLEY MARSH

the largest in the world, it is the nesting area for 18 species of duck, including mallards, pintails, ring-necks, blue teals, shovellers, canvasbacks, and redbacks. You can climb the Breezy Point Observation Tower to view both the wildlife and the sight of the Red meeting the Netley Creek. The creek attracts anglers, who catch northern pike, perch, silver bass, and channel catfish.

To get back to Highway 9, turn around and go to a gravel road, which will take you 6.5 kilometres (4 mi.) west to the village of Clandeboye.

WINNIPEG BEACH

Winnipeg Beach, 76 kilometres (47 mi.) north of Winnipeg on Highway 9, had its beginnings in 1900. The Canadian Pacific Railway was planning to extend its line north of Selkirk and wanted to establish a resort to attract passengers. The company found a beautiful crescent of sand, christened it Winnipeg Beach, and spent $1,000 to purchase the land behind it. The CPR then built a railway station and a dance pavilion. The first passenger train reached the new resort in June 1903.

This started a rush to the beach that reached a peak on Canada Day in 1920, when 13 trains carried passengers from

WINNIPEG BEACH

Winnipeg to the lakeside town. Railway officials estimated that at least 30,000 people travelled to the beach that day.

By that time, Winnipeg Beach had a roller coaster. It was part of a popular amusement park that over the years included penny arcades, dodgem cars, a ferris wheel, and a merry-go-round. During its heyday, the town also had a boardwalk running the length of the beach, a large T-shaped pier, and four hotels.

The two most popular trains were the Moonlight Special and the Daddy Train. The Moonlight Special took young lovers for an evening of dancing at the pavilion, while the morning and evening Daddy Train was full of bread-winning fathers who commuted weekdays while their families spent July and August at the lake.

The early idyllic lifestyle at the beach was brought to an end by the automobile. CPR passenger service to Winnipeg Beach ended in 1961, and the amusement park and dance pavilion were closed in 1964. The Manitoba government subsequently created a beautiful provincial park that runs the length of the Winnipeg Beach waterfront. Town officials are part way through a project to rebuild the historic boardwalk.

Winnipeg Beach is blessed with one of the longest and most attractive sandy beaches in Manitoba. It is also the site of the Boundary Creek Marina. Boundary Creek was the northern boundary of Manitoba from 1870 until 1881. Beyond was the Republic of New Iceland, governed by the first Icelandic immigrants, who had been given powers of autonomy by the Canadian government. New Iceland

GIMLI'S ICELANDIC FESTIVAL

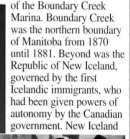

joined Manitoba after a few years and officially became the Rural Municipality of Gimli in 1887. All that remains today is a plaque at Boundary Creek commemorating the former republic.

The Ukrainian Homestead Museum displays artifacts left by the early Ukrainian settlers in the Interlake. The homestead has pioneer buildings, a windmill, a clay bake-oven, and machines and tools used by the settlers in the early 1900s. There are also documents, letters, and photos in the archives section of the museum.

GIMLI

Gimli, 89 kilometres (55 mi.) north of Winnipeg on Highway 9, has made the transition in recent years from a quiet Icelandic fishing village to one of the premier tourist resorts in Manitoba. The community started to change dramatically in 1991 after Gimli's main streets were re-landscaped and the 78-room Country Resort luxury hotel was opened on the waterfront.

In October 1875, the first 200 immigrants from Iceland sailed up the Red River from Winnipeg to make a new home on the shore of Manitoba's biggest lake. They landed at Willow Point, 1.6 kilometres (1 mi.) south of the present Gimli Harbour.

Groups of Ukrainian immigrants started to farm inland in the Interlake around the turn of the century. By 1906, the CPR had arrived in Gimli and the seeds had been planted for a community that is dominated by Icelandic and Ukrainian Canadians.

Gimli's beginnings are commemorated today in the Icelandic section of the Evergreen Library on First Avenue, in the Gimli Museum at the harbourfront, and in a private museum at 127 Fifth Avenue run by retired fisherman Ted Kristjanson.

During World War II, an air base was opened to train British Commonwealth pilots for overseas duty. The base graduated more than 600 pilots who came to Gimli under the Commonwealth Air Training Plan. Today, the main memento of the town's air force past is a T-33 jet trainer mounted on a pedestal near the cenotaph on First Avenue.

The former air force base is the site of the Gimli Motorsport Park, which hosts two music festivals: Sun Country in July and Sun Fest in August. The festivals lure as many as 40,000 weekend visitors with such stars as Tom Cochrane, Pearl Jam, Michelle Wright, Merle Haggard, and Sass Jordan.

GIMLI BEACH

Just as popular is Gimli's annual Icelandic Festival. Always held on the August long weekend, it draws crowds of 30,000 for three days of cultural events, sports competitions, entertainment, rides, and a mammoth parade.

There is a mile (1.6 kilometres) of sandy beach right next to the Gimli Harbour, which boasts the largest wharf in western Canada and is filled with more than 300 pleasure and fishing boats.

A 4.5-metre-tall (15-ft.) Viking Statue on the waterfront at the south end of Second Avenue symbolizes the whole town. It is sculpted in fibreglass. Having a photo taken in front of the statue is a must when you're in Gimli.

GULL HARBOUR RESORT, HECLA PROVINCIAL PARK

HECLA ISLAND

Hecla Island, three hours north of Winnipeg at the end of Highway 8, offers first-class facilities to tourists and boaters. It is the most remote major resort in the Interlake.

The island was settled in the 1870s by the first Icelandic immigrants to Canada. It was the site of a prosperous village until the 1950s. Now it is a provincial park that includes a large hotel, a marina, and a championship-calibre 18-hole golf course.

PELICANS AND GULLS, HECLA PROVINCIAL PARK

The hotel, the Gull Harbour Resort and Conference Centre, offers tennis courts, a miniature golf course, an indoor swimming pool, and a gymnasium. It is close to two white sand beaches set against a background of towering limestone cliffs overlooking Lake Winnipeg. Also in the immediate vicinity are hiking and fitness trails.

Gull Harbour has 213 campground sites and 15 family vacation cabins. The marina arranges boat rentals and water tours of the provincial park, which includes Hecla and a series of other wooded islands with rocky shorelines.

As you approach Hecla, you will arrive first at the pioneer Icelandic fishing village at the south end of the island. Today, the village is a tourist attraction consisting of buildings and homes that have been restored to their original state. These include a general store, a museum, and a fish station where you can learn about the history of the Lake Winnipeg fishing industry.

The Grassy Narrows Marsh, a stop for migrating ducks and geese, is also at the south end of the island. In summer the marsh is the home of 50,000 migrants, including 15 species of ducks, Canada geese, snow geese, and blue geese. The great blue heron and western grebe are also summer residents, as well as the predatory bald and golden eagles. In addition, the marsh provides habitat for muskrats, beavers, foxes, deer, owls, and pelicans. The pelicans nest on granite bedrock about 6 metres (20 ft.) above Lake Winnipeg. Grassy Narrows has a viewing tower where you can spot all these species as well as moose, which roam all over the island.

Hecla is the gateway to Lake Winnipeg's prime cruising areas for pleasure boaters. Within a short distance of Gull Harbour, you can explore hundreds of scenic coves, inlets, and rivers that run into the lake. One of the most interesting spots is nearby Black Island, which is sacred ground to Native people and is well known for its large populations of bears, moose, deer, and red fox.

STONEWALL

Stonewall, just 32 kilometres (20 mi.) from Winnipeg, was served by trolley cars from the capital city in the early

QUARRY PARK, STONEWALL

years of the century. To get there now, drive north on Highway 7 to Highway 67 and turn left.

The community derives its name from the limestone quarries that were the foundation of its economic life from 1882 to 1967. Today the quarries are silent.

The biggest monument to the past is Stonewall Quarry Park at the north end of the main street. Once the site of the major quarries, the park features an interpretive centre where you can see displays about the geology, archaeology, and history of the area. It also has an observation tower from which you can view Canada geese and many other species of birds. The sandy beach at Kinsmen Lake is part of a package of summer attractions that includes nature trails and campgrounds with trailer sites.

GEESE IN LURE CROPS, OAK HAMMOCK MARSH

The past is preserved by the limestone houses, churches, and commercial buildings on many of the town's streets. One of the most impressive buildings is the former post office, which was erected on the main street in 1914. Equally representative of the early days is the Town of Stonewall office, which was built in 1912 as a Manitoba government land titles office.

The flavour of a bygone era can be sampled at the May House Tea Room, 391 Centre Avenue, where you'll find a restaurant and art gallery in a 10-room house that was built in 1896.

Stonewall celebrates its heritage with the Quarry Days festival on the second weekend in August. The town is also the site of a farmers' market that operates on Fridays and Saturdays starting in mid-July.

OAK HAMMOCK MARSH

Oak Hammock Marsh, between Selkirk and Stonewall on Highway 67, is one of the best places in North America to observe marshland wildlife.

The 3500-hectare (8,650-acre) habitat just 30 minutes north of Winnipeg is the home of 260 kinds of birds, 25 species of mammals, and several dozen species of reptiles, amphibians, and fish. It also supports tens of thousands of ducks, geese, and shorebirds during spring and fall migration periods.

SNOWY OWL, OAK HAMMOCK MARSH

The Oak Hammock Marsh Conservation Centre offers wildlife and wetland education programs to the public. It has a 120-seat theatre, large exhibit halls, a craft workshop, and a gift shop. Its programs and courses are changed regularly, and can include everything from bird carving and painting to decoy making and folk art weaving. You can see displays and films and participate in workshops, tours, outdoor programs, and special events.

There are viewing trails, mounds and dikes throughout the marsh, and a long boardwalk takes you to a willow bluff that provides some of the best spots to see songbirds. Added attractions include artesian wells and the largest piece of unbroken tall-grass prairie in Manitoba. To get to the marsh, follow Highway 67 to the Oak Hammock sign. From the sign, there is a four-kilometre (2.5-mi.) drive north into the centre's main parking lot.

INWOOD-NARCISSE

Visitors from many places take Highway 17 to Inwood and nearby Narcisse and Chatfield every spring to see the frenzied mating ritual of the world's largest congregation of garter snakes. Every April, tens of thousands of the red-sided snakes emerge from their winter dens in limestone sinkholes in the district's Narcisse Wildlife Management Area. As many as 12,000 snakes may be seen huddled together in a single pit. Dozens of males twist frantically in "mating balls" around each female. Observation platforms have been erected so you can observe the ritual, which continues until early May. Once it is over, the snakes disperse through the area. They will return in the fall to hibernate for seven months in the sheltered rock crevices below the frozen ground.

RED-SIDED GARTER SNAKE, NARCISSE

Inwood residents have erected a statue of two garter snakes, Sarah and Sam, in a tribute to their principal attraction.

There is plenty of other wildlife in the Narcisse Wildlife Area 116 kilometres (72 mi.) north of Winnipeg. More than 1,100 white-tailed deer gather in winter. If you're patient, you may spot the occasional moose or elk. Common sights are sharp-tailed and ruffed grouse, red-tailed hawks, great horned owls, and scores of songbirds. Hiking trails, open to horse riders, are easily accessible.

Hunters are unwelcome in management areas, but they thrive further north on Highway 17 in the Poplarfield, Fisher Branch, Hodgson, Broad Valley, and Fisherton region, regarded as the best in the Interlake for big game, waterfowl, and upland bird hunting.

THE WEST INTERLAKE

The West Interlake is reached on Highway 6, which runs all the way from Winnipeg to northern Manitoba. Highway

6 is the route to all the Lake Manitoba beaches, which start at St. Laurent only 40 minutes from Winnipeg and run all the way up to Steep Rock.

LIMESTONE CLIFFS AT STEEP ROCK

St. Laurent hosts an annual Métis Days summer festival and is the site of many cottage and beach developments. The next major stop on the highway is Lundar. Close at hand are Lundar Beach and the Swan Creek Fish Hatchery, one of only three in Manitoba.

The Narrows, which connects the south and north basins of Lake Manitoba, offers resorts, camping, and good fishing. Manitoba got its name from The Narrows, which the ancient Cree called "Manitobau" or the "Channel of the Great Spirit."

Ashern is the largest service centre on Highway 6. Northwest of Ashern are the Steep Rock beach and campground, which are being developed into one of the most attractive recreation sites in the Interlake. The first-class beach is set among towering limestone cliffs.

Further north in this excellent fishing and hunting region are the communities of Gypsumville and St. Martin, which offer the last chance for food and fuel before Highway 6 reaches northern Manitoba.

Pembina Valley/ Central Plains

Ellie Reimer

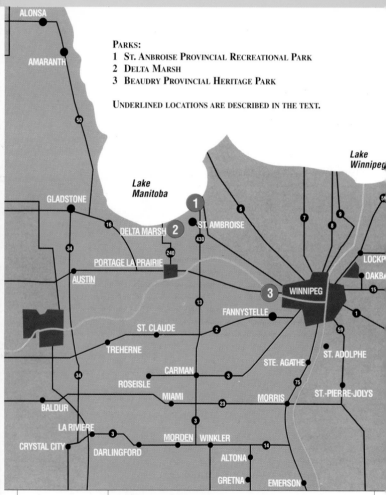

PARKS:
1 St. Anbroise Provincial Recreational Park
2 Delta Marsh
3 Beaudry Provincial Heritage Park

UNDERLINED LOCATIONS ARE DESCRIBED IN THE TEXT.

ALONSA
AMARANTH
GLADSTONE
DELTA MARSH
ST. AMBROISE
PORTAGE LA PRAIRIE
AUSTIN
Lake Manitoba
Lake Winnipeg
WINNIPEG
LOCKP
OAKBA
FANNYSTELLE
ST. CLAUDE
TREHERNE
CARMAN
ROSEISLE
MIAMI
STE. AGATHE
ST. ADOLPHE
MORRIS
ST.-PIERRE-JOLYS
BALDUR
LA RIVIERE
CRYSTAL CITY
DARLINGFORD
MORDEN
WINKLER
ALTONA
GRETNA
EMERSON

PORTAGE LA PRAIRIE

A short drive west of Winnipeg along the Trans-Canada Highway is the city of Portage la Prairie, located near the site of Fort la Reine. The fort was established by French-Canadian explorer Sieur de la Vérendrye in 1738.

Portage la Prairie is very conscious of its place in the history of Manitoba. You can get a sense of that history by visiting Fort la Reine Museum and Pioneer Village, where the fort is a replica of the one built by La Vérendrye. The log

stockade is constructed of round logs 15 to 20 centimetres (6-8 in.) in diameter, standing upright and sunk one metre (3 ft.) into the ground. The stockade encloses a trading post, a blacksmith's shop, and a stable. Surrounding the stockade is the Pioneer Village.

CANOLA FIELDS AND ELEVATOR, DUFRESNE

With a little imagination you can be a trapper, ready to move into the little cabin, typical of many you might have found along the banks of the Assiniboine River. Or you can be a pioneer, newly arrived to settle on the prairie. Several early log and frame houses, a threshermen's

ISLAND PARK

caboose, a school, and other buildings help to recreate the scene for you.

Located in the heart of Portage la Prairie is the scenic area known as Island Park and Crescent Lake. This beautiful park, in an oxbow of the Assiniboine River, is a photographer's haven in summer, with its lush greenery and wildlife. A drive curves around its perimeter and provides access to numerous picnic areas and places to stop and relax or pet the animals. The park is also the home of a sporty 18-hole golf course with grass greens, situated along the shores of Crescent Lake.

Only minutes north of the city is the famous Delta Marsh, one of the most significant natural waterfowl areas in the world. Here, extensive research is conducted on wildlife habitat. International Elderhostel programs run during the spring and fall months at the university field station at Delta Beach.

DELTA MARSH

137

AUSTIN

Situated a short jaunt further west along the Trans-Canada Highway is the town of Austin, home of the Manitoba Agricultural Museum. If you're a steam-engine buff, here's where you can revel in the noise and power of years gone by. Numerous stationary and portable steam engines and other farm-machinery displays are set up on the grounds. At the same site is the Homesteaders' Village, depicting a typical rural community on the prairies.

Walk along the path and enter into a bygone era. You'll come to the railway station, that vital link between prairie communities and the outside world. Life in a rural community revolved around the station, from which flowed mail, necessities, and visitors to the community.

Three houses demonstrate the evolution of housing construction at the turn of the century. The Muir log

VINTAGE TRACTOR AND COMBINES AT THRESHERMEN'S REUNION, MANITOBA AGRICULTURAL MUSEUM

cabin, built in 1879, is the oldest building in the Homesteaders' Village. The Muirhead log house, built in 1885, is more sophisticated than the cabin, and the elegant two-and-a-half-storey Mekiwin Manor, built in 1918, exhibits commendable workmanship and construction for a time when carpentry was still fairly basic.

Reflecting the diversity of religious expression among the pioneers are two church buildings, one Anglican, one Methodist, dating back to the late 1800s. Two schoolhouses, also from the late 1800s, are testimony of the pioneers' emphasis on education.

Other buildings, including a grist mill and an elevator, a post office, a printing shop, a law office, and a harness shop, complete the setting, preserving a vital part of prairie history.

MORDEN

An hour south and west of Portage la Prairie is a pretty little town that the Aboriginals called Pinancewaywinning, meaning "going down to the ford." French fur traders

CANOLA FIELDS

called it Mort Cheval, and the name of the creek running through the town is still the English equivalent, Dead Horse. However, the Canadian Pacific Railway had the last word. It named the town Morden.

Competitive and recreational golfers alike will enjoy the Minnewasta Golf Course in Morden. With its creative landscaping, this 18-hole course provides some of the most challenging golf topography in the province.

Morden's Corn and Apple Festival, held the last weekend in August, is a popular attraction. The free street festival features big-name as well as local entertainment on the outdoor stage, a midway, and free corn on the cob and apple cider for all comers. Vendors and displays line the streets, which are closed to traffic that weekend. Especially popular

CORN AND APPLE FESTIVAL, MORDEN

is the huge farmers' market, where locally grown garden produce, especially corn on the cob and apples, is eagerly purchased.

Morden is home to the Pembina Hills Art Gallery, where local artists display their work. This gallery is part of

CHUCKWAGON RACING, MANITOBA STAMPEDE AND EXHIBITION, MORRIS

Creative Impressions, a self-guided arts and crafts tour featuring galleries in over half a dozen nearby communities.

The Morden and District Museum is a museum of natural history where you will find superbly presented fossil displays, dioramas, skeletal drawings, and artists' conceptions of the birds and animals that existed in this part of the country millions of years ago during the Cretaceous period. Most of the marine fossils were recovered from local bentonite pits.

BULL WRESTLING

Remember the days of one-room schools, oiled floors, double desks, and all grades in the same classroom? Visit the display at the museum for a delightful feeling of *déjà vu*.

Across from the school display you will find an old but well-preserved pump pipe-organ. Your fingers will itch to coax a melody from the keys, but don't touch! It's an authentic church organ, and it's taking a well-deserved rest.

After museums and tours and jostling crowds, it's time to relax. There's no better place than the beautifully landscaped grounds of the Agriculture Canada Research Station, where you can picnic, walk, take pictures or rest, surrounded by manicured lawns, shrubs and hedges, gardens and flower beds.

BRONCO-RIDING

MORRIS

Morris, located 53 kilometres (33 mi.) south of Winnipeg on Highway 75, looks like just another sleepy little prairie town, but watch out! In summer, it comes alive as the host of the Manitoba Stampede and Exhibition, held annually the third week of July. Scheduled attractions include a five-event pro rodeo, ladies' barrel racing, livestock and horse shows, a midway, homecraft displays, a petting zoo, and evening concerts featuring big-name artists as well as local groups.

PARKLAND/ WESTERN REGION

SANDRA FINDLAY

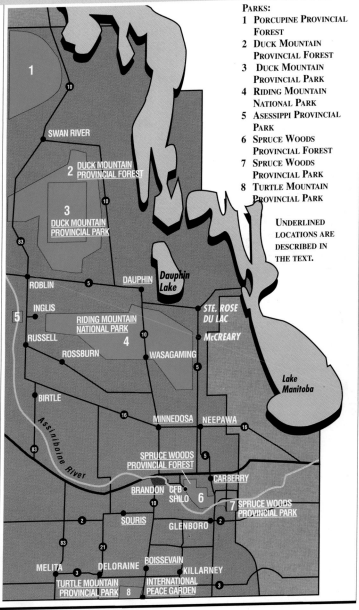

PARKS:
1. PORCUPINE PROVINCIAL FOREST
2. DUCK MOUNTAIN PROVINCIAL FOREST
3. DUCK MOUNTAIN PROVINCIAL PARK
4. RIDING MOUNTAIN NATIONAL PARK
5. ASESSIPPI PROVINCIAL PARK
6. SPRUCE WOODS PROVINCIAL FOREST
7. SPRUCE WOODS PROVINCIAL PARK
8. TURTLE MOUNTAIN PROVINCIAL PARK

UNDERLINED LOCATIONS ARE DESCRIBED IN THE TEXT.

SWAN RIVER

DUCK MOUNTAIN PROVINCIAL FOREST 2

DUCK MOUNTAIN PROVINCIAL PARK 3

ROBLIN

INGLIS

DAUPHIN

Dauphin Lake

STE. ROSE DU LAC

RUSSELL

RIDING MOUNTAIN NATIONAL PARK 4

McCREARY

ROSSBURN

WASAGAMING

Lake Manitoba

BIRTLE

Assiniboine River

MINNEDOSA

NEEPAWA

SPRUCE WOODS PROVINCIAL FOREST

CARBERRY

BRANDON

CFB SHILO 6

SPRUCE WOODS PROVINCIAL PARK 7

SOURIS

GLENBORO

MELITA

DELORAINE

BOISSEVAIN

KILLARNEY

TURTLE MOUNTAIN PROVINCIAL PARK 8

INTERNATIONAL PEACE GARDEN

BRANDON

The major population and service centre for the Parkland/Western region of the province is Brandon. Known as the Wheat City, it was established in 1882. Its location was chosen in 1881 as the first divisional point on the Canadian Pacific Railway west of Winnipeg. The first settlers, Ontario and Maritime Protestants, came by steamboat down the Assiniboine River. The city virtually sprang up overnight.

BRANDON UNIVERSITY

The Bronfman family, one of the world's richest, got its start in Brandon. Ikiel Bronfman began by selling cordwood and frozen fish door-to-door in the city.

A good starting-point for a walking tour of Brandon's historic buildings is the Daly House Museum, located at 122-18th Street, just north of Brandon University. The house is one of the first built in the city. Its owner, Thomas Mayne Daly, was the city's first lawyer and mayor, and the first federal cabinet minister from Manitoba. He arrived in 1881. The house contains period furniture, ornaments, and a collection of 1880s fashions. Also on display are the original furnishings from an old grocery store, furnishings from the original city council chambers, and a beautiful doll's house with miniature furniture dating from the 1880s. The basement houses artifacts and photographs depicting the city's early history. There is a small admission fee, but the museum will give you a feel for the city's history and it's well worth the price. The building is open year-round.

Walk south on 18th Street from the museum and you'll pass two of Brandon's landmark buildings. The old brick structures are the main architectural focus of today's Brandon University. Started as a Baptist Convention of Manitoba college, this school merged with McKee Academy in 1899 to become Brandon College.

Go east on Princess Avenue to 11th Street and you'll pass Brandon's courthouse. It was built in 1908. Just across the street is the old Brandon post office. Built in 1930, it now houses assorted federal government offices. Turn right on 11th Street and about two blocks down you'll come to the Peterson-Matheson house. Painted in the Victorian style, it is a beautiful example of the Eastlake approach to architecture. If you walk back to Princess Avenue and continue east, you'll come to the library building at 638 Princess, which also houses the Art Gallery of Southwestern Manitoba. It's a public art gallery that features changing exhibitions of local, national, and international artists, although the primary focus is on work by Manitoba artists and craftspeople. A donation is the only admission fee, and the gallery is open year-round. During July and August, it's closed on Saturdays.

Just across the street is the city's old fire hall. Built in 1911, it is still in use. From here, walk north to Rosser Avenue. Heading west, back towards 18th Street, you'll pass by the McKenzie Seeds building on 9th Street just north of Rosser. Next is the Fraser building. Built in 1890, it now houses the Soup Kettle. The first classes of what is now Brandon University were held on its second floor. Keep going west and you'll come to the old Merchant's Bank building. Built in 1907, it now houses the city's Chamber of Commerce offices. It is built in the Beaux-Arts Classical style.

After the walking tour, you may want to visit the Commonwealth Air Training Plan Museum. It is best to call ahead and book a tour. Drive north on 1st Street and cross the Trans-Canada Highway. You'll come to Brandon Airport, where the museum is housed. During World War II, pilots and crew from around the Commonwealth were sent to Canada for their flight training, and Brandon was the site of one of the training bases. In one of the original hangars built for the flight-training plan, 13 aircraft are on display. The Harvard, Tiger Moth, Cornell, and Stinson are airworthy, and in the workshop a Hurricane is being reconstructed. Artifacts and displays dedicated to the training programs are on exhibit. Over 18,000 RCAF personnel were killed in the war, and the chapel commemorates these victims. Most of the volunteers at the museum are ex-airmen, and they can give you first-hand

VIEW OF BRANDON

information about the war and what happened during training. The museum is open year-round, and there is a small admission fee.

Brandon hosts several annual exhibitions, and they are some of the city's main tourist attractions. The biggest and best is the Royal Manitoba Winter Fair, always held in late March or early April at the Keystone Centre grounds on 18th Street. It offers a wide variety of exhibits and livestock shows. The horse show is world-class, with international-calibre show jumping and the always-popular heavy-horse-harness classes. Another interesting display features a wide assortment of rabbit and poultry breeds.

Brandon's large Native population celebrates with Winter Tribal Days, held either the last weekend in January or the first weekend in February at the Keystone Centre. It's one of the largest pow-wows in western Canada, attracting 20,000 visitors to the city. The pow-wow competition and the Native arts and crafts displays are popular with the general public. Square dancing, a talent show, and a large Native hockey tournament are also featured.

The Provincial Exhibition, or summer fair, is held in June. It hosts the Budweiser Pro Rodeo, and you'll see some of the best professional cowboys in the world. There is always a large midway on the Keystone Centre grounds.

Another summer attraction is the Brandon Folk Music and Art Festival. Always held the second weekend of August, it includes a daytime workshop stage and an evening main-stage show. The main show can feature everything from bluegrass to world beat to blues. For the kids, there is a family area that features clowns,

SOURIS

storytellers, other performers, and art instructors.

The Brandon area features great golfing at reasonable prices. All five courses in the city are open to the public. The most challenging is probably the 18-hole course at the Brandon Community Recreation and Sports Centre. For the pitch-and-putt set, there are nine holes at Northern Pines.

SOURIS

From Brandon, drive south on Highway 10 for 24 kilometres (15 mi.), then west on Highway 2, and you'll reach the town of Souris. The first permanent settlers came to Souris in 1880, and the town was then called Plum Creek.

SOURIS SWINGING BRIDGE

Like Brandon, Souris had a large Commonwealth Air Training Plan school during World War II. For $100 and up, you can be taken for a ride in one of the old training aircraft or you can fly the plane yourself in a dogfight simulation (always with a trained pilot along). Book ahead by calling Operation Fire Fly.

A well-known Souris attraction is its swinging bridge, one of Canada's longest at 177 metres (581 ft.). It crosses the Souris River, connecting the two sides of town. At one end of the bridge is the Souris Hillcrest Museum, which documents some of the history of the area.

The agate pits at Souris are another attraction worth a visit. To gain access to the quarry, you must visit the rock shop, where the owners will sell you a permit. They'll show you what to look for and direct you to the pits. Then you can take out as many agates and other semi-precious stones as you can carry.

BOISSEVAIN

Drive back to Highway 10, then head south another 50 kilometres (31 mi.), and you'll come to Boissevain. This is one of the must-see places in the area.

To bring visitors to Boissevain, the town commissioned professional artists to paint murals on the sides of buildings. All the murals have themes relating to the history and natural history of the region, and the first group was painted in 1992. One mural depicting the Boundary Commission Trail is painted on the east side of the library. The actual trail, which is south of town, was started in 1873. It was built to supply American and British surveyors who were mapping the 49th parallel from Lake of the Woods to the Rocky Mountains. The North West Mounted Police took this trail in 1874 when they set out to establish and enforce Canadian law in the West.

Another mural, titled Romance of the Railways, is on the Cherry Creek Gallery, and a third, Green Meadows Farm, is on the side of the fire hall, right along Highway 10 (called Mill Road within town limits). There are a number of smaller murals: a winter scene, While Muskrats Slept, on the side of the theatre; Boissevain Saturday Night, a 1950s scene, on

**TURTLE STATUE,
BOISSEVAIN**

Rawlings Food Town on Main Street, or South Railway Street; and a pair of murals depicting an old barbershop and a millinery shop on the ice-cream parlour on the same street. A pair of paintings on both ends of the Garden Motel illustrate the history of the Turtle Mountains. Across the street at the Tommy Turtle site is a huge wetland scene depicting the history of Whitewater Lake. All the murals are within walking distance of one another, and there are guide pamphlets available at some of the sites.

Also on Main Street is the Moncur Gallery. Native artifacts, mostly arrowheads and spear points, are on display. The points tell the story of the earliest people in the Turtle Mountain area and show that the region was inhabited dating back to 10,000 B.C. The Clovis people were the first to live and hunt here. Their quarry were woolly mammoths and later long-horned bison. By the time of white settlement in the 1800s, the Native peoples here were primarily Ojibwa, as well as Plains Cree. Bill Moncur's collection has been meticulously documented and is one of the finest available for reference today. The gallery is located in the civic centre library complex. There is no charge to view the collection, although donations are accepted.

The Beckoning Hills Museum, located along Highway 10, documents the development of the community of Boissevain. Household and small farm artifacts are displayed. Also housed in the museum is a harness collection.

One of the town's more light-hearted attractions is the annual Canadian Turtle Derby, always held the third weekend in July. The festival runs all weekend, with the Canadian and American champion turtles meeting in a final race on Sunday. The turtles are collected from lakes in the area, and after the festivities they are returned to their natural habitat. In addition to the races, the derby features a summer bonspiel and a free family fun night.

TURTLE MOUNTAIN PROVINCIAL PARK

Just south of Boissevain on Highway 10, bordering the Canada-U.S. boundary, is Turtle Mountain Provincial Park. The mountain protrudes from the surrounding prairie, and the park is dotted with small lakes, perfect if you're a canoeist. There are three campgrounds in the park, with both unserviced and serviced sites. Some lakes are stocked with trout, so bring your fishing gear. Wildlife abounds. In the winter months, Adam Lake offers some of the best cross-country ski trails in the area. As well, there are rinks for skating and hockey, a great toboggan hill, and a warming hut.

At William Lake, the Turtle's Back Trail takes you to the summit of the Turtle Mountains. There is a tower at the summit, and the view of the surrounding landscape is quite spectacular. The trail passes through a community pasture, so be on the lookout for cattle roaming freely. To get to William Lake, which isn't within the main park, go east on Highway 341, then south on Highway 444 to the campground. Watch carefully; the sign indicating the turnoff from Highway 10 is small.

INTERNATIONAL PEACE GARDEN

The International Peace Garden borders Turtle Mountain Provincial Park and straddles the 49th parallel. The garden was established in 1932 as a symbol of goodwill between us and our neighbours to the south. It features plantings of ornamental trees and shrubs, and in summer the formal area of the garden is a riot of colour, with perennials and annuals of every kind in full bloom.

When you've finished looking around the formal area, go back to the parking lot and follow the road left. You'll come to a picnic area beside Lake Stormon. Further down the road are two nature trails. As well, there is the Manitoba Horticultural Association's arboretum, where you'll find 100 species of trees and shrubs. The same road takes you near a campground before passing the formal garden area again as you complete the loop on the north side. As soon as you pass the formal area you'll see a huge floral clock, donated by Bulova and planted each year by the garden staff.

INTERNATIONAL PEACE GARDEN

WHITE-TAILED DEER ANTLERS IN THE DUNES AT SPRUCE WOODS PROVINCIAL PARK

CARBERRY

Another day trip out of Brandon means a 42-kilometre (26-mi.) drive east on the Trans-Canada Highway to Carberry and Spruce Woods Provincial Park. Carberry is now home to the new Seton Centre, named for the famous naturalist, artist and author Ernest Thompson Seton, who came to the Carberry area in 1882. Ten years later he was named Manitoba's first provincial naturalist. He wrote and illustrated books about Manitoba's birds and mammals but is probably best known for his nature stories, which were very popular as children's literature in the early 1900s. His best-loved book was *Wild Animals I Have Known*.

Each year the centre features a new exhibit of Seton artwork and artifacts, and it is developing an archival collection. Most of the books written by or about Seton are available for sale. The centre is open from June 1 to the Labour Day long weekend. At other times of the year it is opened by appointment. There is no admission charge.

SPRUCE WOODS PROVINCIAL PARK

Spruce Woods Provincial Park, just south of Carberry on Highway 5, preserves the sandhills produced by Glacial Lake Agassiz. About 12,000 years ago, the Assiniboine River emptied into Lake Agassiz near Brandon. The river

SPIRIT SANDS, SPRUCE WOODS PROVINCIAL PARK

deposited sand and gravel, forming a delta. This delta created the Carberry sandhills and desert that are found in the park today. The Spirit Sands, about 25 square kilometres (10 sq. mi.) of sand dunes, is the only part of the delta that hasn't been reclaimed by spruce forest. This area of the park is a must-see, and is accessible by a self-guided hiking trail. As well, a covered wagon is available to take you through this desert. The area receives too much rainfall to qualify as a real desert, but the dunes do get very hot during the summer, so take plenty of water with you if you're walking. And watch out for poison ivy.

The sandhills are home to a variety of wildlife, including some rare reptiles and amphibians. The plains spadefoot toad, northern prairie skink, and western hognose snake are very rare, and aren't often spotted. Easier to see are elk, moose, and white-tailed deer that populate the park. Many songbirds visit the park in summer. A great campground offers serviced and unserviced sites. Hiking and mountain biking are excellent on the Epinette trail system, and cross-country skiing in the park is terrific during the winter months.

NEEPAWA

For another day's possible tour out of Brandon, head north on Highway 10, travelling 41 kilometres (25 mi.) to Minnedosa. Then drive another 30 kilometres (19 mi.) east on Highway 16, the Yellowhead Route. The town you'll visit is Neepawa, incorporated in 1883. The Fort Ellice Trail, which brought the first settlers to town, ran from the Red River Settlement to Fort Edmonton. Neepawa has earned a reputation as one of Manitoba's most beautiful communities.

THE STONE ANGEL, RIVERSIDE CEMETERY

Probably the most famous resident of the town was Margaret Laurence, one of Canada's great authors. She is known for the Manawaka (a fictional Neepawa) series: *The Stone Angel*, *The Fire Dwellers*, *A Bird in the House*, and *The Diviners*. The home where she grew up, on the corner of Brydon Street and First Avenue, has been turned into a museum documenting her life and career. The museum houses artifacts that belonged to her, as well as a resource and research area containing books on her life, magazines, videos, and tapes of various radio interviews she gave. All her books are available for sale, and you can buy items crafted by local and Manitoba artists in the Manawaka Souvenir and Gift Shop.

MARGARET LAURENCE HOME

Laurence died January 5, 1987, and her ashes are interred at Riverside Cemetery, where the town plants flowers on every grave. The Davidson monument in that cemetery may be the "stone angel" she describes in her book of the same name.

Besides the Margaret Laurence Home, two other buildings in Neepawa have earned historic designations. The Beautiful Plains County Court building was constructed in 1884 and is the fifth-oldest substantial public building remaining in Manitoba. It is also the second-oldest courthouse in western

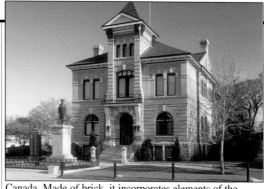

THE BEAUTIFUL PLAINS COUNTY COURT BUILDING

Canada. Made of brick, it incorporates elements of the Queen Anne style of architecture.

The other historic building is Knox Presbyterian Church, on the corner of First Avenue and Mill Street.

Constructed in 1892, this brick building was designed in the Romanesque style. It has a unique bell tower and a pyramid roof with pinnacles at each corner. The interior was renovated in 1992, but the original pews, choir loft and pulpit remain. You are invited to go in and look around.

Beautiful Plains Museum is housed in the town's old CN station. Artifacts dealing with agriculture and farm life are displayed in the basement. The museum features a large collection of early newspapers, scrapbooks and photos depicting life in the district. There is a large collection of Bibles in the chapel area, and some rooms are dedicated to the early Polish and Ukrainian settlers in the region.

If you want to stay at Neepawa overnight, there is a beautiful campground in Lions Riverbend Park with serviced and unserviced sites and a swimming pool.

KNOX PRESBYTERIAN CHURCH

RIDING MOUNTAIN NATIONAL PARK

Now take Highway 16 back to Highway 10. Head north for 50 kilometres (31 mi.), and you'll be in Riding Mountain National Park. The park was established in 1929, when 2970 square kilometres (1,147 sq. mi.) of land was set aside. The Riding Mountain is actually part of the Manitoba Escarpment, and it dominates the eastern half of the park. The western part is mostly open woodland. Boreal forest, prairie, and mixed deciduous forest are all present within the park's borders. The main townsite is Wasagaming, which borders the deep, blue waters of Clear Lake. The town has an assortment of shops, restaurants, and hotels, with a beautiful beach-front for swimmers. Also in Wasagaming are the park headquarters and interpretive centre, where you can get information on the park's many hiking and back-country trails. These double as excellent cross-country ski trails in winter. The lakes in the park present good angling opportunities. Some of the species you can try to catch are trout, pike, pickerel, and whitefish.

The main campground is just inside the park gates. It offers serviced and unserviced sites. Unserviced campgrounds are located at Moon Lake, Whirlpool Lake, and Lake Audy.

There is plenty of wildlife in the park. Birds are numerous (233 species of regular residents have been identified), and there are 60 species of mammals. If you're lucky, you may see a black bear by the side of the road, or hear the call of a bull elk.

Riding Mountain is also home to one of the last free-ranging bison herds in the West. The buffalo compound is on the Lake Audy road, just before the campground there. The bison don't always make themselves visible, but if you're lucky you may get a close-up view of some of these rare animals.

BALD EAGLE AT MOON LAKE, RIDING MOUNTAIN NATIONAL PARK

ASPEN PARKLAND

Back-country hiking opportunities are great. The Ochre River trail will take you back to some generally deserted campsites, and the trail network running south of Dead Ox Gorge winds through some spectacular

valleys. West of the escarpment, on more gently rolling terrain, is a network of more than 160 kilometres (100 mi.) of trails where you can get a glimpse of how the land surrounding the park must have looked before it was cleared for agriculture.

Grey Owl's cabin (see pp. 20-21) is an eight-kilometre (5-mi.) trek from Highway 19.

If you're a golfer, you'll want to play the scenic and challenging 18-hole Clear Lake Golf Course, one of the best in the province. It's wise to book your tee time.

INDIAN PAINTBRUSH

BISON

UKRAINIAN ORTHODOX CHURCH, SANDY LAKE

WHIRLPOOL LAKE

DAUPHIN

If you continue north on Highway 10, you'll come to the town of Dauphin. La Vérendrye, who is famous for leading the first European exploration across the Missouri River into the Great Plains, first visited the area in the 1730s. He gave the name Dauphin, after the oldest son of the king of France, to a trading post in the region in 1741.

The town is home to a large Ukrainian community. The first Ukrainians arrived in the area in 1896. To celebrate their heritage, Canada's National Ukrainian Festival is held in early August at the Selo Ukraina site, which is 12 kilometres (7.5 mi.) south of town on Highway 10, and one kilometre (0.6 mi.) west. Grandstand shows feature the best in Ukrainian dance and music. You can buy Ukrainian handicrafts, and when you get hungry you can feast on

cabbage rolls, perogies, and kolbasa (garlic sausage). The site is also the permanent home of a Ukrainian folk art centre and museum. An original Ukrainian homestead house stands here. Built of logs, it has a straw thatched roof. As well, a restored Ukrainian Orthodox church is open to visitors.

Countryfest, a major country music festival, is held on the Canada Day long weekend at the same site. It manages to book some of the top names in country music, such as Travis Tritt, Chelly Wright, and Martina McBride. Camping is available on-site, but plan ahead because tickets and accommodations sell out quickly.

An architectural walking tour of Dauphin has been organized. It features the Dr. Vernon Allied Arts Centre, the fortress-like CN station, and one of the beautiful Ukrainian Catholic churches in the area, the Church of the Resurrection (open by arrangement). The Fort Dauphin Museum complex is a replica of a North West Company trading post.

RAILROAD STATION, DAUPHIN

Camping is available in Dauphin, or you can drive to Rainbow Beach Provincial Park or Stoney Point Beach. Both campgrounds are on Dauphin Lake, and there are serviced and unserviced sites.

NORTH OF 53°

DONNA HENRY

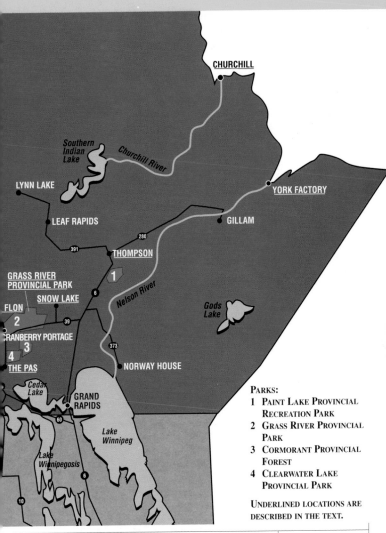

PARKS:
1 PAINT LAKE PROVINCIAL RECREATION PARK
2 GRASS RIVER PROVINCIAL PARK
3 CORMORANT PROVINCIAL FOREST
4 CLEARWATER LAKE PROVINCIAL PARK

UNDERLINED LOCATIONS ARE DESCRIBED IN THE TEXT.

In 1912 the Government of Canada transferred 500,000 square kilometres (193,000 sq. mi.) of real estate to the Province of Manitoba. This vast area that stretched north of the 53rd parallel to the 60th was a rugged land of forests, lakes, and tundra. The people who lived here were trappers, traders, fishermen, freighters, prospectors, and woodsmen.

Much of northern Manitoba has only recently entered the industrial age. The greatest agents of change have been mining and the development of hydroelectric power dams along the rivers.

CHURCHILL

"Churchill." Around the world the word conjures up images of Canada's north: polar bears, beluga whales, caribou, seals, wolves, foxes, nesting and migratory birds, delicate Arctic wildflowers, scrubby 400-year-old one-sided trees, and the northern lights dancing across the evening sky.

The world's largest concentration of polar bears is found near Churchill (see pp. 16-17). Polar bears and caribou are

frequently seen along the coastal tidal flats during the summer.

Hudson Bay is home to beluga whales and four species of seal. Each summer the whales return to the estuaries of the Nelson, Churchill and Seal rivers to feed and calve. In July and August, pods of these snowy white mammals swim in and out of the Churchill harbour with the tides. In late June bearded and ringed seals bask on the ice floes. Whales, seals, and many species of waterfowl and shorebirds can be observed from Cape Merry National Historic Site at the mouth of the Churchill River or from a tour boat. Sea North tour boats are equipped with hydrophones that enable you to eavesdrop on the belugas' underwater conversations.

CHURCHILL WILDLIFE: GOLDEN PLOVER, HORNED GREBE, AND BELUGA WHALES

Churchill is a bird-watcher's paradise; over 200 species have been observed. Here you can see birds that are associated with the boreal forest alongside typical Arctic species. During the brief subarctic summer, millions of

birds migrate to the Churchill region to breed. In May and June the air is filled with the courtship calls of shorebirds, songbirds, and waterfowl. Since 1980 a small number of Ross' gulls have come to nest annually in ponds near Churchill. Arctic terns return from as far away as Antarctica. The tidal flats, salt marshes and willows of La Perouse Bay are home to Manitoba's only snow goose colony, where upwards of 6,000 geese nest alongside a

colony of eiders. Raptors include osprey, rough-legged hawks, and the peregrine falcon, globally considered an endangered species.

The rich culture and traditions of the Inuit are interpreted at the Eskimo Museum, one of the finest repositories of Inuit art and artifacts in the world. The museum displays 800 contemporary sculptures and houses 3,000 historic and prehistoric artifacts as well as wildlife specimens. The original pieces in the museum were acquired by Oblate priests who worked in the central Canadian Arctic after

1912 and collected stone and ivory sculptures. Contemporary sculptures created since 1930 are the main focus of the display area. Some of the most exquisite pieces are from Pelly Bay, an isolated community in the high Arctic famous for its unique, very beautiful stone and ivory miniatures. Most pieces are from the central and eastern Arctic, including northern Quebec.

POLAR BEAR SOW AND CUB ON TIDAL FLATS

Churchill is the oldest community in Manitoba. The Hudson's Bay Company (HBC) built the first Prince of Wales' Fort, a trading post, on the west bank of the Churchill River in 1717. The site is accessible by boat. A five-kilometre (3-mi.) hiking trail along the peninsula leads from this site to the second Prince of Wales' Fort, an imposing stone fortress at the harbour entrance. It is generally a full day's trip because access to the peninsula is affected by the tides. Ancient campsites, graves, and

CANADA DAY
parade, CHURCHILL

155

WINDSURFING AMONG ICEBERGS, CHURCHILL

S. HEARNE ETCHED HIS NAME ON A ROCK IN SLOOP'S COVE IN JULY, 1767

NORWAY HOUSE CANOEISTS IN TRADITIONAL CLOTHING AT YORK FACTORY DEPOT

signatures carved in the rock are reminders of the Aboriginals and Europeans who have lived here over the centuries. Guided tours are available. Several plants that grow on the peninsula are found nowhere else in Churchill.

The second Prince of Wales' Fort was designed to be a bastion where all bayside employees could retreat in case of attack. The distinctive greywacke rock used to build walls six metres (20 ft.) high and 12 metres (39 ft.) thick was quarried nearby. The fort took 40 years to build. The HBC installed 40 cannon for defence. But in 1782 the mighty fortress was surrendered without a fight. It was destroyed by the French, but has been partially restored.

Directly across the mouth of the river is Cape Merry National Historic Site, where the stone battery, cannon, and powder magazine are further evidence of the HBC's determination to defend Prince of Wales' Fort at any cost. The cape offers a series of microclimates where diverse bird and plant life flourishes.

The Parks Canada Visitor Centre in Churchill specializes in presentations on the history of northern Manitoba.

You cannot drive to Churchill. There is scheduled plane and rail service from Winnipeg, Thompson, and Gillam. Book accommodation and tours in advance, especially during polar-bear season.

YORK FACTORY
In the late 1600s the Hudson's Bay Company began trading for furs on the coast of Hudson Bay. The Native people of the interior transported their furs by canoe along the northern rivers to the bayside post of York Factory, the

main HBC depot in the region. There they traded the pelts for pots and pans, guns and ammunition, and other modern European conveniences that arrived on ships from England each summer. These ships transported the furs to the fashion houses of Europe.

FISHING BY FLOAT PLANE, THOMPSON

York Factory was the original gateway to the interior for explorers and settlers, and the largest community in western Canada. In its heyday it boasted over 50 buildings, including a school, a library, churches, boathouses, and shops where trade goods were manufactured for inland posts. Today only the great white depot, the clerk's quarters, the ruins of a powder magazine, and the cemetery with its markers dating back to the 1800s remain. The majestic depot, built in 1831, is the largest and oldest wooden building constructed on permafrost in Canada. On its walls are etched the names of many people who brought York Factory to life.

Transportation to York Factory by chartered aircraft or helicopter can be arranged from Churchill, Gillam, or Thompson. The 600-kilometre (375-mi.) three-week canoe trip from Norway House down the historic Hayes River route to York Factory is popular with canoeists. If you canoe to York Factory, be sure to make prior arrangements with a chartered aircraft company for the trip out. Camping is not permitted at York Factory because of the danger of polar bears. You must book well in advance at Silver Goose Lodge to ensure that you will have accommodation. Contact the owners at Box 322, Gillam, Manitoba, R0B 0L0 (204-652-2776). There is no community at York Factory and no stores or services. Be prepared to stay longer than planned; the coast is famous for its fog and inclement weather. York Factory National Historic Site is open from June 1 to mid-September. Tours must be booked in advance.

THE PAS TRAPPERS FESTIVAL

THE PAS AND OPASKWAYAK CREE NATION

Opaskwayak Cree Nation and the town of The Pas lie on opposite banks at the confluence of the Pasquia, Carrot, and Saskatchewan rivers. In 1750 the La Vérendrye family of French voyageurs chose this strategic spot to build Fort Paskoyac.

In the 1800s The Pas became a centre for missionary service. The first mission was established on Devon Island in 1840. Devon Island has now become part of the mainland. Much of the community's history is commemorated on plaques and cairns at Devon Park.

A short walk from Devon Park stands Christ Church Anglican. Constructed in 1896, it is the oldest building in The Pas. The pews, baptismal font, pulpit, and four tablets inscribed with Cree syllabics were used in the first Christ Church, which was founded in 1847 and demolished in 1895.

FOG AND BLACK SPRUCE NEAR FLIN FLON

The Roman Catholic Church established its mission in 1843. The First Catholic Church was built in 1897. Inquire at the rectory east of the cathedral if you wish to visit the church.

The newly renovated Court House-Community Building is an architectural rarity in the north, one of only a handful built of brick. After The Pas became part of the newly expanded province of Manitoba in 1912, the building was designed to be the administrative centre for the vast "new north." It opened in 1917. It housed not only the court, but also a jail. It also housed municipal, land registry, and game warden offices, the office of the commissioner of the North West Territories, and an assembly hall.

The Sam Waller Museum, located in this building, is one of the finest in the province. Artifacts and specimens that reflect the human and natural history of The Pas and northern Manitoba are well represented, but the eclectic collection goes well beyond this region. The library holds many rare, out-of-print books. During the summer, the museum offers historic walking tours of the community.

Look for Native arts and crafts at the Friendship Centre and at shops in Opaskwayak Cree Nation's Otineka Mall.

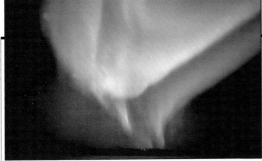

FLIN FLON

An ore body was discovered on the shores of Ross Lake in 1915. This led to the construction of one of the most productive copper mines in Manitoba. The town of Flin Flon sprang up around it.

Hudson Bay Mining and Smelting is still mining copper, but these days it's also growing roses and orchids in a subterranean greenhouse down in the mine. The constant year-round temperature and humidity are ideal for many plants, including the western yew whose bark and roots are used to produce an important cancer drug.

The Provincial Building on Main Street was designed and built by Ikoy in 1985. Its unusual kinetic design has won architectural awards, but the building has generated local controversy because its functional parts are prominently displayed. The building's northern art collection was selected through a special competition.

Two Flin Flon galleries worth a visit are Sarah's Studio Gallery and the Hanging Wall Gallery.

THE GRASS RIVER REGION

You can trace much of the route of famous 18th-century explorer Samuel Hearne by canoeing the Grass River. It is ideal for beginners, families, or those who want to stay relatively close to "civilization." The highway runs parallel to it, providing a number of "in" and "out" points. Towns and lodges allow for resupply on a regular basis. The rivers and lakes are well known for trout, pickerel and pike fishing.

Highways 39 and 6 follow the river from the headwaters at the Manitoba-Saskatchewan border north to Gillam. The highway passes some of the most scenic spots in the north, such as Sasagui Rapids and Pisew Falls, the highest accessible waterfall in Manitoba. The heritage of the Grass River region is interpreted in the parks and communities along the way.

SNOW LAKE

This small mining community is a scenic half-hour drive north of Highway 39 on Provincial Road 392. The road

WEKUSKO FALLS NEAR SNOW LAKE

skirts Wekusko and Tramping lakes and crosses over Wekusko Falls, one of the prettiest spots along the Grass River. The community, which sits on the shore of Snow Lake surrounded by wilderness, is an idyllic spot for wildlife photographers and artists. Snow Lake is home to wildlife artist Audrey Casey and to Annabelle Ayres, who creates beautiful birch-bark bitings, a traditional craft of Manitoba's Native women.

A trip to the Snow Lake Art Gallery, which specializes in northern Manitoba artists, is a highlight for many visitors. Local artists have captured the history of the early Aboriginal people and the map-makers, prospectors and miners in wall murals on many buildings in downtown Snow Lake.

SKIING TRAILS IN THOMPSON

THOMPSON

Thompson, with a population of 16,000, is the largest city and one of the youngest communities in northern Manitoba. It came into existence after a major nickel ore body was discovered in the Thompson Nickel Belt in 1956. Its history is interpreted at Heritage North Museum.

The Hudson Gallery at 60 Hemlock Crescent is committed to developing Aboriginal and non-Aboriginal art of the region. Another gallery of high quality is the Northern Creations Art Gallery in the City Centre Mall.

The Inco mine offers guided walking tours of Inco's surface area (headframe, mill, smelter, and refinery). Thompson's zoo specializes in northern birds and animals.

Eastern Manitoba

Joyce Meyer

Victoria Beach

Victoria Beach occupies a promontory on the east shore of Lake Winnipeg. It is on the Laurentian extension of the Canadian Shield, the oldest rock in the world, and is dotted with many coves and bays of fine sand. You can reach it by driving to the northern end of Highway 59.

The northernmost beach is two kilometres (1.25 mi.) long, and consists of fine white sand that stretches into a sandbar which, in low water, can be walked to Elk Island. This island, now a provincial heritage park, was one of the first sights to greet the brigades of voyageurs, clerics and fur-trade employees who emerged at the western end of the onerous 3200-kilometre (2,000-mi.) canoe route from Montreal.

By the early 1900s a small colony of cottages had been built at Victoria Beach by Winnipeg's prosperous citizens. At first, visitors came to the beach from Winnipeg by the steamer *Pilgrim*. In 1916 the Canadian Northern Railway was persuaded to build a line from Winnipeg to the beach, and this became the usual mode of travel. It was common for women and children to live at the beach all summer. Husbands would arrive by train on weekends to join their families.

The Victoria Beach Inn and the Pinehurst Inn once hosted illustrious Winnipeggers. No hotel now exists at Victoria Beach, and train service is long since gone. A nine-hole, par-32 golf course is still in operation and open to the public.

From the beginning, automobiles were prohibited, to ensure quiet and privacy. They are still banned in July and August. Cottagers must leave them in a parking lot at the edge

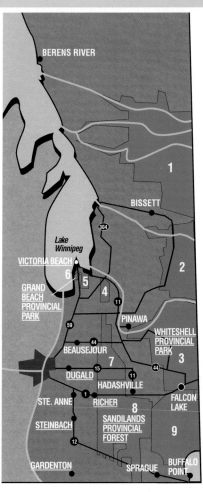

PARKS:

1. **Atikaki Provincial Wilderness Park**
2. **Nopiming Provincial Park**
3. **Whiteshell Provincial Park**
4. **Grand Beach Provincial Park**
5. **Belair Provincial Forest**
6. **Victoria Beach**
7. **Agassiz Provincial Forest**
8. **Sandilands Provincial Forest**
9. **Northwest Angle Park**

Underlined locations are described in the text.

of the community and walk, or bicycle, to their summer homes. Taxi service is available.

GRAND BEACH PROVINCIAL PARK

Of the beaches along the east shore of Lake Winnipeg, Grand Beach is the best known. It's less than 90 kilometres (56 mi.) from the centre of Winnipeg, and about 25 kilometres (16 mi.) south of Victoria Beach. If you don't mind crowds, this is the place to be on a summer Sunday. The sand, deposited by retreating glaciers, is talc-fine, and there are three kilometres (almost 2 mi.) of it, with grass-topped dunes that reach as much as nine metres (30 ft.) high. The dunes are bordered by trees. It's perfect for families with little children: the lake is so shallow and the gradient so gradual that parents can easily keep an eye on them as they paddle near the shore.

GRAND BEACH, LAKE WINNIPEG

A merry-go-round, concession stands, a restaurant, and beach kiosks were built long ago. A boardwalk extended along the beachfront from the train station to the lagoon. The grandest of all the buildings was the dance pavilion, built in 1915 and reputed to be the largest dance hall in the Commonwealth. Taking the railway's "Moonlight Special" (50 cents round trip, leaving Winnipeg after supper) was soon the acme of summertime thrills for Winnipeg youth. But it all ended suddenly on Labour Day, 1950, when fire destroyed the hall.

Inland from the dunes is a lagoon where pelicans and cranes feed. More than 100 species of birds frequent this provincial park. Living in the nearby forest are deer, bears, chipmunks, squirrels, skunks and badgers. Whitefish,

northern pike, perch, walleye, bullhead and bass inhabit Lake Winnipeg.

Where once a lone Indian trail meandered, a well-developed campground now exists, with 104 electrical and 295 unserviced sites. Boats, sailboards and canoes can be rented.

The nearest indoor accommodation is at Grand Marais, just south of Grand Beach. There are seven inns, motels, cottages, and cabin lodges, all modestly priced and correspondingly modest in decor and comfort.

PRAIRIE CROCUS, SANDILANDS PROVINCIAL FOREST

Grand Beach has been named as one of the top ten in North America by two large-circulation magazines. To avoid crowds, go mid-week or off-season.

DUGALD

To reach Dugald from Winnipeg, take Lagimodiere Boulevard to Dugald Road and turn east. Just west of the

DUGALD COSTUME MUSEUM

town on Provincial Road (PR) 206 is The Costume Museum of Canada. It is the only Canadian museum solely dedicated to antique clothing and textiles. It houses more than 20,000 items dating from 1765 to the present.

Displays are done in a *tableau vivant* style, with mannequins posed in period settings. A visual storage room adjacent to the main gallery holds plexiglass-topped drawers that slide out for close-up viewing. Here, you can see hair accessories, gloves, hats, shoes and jewellery from times past.

FLAX, PEMBINA HILLS

Also in the museum are a tearoom and a gift shop. Next door is an authentic restored farmhouse built around 1866, which depicts pioneer life in the rugged 19th century.

RICHER AND AREA

When you're satiated on beautiful clothing, travel about 20 kilometres (12 mi.) south to the Trans-Canada Highway (#1) and turn east past long stretches of flat but fertile farmland. If

RED FOX AT SANDILANDS

you're lucky, there will be fluorescent-yellow fields of canola, or patches of lake-blue flax, or a stretch of chrome-yellow sunflowers tilting their faces eastward. At 61 kilometres (38 mi.) from Winnipeg, you'll see the Richer Inn on the south side of the highway. It has a good coffee shop where you can buy a "Lord Selkirk," a quarter-pound burger made with buffalo meat.

Kayser's farmers' market, on the north side of the road about eight kilometres (5 mi.) farther east, is a quirky place whose courtyard is decorated with the owner's wood carvings, including a big hand with forefinger raised. The owners' house was once a small church. On sale are fresh produce, frozen chickens, eggs, homemade jams, honey, and wild blueberries.

SANDILANDS PROVINCIAL FOREST

As you continue east, you'll soon see the first outcrops of granite that signal the start of the Precambrian Shield, which underlies almost half of Canada. You'll also note the start of evergreens at the edge of the Sandilands Provincial Forest. Turn south at the junction of Highway 11 for a visit to the Sandilands Forest Centre. About two kilometres (1.2 mi.) into the woods, the road turns west. Go west for about 0.4 kilometre (0.25 mi.), then turn south and drive about 0.8 kilometre (0.5 mi.) to the gates of the centre. The 120 hectares (296 acres) of land are on sandy terrain that was a beach of Lake Agassiz, a huge glacial lake that stretched as far west as Riding Mountain National Park after the Ice Age of 6,000 to 12,000 years ago.

BIG WHITESHELL LAKE

The tree-planting car at the Forest Centre supplants an older wooden car that travelled around Manitoba and was

seen by more than 1.5 million people representing four generations. Displays tell how a tree grows, how to tell its age, and how to prevent forest fires. In the tree identification building are cross-sections of trunks, twigs and leaves of various trees. School groups are taught the signs and control of Dutch elm disease, which struck Manitoba just over a decade ago. Outside, a suspension bridge leads across the Whitemouth River to a self-guiding trail through aspens and patches of fern, past a spot on the river where deer drink (watch for their hoofprints). The Old Dawson Ranger Station has a fire tower and weather station.

If all this has made you hungry, drive a bit farther east on the Trans-Canada and watch for a sign, "Nelda's Giant Homemade Cinnamon Buns" (north side of the highway, near McMunn). Still farther along, near East Braintree, the K&B Kitchen sells homemade perogies (Ukrainian

dumplings stuffed with potato and cheese or sauerkraut).

WHITESHELL PROVINCIAL PARK

At about 125 kilometres (78 mi.) from Winnipeg you'll reach Falcon Lake, just inside Whiteshell Provincial Park. The townsite has a shopping centre, riding stable, miniature golf, and Manitoba's largest sailing club. Nearby is one of the best 18-hole golf courses in the province.

BANNOCK POINT PETROFORM, WHITESHELL PROVINCIAL PARK

Whiteshell is the oldest and one of the biggest of Manitoba's provincial parks (2590 square kilometres/1,000 sq. mi.). It contains 200 lakes, a quarter of the province's fishing lodges, a picture-perfect waterfall (Rainbow Falls near White Lake off PR 307), and many resorts. Travel Manitoba information centres are located at both the western and eastern entrances to the park.

Near the town of Rennie on Highway 44 (north of the Trans-Canada) is a small lake that's a sanctuary for Canada geese. It was established in the late 1930s by a local mink rancher and outdoorsman, Alfred A. Hole. A railroad worker had found four abandoned giant Canada goslings, and he made a bet with Hole, who had a soft spot for wildlife, that Hole couldn't keep them alive for six weeks.

Hole won the bet. He built a wire pen and fed the goslings hand-picked dandelions for most of the summer. That winter the geese were pinioned and kept indoors. During their second summer, Hole obtained an old gander from a park and got it to mate with the lone female in the brood. The female laid four eggs, and the resulting goslings were banded and turned loose on the pond. When they were fully grown they joined the geese flying south and left their parents behind. But all four returned the next spring and each year thereafter. These were the forebears of the flock of more than

200 giant Canada geese that now spend their summers at the sanctuary. Unwittingly, Hole had become the saviour of a race of geese that was believed to be extinct. The flock at the sanctuary is, to this day, the major reservoir for the race.

These geese spend their winters at the Rock Prairie Refuge in Wisconsin, 1000 kilometres (600 mi.) to the southeast. With a wingspan of more than two metres (6.5 to

MANTARIO HIKING TRAIL

WHITESHELL NATURAL HISTORY MUSEUM

7.5 ft.), they can make this flight non-stop in 20 hours.

Now, besides the permanent summer residents, some 2,500 other migrating geese use the pond as a staging area on their way to and from their northern nesting grounds. Spring and fall are the best viewing times, when as many as 1,500 birds can be seen at once. There's a 1.5-kilometre (1-mi.) self-guiding trail around the pond, with benches and interpretive signs.

Another highlight of Whiteshell Park is Bannock Point, just north of Betula Lake on PR 307, where you'll see petroforms — stones laid on the ground in the shapes of snakes, fish, turtles and birds. They're believed to have been laid down centuries ago by Natives for initiation ceremonies.

Whiteshell Park is a haven for hikers, with 15 trails ranging from easy two-kilometre (1.2-mi.) strolls to the granddaddy of them all, the 66-kilometre (41-mi.) Mantario Trail. It's the longest hiking trail in western Canada's Precambrian Shield country. It crosses some very rough terrain and goes up and down rock ridges and through swamps and thick forest. Moose, hawks and bald eagles are abundant, and you'll see many beaver dams. There are lots of black bears in this forest, but sightings are relatively rare. You must be in good shape and well organized to manage the Mantario Trail. In places it's likely to be almost grown over and the path easily lost. Water can be waist-deep in places. Covering the entire distance takes at least three days, and at the end you'll have to rough it in a spartan cabin with no modern amenities. Still, people who have survived it come back raving about the silence, the star-spangled skies, and the healing effect of close contact with nature.

Of the other trails, the most popular and perhaps most scenic is the Pine Point Self-guiding Trail, which can be hiked in summer and skied in winter. It's located southeast of Nutimik Lake off PR 307. Total distance for the two loops of the trail is 9.6 kilometres (6 mi.), a four-hour round trip.

There are lodges and resorts on more than a dozen of the lakes in this park. Two that this writer knows personally are the Inverness Falls Resort on Brereton Lake just north of Rennie and the Jessica Lake Lodge, named after the lake on which it's situated. Inverness Falls Resort is open year-round and is run by a friendly and accommodating couple, Judy and Stewart Cornell. Their resort has 12 housekeeping cabins. It's a beautiful spot in the woods, with a murmuring waterfall near the cabins where Brereton Lake empties into the Rennie River.

At Jessica Lake Lodge, you can sit tranquilly in a screened veranda and look out at the pretty lake, which is surrounded by evergreen forest. There are 10 light-

housekeeping cabins, most with saunas and whirlpools, and there's a barbecue outside each cabin.

If camping is more your style, there are private or government-run campgrounds at Betula, Big Whiteshell, Brereton, Caddy, Falcon, Nutimik, West Hawk, and White lakes. Falcon Beach Campground is the biggest. West Hawk Lake is thought to have been formed by a meteorite crashing to earth, and is so deep the bottom hasn't been found in certain spots.

If you're near Nutimik Lake, visit the Whiteshell Natural History Museum on PR 307. It contains displays of local animals. There's a reference room, and information is available on back-country hiking and recreation. It's all housed in a log cabin of the typical Red River post-on-sill construction.

Sailing is a big sport in Whiteshell Park, with sailing clubs at Pinawa, Big Whiteshell Lake, and Falcon Lake. And the park is a great place to see wildlife such as great gray owls, common loons, bald eagles, and osprey.

THE MENNONITE HERITAGE VILLAGE, STEINBACH

STEINBACH

If you're in the mood for some 19th-century Mennonite atmosphere, take the Trans-Canada Highway out of Winnipeg to the turnoff about 30 kilometres (19 mi.) east of the city. Turn south on Highway 12 and travel about 20 kilometres (12 mi.). On the horizon to your left you'll see the sails of a big windmill, the focal point of the Mennonite Heritage Village (Canada) Ltd., a complex of authentic century-old farmhouses and rural buildings that have been assembled from the area into a replica of an early Mennonite village. The windmill grinds wheat into the flour used in baking the delicious bread sold here. You can climb up a timber staircase to the milling floor and watch the great millstones being turned by the sails; or step out onto the deck where the 20-metre (60-ft.) sails are wheeling in the wind. In the nearby Livery Barn restaurant, women in 19th-century dress serve such authentic Mennonite fare as borscht, farmer's sausage, varenyky (a Mennonite version of perogies) with cream gravy, and a rhubarb dessert called platz. Visit the village church, where men sat on one side,

women on the other. A general store sells locally crafted items, the stone-ground flour, old-fashioned candy and souvenirs. If you're there during Pioneer Days, held on the August long weekend, you can see steam-driven machines sawing wood and threshing grain, as well as sheep being sheared, butter being churned, and bread being baked in outdoor ovens. In the interpretive building you can read about the appalling persecution suffered by the Mennonites in their flights from one European country to another. The overall mood of the place, however, is one of industry, harmony and achievement.

GARDENTON AREA

Before the arrival of European settlers, the Red River Valley was a vast sea of tall-grass prairie, a complex ecosystem with an astonishing variety of grasses, flowers and wildlife. Intensive cereal farming has greatly modified the region, but a 2023-hectare (5,000-acre) remnant of tall-grass prairie has been conserved near the towns of Tolstoi and Gardenton — the largest area of protected tall-grass prairie in Canada today. Manitoba is the only prairie province in which it still survives.

From April to October, tall-grass is in constant metamorphosis. During mid-June, this area displays the endangered small white lady's slipper. In early July the rare western fringed prairie orchid is in bloom; it grows up to 0.6 metre (2 ft.) tall. In August, the threatened lady's tresses appear. Also in August the sacred sweet grass of the Aboriginal people is mature, while big bluestem and Indian grass dominate the horizon. Big bluestem grass reaches a height of about 1.8 metres (6 ft.) by the end of summer, and turns a deep magenta.

The tall-grass prairie supports more than 150 native floral species and is an excellent ecosystem for songbirds, sandhill cranes, wild turkeys, hawks, falcons, white-tailed deer, and even the occasional moose. Seven organizations, including the World Wildlife Fund, are working with the Manitoba Naturalists Society to ensure that the preserve in southern Manitoba is protected.

To reach it, drive south on Highway 59 to Tolstoi, near the Canada-U.S. border, and turn east on PR 209 to Gardenton. You can pick up brochures and a map at the Gardenton Ukrainian Museum. The main preserve (there are three) is between Gardenton and Tolstoi. There's a sign, plus a picnic site and washrooms.

FRINGED ORCHID, TALL-GRASS PRAIRIE, TOLSTOI

TALL-GRASS PRAIRIE

CONTENTS

GETTING THERE

BY LAND

Visitors from the United States must pass through Canada Customs checkpoints before entering the country.

Greyhound Bus Lines (204-783-8840 or 1-800-661-8747) and Grey Goose Bus Lines (204-784-4500) offer daily transportation to and from Winnipeg and dozens of Manitoba's smaller centres.

VIA Rail Canada (1-800-561-8630 for reservations and fares; 204-944-8780 for arrival and departure information) arrives and departs daily from Winnipeg and many smaller communities.

BY AIR

Air Canada (204-943-9361), Canadian Airlines International (204-632-1250), and Northwest Airlines (1-800-225-2525) feature regular flights to and from the Winnipeg International Airport, with connecting flights to any destination in the world. Regional carriers Air Manitoba (204-783-2333 or 1-800-665-1415), Calm Air International (204-778-6471 or 1-800-839-2256), and Perimeter Airlines (Inland) Ltd. (204-783-8000) also fly to and from the Winnipeg International Airport regularly, and offer service to various points within Manitoba. Some of the regional airlines do not use the main airport terminal.

The Winnipeg International Airport is situated eight kilometres (5 mi.) northwest of downtown Winnipeg. Taxis are available at the main terminal, and limousine service to and from the airport is offered by major hotels. Transit bus route #15 (Sargent/ Mountain) provides service between the main terminal and downtown Winnipeg from approximately 6:15am until 12:45am (times vary depending on the day of the week). Bus drivers do not carry change.

CUSTOMS

Arriving

Visitors to Canada may bring certain goods into the country duty-free as part of their personal baggage, as long as these items are declared to Canada Customs on arrival. Such goods include 50 cigars, 200 cigarettes, and one kilogram (2.2 lbs.) of manufactured tobacco. Visitors are also permitted 1.1 litres (40 fl. oz.) of liquor or wine or 24 12-ounce cans or bottles (or its equivalent 8.5 litres or 288 fl. oz.) of beer or ale.

Gift items for Canadian residents are also duty-free, provided the value of each gift does not exceed $40 (Canadian funds) and the gifts do not consist of tobacco products, alcoholic beverages, or advertising material.

Boats, trailers, sporting equipment, cameras, and similar big-ticket items may enter Canada free of duty. However, Canada Customs may occasionally require a refundable deposit to ensure that these goods are taken out of Canada at the conclusion of the visit.

You may import food for your own use without duty payment, provided the quantity is consistent with the duration and nature of your stay in Canada. Certain fruits, vegetables, and meat from countries other than the U.S. may be prohibited. All importations of meat over 20 kilograms (44 lbs.) must be inspected.

Dogs and cats from the U.S. must be accompanied by a veterinarian's certificate stating that the animal has been vaccinated against rabies within the last three years. Pets arriving from countries other than the U.S. may require quarantine.

All weapons must be declared upon arrival. If you are planning to bring into Canada any weapons other than ordinary rifles or shotguns, it's best to check the detailed restrictions and limitations before leaving home. Some weapons are prohibited.

For further information, contact Canada Customs, 401-266 Graham Avenue, Winnipeg, MB, R3C 0J8; 204-983-6395.

Departing

After more than 48 hours in Canada, U.S. residents may take back merchandise to the value of US$400 duty-free (provided no part of this exemption has been used within the previous 30 days). Family members may pool their exemptions. Up to 100 non-Cuban cigars, 200 cigarettes (one carton), and one litre (33.8 fl. oz.) of alcoholic beverage per person may be included in the duty-free exemption.

To find out more about U.S. customs regulations, contact your local customs office or the U.S. Customs Service, P.O. Box 7407, Washington, DC 20044. Ask for a copy of Know Before You Go.

Visitors from other countries should also check on customs regulations before leaving home.

GETTING ACQUAINTED

TIME ZONE

Manitoba falls within the Central Time Zone, which is one hour behind the Eastern Time Zone. Daylight Saving Time, when the clocks are advanced one hour, is in effect from the first Sunday in April until the last Sunday in October.

CLIMATE

Average daily maximum temperatures for Winnipeg:
Jan. -13°C (7°F)   July 26°C (79°F)
Feb. -10°C (14°F) Aug. 25°C (77°F)
Mar. -2°C (27°F)   Sept. 19°C (64°F)
Apr. 10°C (48°F)   Oct. 11°C (54°F)
May 19°C (64°F)   Nov. 0°C (32°F)
June 23°C (73°F)   Dec. -10°C (16°F)
Average daily maximum temperatures for Churchill:
May 3°C (36°F)   Aug. 16°C (59°F)
June 11°C (52°F)   Sept. 9°C (48°F)
July 17°C (63°F)   Oct. 1°C (34°F)

METRIC SYSTEM

Manitoba, like the rest of Canada, has converted to the metric system of weights and measures. Some useful conversions:

1 kilometre = 0.62 miles
100 kilometres per hour =
62 miles per hour
1 litre = 0.264 U.S. gallon
1 litre = 0.22 imperial gallon
1 metre = 3.28 feet
1 centimetre = 0.39 inch
1 kilogram = 2.2 pounds
20 degrees Celsius =
68 degrees Fahrenheit

To convert degrees Celsius to Fahrenheit, multiply by 2 and add 30 (accurate within 2 degrees).

LAWS

The use of seatbelts, child restraints, and motorcycle helmets is compulsory within Manitoba. The possession and use of radar detection devices is illegal. It is suggested that such devices be detached and placed inside a piece of luggage.

The legal minimum age for the purchase or consumption of alcoholic beverages is 18. Open liquor must not be transported in a vehicle unless stored in the trunk or space designed for baggage.

TRAVEL INFORMATION CENTRES

Manitoba

You can obtain free travel literature on the province by writing to Travel Manitoba, Department SP5, 7th floor - 155 Carlton Street, Winnipeg, MB, R3C 3H8; phone 204-945-3777 ext. SP5, or 1-800-665-0040 ext. SP5. For a 24-hour recorded message that provides current information on attractions and events, call 204-942-2535.

Free travel literature and personalized travel counselling are available at Travel Manitoba's seven Travel Information Centres (watch for the "?" symbol):

- Explore Manitoba - Travel Idea Centre, located adjacent to the Johnston Terminal at The Forks in Winnipeg. Supplies information on Winnipeg, Manitoba, and Canada. Open daily.
- Legislative Building, at the corner of Broadway and Osborne in Winnipeg. Open Monday to Friday.
- Canada/U.S. border, Hwy. 75. Mid-May to Labour Day, open daily 8am-9pm; September to mid-May, open 9am-5pm Thursday to Monday.
- Canada/U.S. border, Hwy. 10. Mid-May to Labour Day, open daily 8am-5pm.
- Manitoba/Ontario boundary, Hwy. 1. Mid-May to Labour Day, open daily 8am-9pm.
- Manitoba/Saskatchewan boundary, Hwys. 16 & 83. Mid-May to Labour Day, open daily 8am-9pm.

• Manitoba/Saskatchewan boundary, Hwy. 1. Mid-May to Labour Day, open daily 8am-9pm.

Among the many useful publications available from Travel Manitoba are the Manitoba Explorer's Guide, Manitoba Accommodation & Campground Guide, Manitoba Travel Values Guide, Manitoba Events Guide (winter and summer editions), Manitoba Magic: Provincial Parks Guide, Manitoba Fishing & Hunting Adventures, and the Manitoba Sport Fishing Guide.

Parks Canada

The Forks National Historic Site office in the Children's Museum at The Forks in Winnipeg features displays and literature on the national parks and national historic sites in Manitoba, Saskatchewan, and the Northwest Territories. Parks Canada staff are available to answer your questions. The office is open 8:30am-4:30pm Monday to Friday. The mailing address is 45 Forks Market Road, Winnipeg, MB, R3C 4T6; phone 204-983-2290.

Winnipeg

Free travel literature about Winnipeg is available from Tourism Winnipeg, 320-25 Forks Market Road, Winnipeg, MB, R3C 4S8; phone 204-943-1970 or 1-800-665-0204. The office is located on the third floor of the Johnston Terminal at The Forks and is open 8:30am-4:30pm Monday to Friday.

There is a Tourism Winnipeg Information Centre at the north end of the main level of the Winnipeg International Airport. It is open 8:30am-10pm daily. Phone 204-774-0031.

Some of the publications available from Tourism Winnipeg are the Official Visitor's Guide; Passport to Winnipeg, an events guide; Taste, a restaurant guide; and "Walk Winnipeg: A Visitor's Guide to Winnipeg's Historic & Architectural Downtown Area."

STAYING HEALTHY

Medical care in Manitoba is first-rate but costly. Visitors are urged to obtain travel health insurance before leaving home.

EMERGENCIES

Within Winnipeg, emergency 911 service is available. In life-threatening situations only, you should call 911 and ask for ambulance, fire, police, or poison treatment. Then give the location of the emergency.

In other parts of Manitoba, you can dial zero in any emergency if you don't know the phone number for the emergency service you require. Tell the operator what type of emergency you are reporting and give brief details, including the exact location where help is needed.

LODGING

For a complete listing of accommodations in the province, including campgrounds, fly-in lodges, bed and breakfasts, and country vacation farms, consult Travel Manitoba's Accommodation & Campground Guide. Travel Manitoba's Fishing & Hunting Adventures provides detailed information on lodges. Bed and Breakfast of Manitoba publishes a listing of its members and offers a reservation service. You can contact Bed and Breakfast of Manitoba at 533 Sprague Street, Winnipeg, MB, R3G 2R9; 783-9797. Hostellers should contact Hostelling International, 194A Sherbrook Street, Winnipeg, MB, R3C 2B6; 784-1131. If you are interested in Backpackers Resorts accommodation, you may wish to contact Guest House International, 168 Maryland Street, Winnipeg, MB, R3G 1L3; 772-1272.

In general, the accommodations listed below are some of the best of their kind in Manitoba. Approximate prices are indicated, based on the average cost, at time of publication, for two persons staying in a double room (excluding taxes): $ = under $70; $$ = $70-$100; $$$ = more than $100.

WINNIPEG

• Bannerman East Bed & Breakfast, 99 Bannerman Ave., Winnipeg,

R2W 0T1; 589-6449. Georgian-style home in North-End Winnipeg near the Red River and St. John's Park. Advance notice. $

- Comfort Inn South by Journey's End, 3109 Pembina Hwy., Winnipeg, R3T 4R6; 269-7390 or 1-800-228-5150. Just north of the Perimeter Hwy. in south Winnipeg. Complimentary morning coffee and newspaper. Seniors' and CAA rates available. $-$$

- Delta Winnipeg, 288 Portage Ave., Winnipeg, R3C 0B8; 1-800-268-1133 (Cdn) or 1-800-877-1133 (US). Downtown, connected to many shops and services. Indoor pool, whirlpool, exercise room, sauna, restaurant, lounges. $$$

- Holiday Inn Crowne Plaza, 350 St. Mary Ave., Winnipeg, R3C 3J2; 942-0551 or 1-800-465-4329. Downtown, adjacent to shopping malls. Indoor and outdoor pools, sauna, whirlpool, fitness centre, two restaurants. $$-$$$

- Hotel Fort Garry, 222 Broadway, Winnipeg, R3C 0R3; 942-8251 or 1-800-665-8088. This hotel, built in 1913, offers Victorian-style guest rooms and luxury suites. Features an in-house European-style casino, restaurants, lounge, and cabaret. Downtown, minutes from the historic Forks Market. $-$$

- Radisson Suite Hotel Winnipeg Airport, 1800 Wellington Ave., Winnipeg, R3H 1B2; 783-1700 or 1-800-333-3333. Each suite features a bedroom and separate living room. Microwave ovens and refrigerators available. Restaurant, lounge, exercise room, indoor and outdoor pools, sauna, whirlpool. $$-$$$

- Sheraton Winnipeg, 161 Donald St., Winnipeg, R3C 1M3; 942-5300 or 1-800-325-3535. One block from shopping centres and the downtown skywalk system. Weekend entertainment in Windows Lounge. Restaurant and indoor pool. $$-$$$

- The Westin Hotel Winnipeg, 2 Lombard Place, Winnipeg, R3B 0Y3; 957-1350 or 1-800-228-3000. At the historic corner of Portage and Main downtown. Connected via indoor skywalk to many shops and attractions. Restaurants, indoor pool, fitness centre. $$-$$$

INTERLAKE REGION

- Country Resort by Carlson, 10 Centre St., Box 1860, Gimli, MB, R0C 1B0; 642-8565 or 1-800-456-4000. Located on the Lake Winnipeg beachfront. Guest rooms and two-room suites available. Indoor and outdoor pools, sauna, whirlpool, restaurant and lounge. $-$$

- Daerwood Motor Inn, 162 Main St., Selkirk, MB, R1A 1R3; 482-7722. Air-conditioned rooms and kitchenettes. Restaurant and lounge next door. $-$$

- Gull Harbour Resort & Conference Centre, Hecla Provincial Park; 475-2354 or 279-2041. Mailing address: General Delivery, Riverton, MB, R0C 2R0. Indoor pool, whirlpool, sauna, gymnasium, miniature golf, dining room, and lounge. Beaches, an 18-hole golf course and trails nearby. $$

- Rockwood Motor Inn, 376 Main St., Box 1428, Stonewall, MB, R0C 2Z0; 467-2354. Licensed dining room, beverage room, live entertainment. Wheelchair access. $

- Viking Motor Hotel, 78 - 7th Ave., Box 131, Gimli, MB, R0C 1B0; 642-5168. Dining room, cocktail lounge, nightclub. Fridges in all rooms. $-$$

PEMBINA VALLEY/CENTRAL PLAINS

- Holiday Mountain Resort, Box 89, La Riviere, MB, R0G 1A0; 242-2172. Motel units and a chalet with a licensed dining room, coffee shop, and cocktail lounge. Ten ski slopes and a 9-hole golf course. $

- Manitoba Inn, Hwy. 1, Box 867, Portage la Prairie, MB, R1N 3C3; 857-9791 or 1-800-214-6655. Indoor pool, hot tub, sauna, tennis and volleyball courts, walking trails, licensed dining room and lounge, seniors' rates. $$

- Morden Motor Inn, 780 Thornhill Ave., Box 1177, Morden, MB, R0G 1J0; 822-6272. Licensed dining room, coffee shop, pub. Wheelchair access. $

- Pembina Crossing Guest Ranch, Box 490, Manitou, MB, R0G 1G0;

242-2059. Located 12 km/7 mi. south of Manitou. Fully equipped guest house, restaurant, store, and walking trails. Also serviced lots for camping. $

- Westward Village Inn, 2401 Saskatchewan Ave. W., Portage la Prairie, MB, R1N 3L5; 857-9745. Fitness complex, indoor pool and whirlpool, nightclub, licensed dining room, cafeteria, and lounge. $
- Winkler Inn, 851 Main St. N., Box 968, Winkler, MB, R6W 4B1; 325-4381. Indoor pool, whirlpool, licensed dining room, beverage room, Sunday smorgasbord. $-$$

PARKLAND/WESTERN REGION

- Blue Jewel Inn (bed & breakfast), 401 Mill Road, Box 445, Boissevain, MB, R0K 0E0; 534-6258. A quaint century-old home located a 15-minute drive from the Turtle Mountains. Gift shop and tearoom. $
- Casa Maley (bed & breakfast), 1605 Victoria Ave., Brandon, MB, R7A 1C1; 728-0812. This European-style three-storey Tudor home, built in 1912, is a designated heritage site. Beautiful oak interior. Advance notice. $
- The Castle Bed & Breakfast, 149 - 2nd Ave. S.W., Box 1705, Minnedosa, MB, R0J 1E0; 867-2830. A restored two-turret 1901 Queen Anne heritage site on the river. Large honeymoon suite available. Advance notice. $-$$
- Elkhorn Resort & Conference Centre, Box 40, Wasagaming, MB, R0J 2H0; 848-2802. Adjacent to Riding Mountain National Park. Nine-hole golf course, indoor pool, jacuzzi, sauna, exercise room, licensed dining room, lounge. $$-$$$
- Royal Oak Inn, 3130 Victoria Ave. W., Brandon, MB, R7A 5Z7; 728-5775 or 1-800-852-2709. Indoor pool and hot tub complex, 1930s theme restaurant, country nightclub. $$
- Russell Inn Hotel & Conference Centre, Box 578, Highway 16, Russell, MB, R0J 1W0; 773-2186 or 1-800-665-0678. Licensed restaurant, indoor and outdoor hot tubs, sauna. Several theme suites with private hot tubs. $-$$$

- Trails West Motor Inn, 210 - 18th St. N., Brandon, MB, R7A 5Z8; 727-3800. Indoor pool and waterslide, licensed dining room and lounge, saloon. $
- Victoria Inn, 3550 Victoria Ave. W., P.O. Box 458, Brandon, MB, R7A 5Z4; 725-1532 or 1-800-852-2710. Located next to a shopping plaza. Health club facilities, solarium, pool, hot tub and saunas, licensed restaurant and lounge. $-$$

NORTHERN REGION

- Anna's Bed & Breakfast, 204 Wolf St., Thompson, MB, R8N 1J7; 677-5075. Completely private quarters. Pick-up at airport and train station. Advance notice. $
- Big Sand Lake Lodge, Big Sand Lake; 774-6666. Mailing address: Room 1, 1808 Wellington Ave., Winnipeg, MB, R3H 0G3. Fly-in fishing and hunting lodge with licensed dining room, lounge, hot tub, sauna, and exercise room. Open June to September. American package plan includes return airfare from Winnipeg.
- Country Inn & Suites, 70 Thompson Dr., Thompson, MB, R8N 0C3; 778-8879 or 1-800-456-4000. Guest rooms and two-room suites available. Indoor pool, whirlpool, sauna, free Continental breakfast. $$
- Knee Lake Resort Inc., Knee Lake; 632-6098 or 1-800-563-7151. Mailing address: 3-1791 Dublin Ave., Winnipeg, MB, R3H 1A9. Fly-in fishing lodge with licensed dining room and lounge. Modern lakeview cabins have Franklin fireplaces and verandas. Open late May to mid-September. All-inclusive package plans include transportation from Winnipeg.
- Nejalini Lake Resort, Nejanilini Lake; 775-2229 or 1-800-387-5090. Mailing address: 814-1661 Portage Ave., Winnipeg, MB, R3J 3T7. Fly-in fishing and hunting lodge with fully modern units, licensed dining room, cocktail lounge, and sauna. Open late June to September. American package plans include transportation from Winnipeg.
- Nueltin Fly-In Lodges, Nueltin Lake; 767-2330 or 1-800-361-7177.

Mailing address: Box 500, Alonsa, MB, R0H 0A0. Manitoba's northernmost fishing lodge. Licensed dining room, lounge, and fully modern cabins with fireplaces. Open mid-June to end of August. American package plans include transportation from Winnipeg.

• Seaport Hotel, 299 Kelsey Blvd., Box 339, Churchill, MB, R0B 0E0; 675-8807. Airport limousine service, licensed restaurant and dining room, cocktail lounge, gift shop. $$

• Victoria Inn, 160 Hwy. 10, Box 220, Flin Flon, MB, R8A 1M9; 687-7555. Indoor pool, licensed dining room and lounge, saunas, whirlpool. $

• Wekusko Falls Lodge, P.O. Box 705, Snow Lake, MB, R0B 1M0; 358-2341. Located south of Snow Lake, at Wekusko Falls on the Grass River. Modern kitchenette cabins, store, dining room and lounge, coffee shop, laundromat, boats. Fishing and hunting. $

• Wescana Inn, 439 Fischer Ave., P.O. Box 2519, The Pas, MB, R9A 1M3; 623-5446 or 1-800-665-9468. Licensed dining room and lounge, laundry room, small fridges available, coffee makers in rooms. $

EASTERN REGION

• Aikens Lake Wilderness Lodge, Aikens Lake; 237-5253 or 1-800-565-2595. Mailing address: Box 98, St. Boniface P.O., Winnipeg, MB, R2H 3B4. Fly-in fishing lodge with cabins, modern motel units, and luxury suites. Unlicensed dining room. Open May to September. All-inclusive American-plan fishing packages available.

• Barrier Bay Resort, Dorothy Lake, Whiteshell Provincial Park; 348-7755. Mailing address: Box 116, Seven Sisters Falls, MB, R0E 1Y0. Modern light-housekeeping cabins and motel units. Heated outdoor pool, restaurant, store, fishing. Open May to October. $-$$$. Weekly summer rates.

• Eagle Nest Landing, Winnipeg River, Whiteshell Provincial Park; 884-2301 or 1-800-665-0232 (U.S.). Mailing address: Box 25, Pointe du Bois, MB, R0E 1N0. Modern kitchenette cabins with whirlpools and fireplaces. Fishing for northern pike, walleye, smallmouth bass, sturgeon, lake trout, and goldeye. Package plans available.

• Grand Marais Inn, Hwy. 12, Box 143, Grand Marais, MB, R0E 0T0; 754-2141. Air-conditioned rooms, TVs, licensed restaurant, saloon. Wheelchair access. $

• Inverness Falls Resort, Brereton Lake, Whiteshell Provincial Park; 369-5336. Mailing address: Rennie, MB, R0E 1R0. Modern kitchenette cottages with fireplaces, some with whirlpools. Hiking trails, complimentary canoes and bicycles. Fishing for walleye, northern pike, and perch. $-$$$. Weekly summer rates.

• Jessica Lake Lodge, Jessica Lake, Whiteshell Provincial Park; 348-7544. Mailing address: Rennie, MB, R0E 1R0. Modern lakefront kitchenette cottages, some with whirlpool and sauna. Free use of canoes and bicycles. Fishing for walleye, northern pike, and perch. $$-$$$. Weekly summer rates.

• Riverview Lodge, Eleanor Lake, Whiteshell Provincial Park; 348-7607. Mailing address: Box 114, Seven Sisters Falls, MB, R0E 1Y0. Luxury cottages and modern lakefront cabins. Restaurant, store, sauna. Fishing for pickerel, northern pike, bass, and goldeye. $$-$$$. Weekly rates available.

• Tallpine Lodges, West Hawk Lake, Whiteshell Provincial Park; 349-2209. Mailing address: Whiteshell P.O., West Hawk Lake, MB, R0E 2H0. Light-housekeeping lodges with fireplaces, most with saunas. Heated outdoor pool. $$-$$$

DINING

A free guide to restaurants in Winnipeg, titled Taste, is available from Tourism Winnipeg.

Listed below are some recommended restaurants in the various regions of the province. Approximate prices are indicated, based on the average cost, at time of publication, of one dinner including soup or salad, main course, dessert and beverage (excluding wine or liquor, taxes, and gratuity): inexpensive = under $15; moderate = $15-$25; expensive = over $25.

The list of restaurants in the Winnipeg area was compiled by Marion Warhaft, restaurant critic for the Winnipeg Free Press and author of Dining Out with Marion Warhaft: A Guide to Over 80 Winnipeg Restaurants (Turnstone Press).

WINNIPEG AND AREA

- Amici, 326 Broadway; 943-4997. Fine North Italian cuisine in elegant surroundings. Linguine with lamb, lobster agnolotti. Dinner Monday to Saturday, lunch Monday to Friday. Expensive.
- Bangkok Thai, 100 Osborne St.; 474-0908. Fiery, flavourful Thai cuisine. Dinner daily, lunch Monday to Friday. Moderate.
- Le Beaujolais, 131 Provencher Ave.; 237-6276. Lovely French food, seductive setting. Salmon in basil sauce, rib steak in beaujolais. Dinner daily. Expensive.
- Between Friends, 1480 Pembina Hwy.; 284-8402. Excellent French-Italian food. Crab ravioli, lime-honey veal. Dinner daily, lunch Monday to Saturday. Expensive.
- Between Friends, Holiday Inn Crowne Plaza, 350 St. Mary Ave.; 946-5200. Same owners as above. Elegance and delicious French and Southwestern food. Mussels marinière, beef in cabernet. Dinner Monday to Saturday, lunch Monday to Friday, Sunday brunch. Expensive.
- Bistro Bohemia, 159 Osborne St.; 453-1944. Czech and other European dishes, luscious desserts. Dinner and lunch Monday to Saturday. Moderate.
- Bistro Dansk, 63 Sherbrook St.; 775-5662. Owned by the same family and serves many of the same dishes as Bistro Bohemia. Dinner and lunch Monday to Saturday. Moderate.
- Bombolini, 326 Broadway; 943-5066. Amici's downstairs cafe (see Amici above). Serves some of the same dishes. Lunch and dinner Monday to Saturday. Moderate.
- Cafe Carlo, 243 Lilac St.; 477-5544. Excellent, informal, eclectic food. Pastas, seafood chowder, jerk chicken. Dinner and lunch Monday to Saturday. Expensive.
- Edohei, 355 Ellice Ave.; 943-0427. Sushi and cooked Japanese dishes. Dinner Wednesday to Monday; lunch Monday, Wednesday, Thursday and Friday. Moderate.
- Grand Garden, 268 King St.; 942-1878. Chinese dinners and dim sum lunches. Lunch and dinner daily. Inexpensive.
- India Gardens, 764 McDermot Ave.; 783-0306. Fine Indian cooking amid beautiful Indian art. Dinner Monday to Saturday, lunch Monday to Friday. Moderate.
- Kum-Koon Garden, 257 King St.; 943-4655. Good dinners and a huge variety of dim sum. Lunch and dinner daily. Inexpensive.
- Mandarin restaurants. Two under the same management, both offering fine cuisine. (1) Mandarin, 613 Sargent Ave.; 775-7819. North Chinese cooking. Dinner Tuesday to Sunday. Inexpensive. (2) River Mandarin, 252 River Ave.; 284-8963. Original dishes of North Chinese inspiration. Dinner daily, lunch Monday to Friday. Moderate.
- Orlando's, 709 Corydon Ave.; 477-5899. Seafood and Portuguese dishes. Dinner Monday to Saturday, lunch Thursday and Friday. Expensive.
- Peppoli, 454 River Ave.; 284-3996. Fine pastas and fresh fish. Dinner Monday to Saturday, lunch Monday to Friday. Expensive.
- Prairie Oyster, The Forks; 942-0918. Fine North American cafe food, and yes, they serve prairie oysters. Monday to Thursday 11am-10pm; Saturday to midnight; Sunday to 9pm. Moderate.
- Rae and Jerry's, 1405 Portage Ave.; 775-8154. Beef is king and martinis the tipple of choice in this Winnipeg landmark. Lunch and dinner daily. Expensive.
- Roma, 166 Provencher Ave.; 231-5757. Excellent little trattoria. Monday to Friday 11:30am-10:30pm; Saturday 5pm-10:30pm. Inexpensive.
- Sandpiper, The Forks; 942-0918. Fine steaks and fresh seafood in one of the city's best. Lunch and

dinner daily. Expensive.
- Settebello, 788 Corydon Ave.; 477-9105. Busy, trendy, crowded, with good dinner pastas and appetizers. Monday to Thursday 11:30am-10pm; Friday and Saturday to 2am; Sunday 5pm-11pm. Moderate.
- Tokyo Joe's, 132 Pioneer Ave.; 943-5796. Delicious Korean tartar steak and Japanese shrimp tempura. Dinner daily. Moderate.
- Tre Visi, 173 McDermot Ave.; 949-9032. Fine, authentic Italian food in attractive setting. Dinner Monday to Saturday, lunch Monday to Friday. Moderate.
- Viva, 505 Sargent Ave.; 772-3167. Excellent Vietnamese cuisine. Lunch and dinner daily. Inexpensive.

The Forks has several ethnic food booths serving Greek, Italian, Jamaican, Sri Lankan, and Ukrainian food.

Four charming tearooms within a short drive of Winnipeg:
- Captain Kennedy House, Lot 63 River Rd., St. Andrews; 334-2498. An 1866 riverside house that has been converted to a tearoom and museum, with spectacular gardens. Seasonal hours. Inexpensive.
- May House, 391 Centre Ave., Stonewall; 467-2289. A restored 1896 house. Seasonal hours. Inexpensive.
- Rose Lane, 31 Rose Lane, Rosenort; 746-6196. A restored turn-of-the-century farmhouse. Seasonal hours. Inexpensive.
- Walnut Street Tearoom, 77 - 2nd Ave. S.W., Carman; 745-6787. A century-old church. Seasonal hours. Inexpensive.

INTERLAKE REGION

- Brennivins, 70 - 1st Ave., Gimli; 642-5555. Pizza, ribs, shrimp, pasta. Some Icelandic alcoholic beverages. Dinner Wednesday to Sunday; also lunch during the summer. Inexpensive.
- Bronze Boot Steakhouse, 380 Eveline St., Selkirk; 482-6212. Specializes in steak and ribs, and features an open steak pit. Licensed outdoor patio. Lunch and dinner daily. Moderate.

- Grrrumpy's, 635 Morris Ave., Selkirk; 482-9104. Steaks, chicken, shrimp, burgers. Lunch and dinner daily. Moderate.
- Jane & Paula's Dunnottar Inn, 30 Gimli Rd., Matlock; 389-5303. Steaks, prime rib, veal, chicken, barbecued ribs, salmon, shrimp. Homemade soups and desserts. Seasonal hours. Inexpensive.
- Jane & Walter's, Hwy. 9 and Congdon Rd., Sandy Hook; 389-5473. Prime rib, steak, lamb, chicken, fishermen's platters, pastas. Seasonal hours. Inexpensive.
- Jimmy's Cafe, 129 Hwy. 9, Gimli; 642-4424. A family restaurant serving Greek specialties and Canadian dishes. All-day breakfast, homemade fries. Breakfast, lunch and dinner daily. Inexpensive.
- Niakwa Family Restaurant, Boardwalk Mall, Winnipeg Beach; 389-2299. Veal, ribs, steaks, seafood, pizza, pasta, burgers and sandwiches. Lunch and dinner daily. Inexpensive.
- Royal Quarry Restaurant & Lounge, Westside Plaza, Stonewall; 467-5321. Perogies, fish, veal cutlets, shrimp, steak. Italian, Ukrainian or Chinese smorgasbords for Friday dinner. Breakfast, lunch and dinner daily. Inexpensive.
- Valentino Restaurant & Lounge, 46 Main St., Winnipeg Beach; 389-2223. Authentic Italian cuisine. Homemade soups, children's menu, outdoor patio. Seasonal hours. Lunch and dinner daily in summer. Moderate.

PEMBINA VALLEY/CENTRAL PLAINS

- Four C Dining Room and Coffee Shop, 28 Main St. at Hwy. 3, Manitou; 242-2858. Full menu includes everything from hamburgers to steak and lobster, with daily noon specials. Breakfast, lunch and dinner daily. Inexpensive.
- Log Cabin Restaurant, 10 Thornhill St., Morden; 822-6681. Unique log cabin ambience with a stone fireplace in the centre. Steak, chicken, seafood, ribs, pasta. Good wine cellar. Lunch and dinner

daily; also breakfast Saturday and Sunday. Moderate.

- Manitobah Inn restaurant, at the junction of the Trans-Canada Hwy. by-pass and Yellowquill Trail, Portage la Prairie; 857-9791. Steaks, burgers, children's menu, breakfast buffet. Breakfast, lunch and dinner daily. Inexpensive.

- Triangle Oasis restaurant, 880 Centennial St. at the junction of Hwys. 14 and 32, Winkler; 325-8922. Famous for its Mennonite dishes as well as its homemade soups and pies. Breakfast, lunch and dinner daily. Inexpensive.

- Twister's Burgers, Fries & Malts, 400 Memorial Dr., Winkler; 325-1957. Full meals as well as the signature homemade-style burgers and real old-fashioned chocolate malts. Full of 1950s atmosphere. Breakfast, lunch and dinner daily. Inexpensive.

- Valley Gardens Family Restaurant and Heritage Gardens Dining Room, 230 Roblin Blvd., Winkler; 325-5010. Valley Gardens, the main area in the restaurant, serves chicken, steaks, seafood, sandwiches and pasta. Breakfast, lunch and dinner daily. Inexpensive. Heritage Gardens is a formal dining room for special candlelight dinners, with its own menu. Lunch and dinner daily. Moderate.

PARKLAND/WESTERN REGION

- Brede's, 121 Main St. S., Minnedosa; 867-2162. German, Austrian and French cuisine. Dinner Wednesday to Sunday. Moderate.

- Casteleyn Belgian Chocolatiers & Cappuccino Bar, 908 Rosser Ave., Brandon; 727-2820. Serves desserts and Belgian chocolates made in the building. Also Italian ice cream and a full range of coffees. No full meals. Open Tuesday to Sunday.

- Harry's Ukrainian Kitchen, Trans-Canada Hwy., Brandon; 725-4020. Ukrainian and Canadian dishes. Breakfast, lunch and dinner daily. Inexpensive.

- Jerry's Bistro, upstairs at 926 Rosser Ave., Brandon; 727-7781. Seafood is a specialty here. Continental cuisine, fondues, pickerel, souvlaki. Lunch and dinner Monday to Saturday. Expensive.

- Kokonas, 1011 Rosser Ave., Brandon; 727-4395. Greek dishes, char-broiled steaks, lamb, poultry, seafood. Well known for its prime rib. Dinner daily, lunch Monday to Saturday. Moderate.

- Kurt's Schnitzel House, 123 - 4th St., Wawanesa; 824-2472. German specialties, steaks, seafood, prime rib, chicken, homemade bread, imported beers. Reservations required. Dinner Wednesday to Sunday. Moderate.

- Old Hotel Cafe, Hwy. 10, Onanole; 848-2966. A family restaurant full of antiques that's known for its fish and chips, ribs, burgers, homemade fries, and large salads. Seasonal hours. Inexpensive.

- Sommer Kitchen, 608 Rosser Ave., Brandon; 728-1495. Specializes in Mennonite food and also offers Canadian dishes. Known for its soups and homemade breads. Breakfast, lunch and dinner Monday to Saturday. Inexpensive.

NORTHERN REGION

- Adventurers North Dining Room, Mystery Lake Motor Hotel, Cree Rd. and Selkirk Ave., Thompson; 677-3662. A full range of menu items, from hamburgers to lobster. Daily specials and a Sunday smorgasbord. Breakfast, lunch and dinner Monday to Saturday; breakfast and lunch Sunday. Moderate.

- Gypsy's, 253 Kelsey Blvd., Churchill; 675-2322. A good bakery and cafe that displays local wildlife photos. Menu items include pizza, steaks, and burgers. Breakfast, lunch and dinner Monday to Saturday. Inexpensive.

- Mr. Ribs, at the Riverbase on the north bank of the Burntwood River, Thompson; 778-7111. You can watch the float planes take off and land. Northern art is on display and for sale. Greek and Canadian cuisine. Lunch and dinner daily. Moderate.

- Trader's Table, Arctic Trading Co., 141 Kelsey Blvd., Churchill; 675-8804. Good home-cooked meals and great ambience. Arctic char is a specialty. Artifacts and art are on display. Seasonal hours. Inexpensive.

- Victoria Inn dining room, 160 Hwy. 10, Flin Flon; 687-7555. Chicken, seafood, steaks, light dinners, sandwiches. Breakfast, lunch and dinner daily. Moderate.
- Wescana Inn dining room, 439 Fischer Ave., The Pas; 623-2777. Canadian cuisine, with nightly specials. Breakfast, lunch and dinner Monday to Saturday; breakfast and lunch Sunday. Inexpensive.

EASTERN REGION

- Dutch Connection, 88 Hwy. 12 S., Steinbach; 326-2018. French Continental cooking, with some Dutch dishes. Breakfast, lunch and dinner Tuesday to Sunday. Moderate.
- G'News, 544 Main St., Oakbank; 444-3424. A family restaurant with an extensive menu, including T-bone steak and ribs. Breakfast, lunch and dinner daily. Inexpensive.
- Grand Beach Road Cafe, Grand Marais. Known for its roast beef and hot beef sandwiches. Seasonal hours. Breakfast, lunch and dinner daily in summer. Inexpensive.
- Jennifer's, Seven Sisters Falls; 348-7135. Fine European dining in a very relaxed atmosphere. Lunch and dinner daily. Inexpensive.
- The Jenny Wren, Hillside Beach Road and Hwy. 59 N., Victoria Beach; 756-3762. British decor and menu, including scones, Cornish pasties, and English desserts. Also hamburgers and sandwiches. Seasonal hours. Inexpensive.
- The Lakeview restaurant, 57 Park Ave., Lac du Bonnet; 345-8661. Roasts, sandwiches, shrimp, chicken, ribs. Features a steak pit and salad bar Wednesday to Saturday evenings. Breakfast, lunch and dinner Monday to Saturday. Inexpensive.
- The Livery Barn, Mennonite Heritage Village, Steinbach; 326-9661. Hearty Mennonite food. Seasonal hours. Inexpensive.
- Papertown Motor Inn dining room, 1.6 km/1 mi. east of Pine Falls at Hwys. 304 & 11; 367-2261. Salads, sandwiches, steak, chicken, burgers. Breakfast, lunch and dinner daily. Inexpensive.

- White Lake Resort restaurant, off Hwy. 307 at White Lake; 348-7605. Hot beef sandwich platters, schnitzel, chicken, perogies, fish and chips. Homemade, traditional European sweet treats such as black forest cake. Seasonal hours. Inexpensive.

ATTRACTIONS

The Manitoba Explorer's Guide, published by Travel Manitoba, contains extensive information about the province's attractions. A free booklet that provides details about museums, titled Museums in Manitoba, is available from the Association of Manitoba Museums, Suite 422, 167 Lombard Avenue, Winnipeg, MB, R3B 0T6; 947-1782. Here we provide a selective listing of many of the points of interest. Also see "Parks and Natural Attractions," pp.188-190.

WINNIPEG

- Air Force Heritage Park, Sharpe Blvd. north of Ness Ave., and at Ness Ave. and Conway St.; 833-2212.
- Assiniboia Downs, 3975 Portage Ave. at the Perimeter Hwy.; 885-3330.
- Assiniboine Park Conservatory (park entrance at Corydon Ave. and Shaftesbury); 986-5537.
- Assiniboine Park Zoo (park entrance at Corydon Ave. and Shaftesbury); 986-6921.
- Crystal Casino, Hotel Fort Garry, 7th floor, 222 Broadway; 957-2600.
- Dalnavert Museum, 61 Carlton St.; 943-2835.
- The Forks National Historic Site, south of Water Ave. and east of Main St.; 983-2007 or 983-5988.
- The Forks Public Market, east of Main St. at York Ave.; 942-6309.
- Gabrielle Roy House, 375 rue Deschambault.
- Grant's Old Mill, 2777 Portage Ave.; 986-5613 or 837-1775.
- IMAX Theatre, Level 3 - 393 Portage Ave.; 956-4629.
- Manitoba Children's Museum, at The Forks (east of Main St. at York Ave.); 956-5437 or 956-1888.
- Manitoba Legislative Building,

Broadway at Osborne St.; 945-5813.
- Museum of Man and Nature, 190 Rupert Ave.; 943-3139 or 956-2830.
- Planetarium, 190 Rupert Ave.; 943-3139 or 956-2830.
- Prairie Dog Central (steam train rides), CNR St. James Station, 1661 Portage Ave.; 832-5259.
- Rainbow Stage, Kildonan Park; 784-1280.
- Riel House National Historic Site, 330 River Rd. (St. Vital); 257-1783.
- River Rouge & M.S. Paddlewheel Queen (river cruise ships); 942-4500.
- Ross House, in Joe Zuken Heritage Park, west side of Meade St. between Sutherland and Euclid; 943-3958 or 943-2835.
- Royal Canadian Mint (tours), 520 Lagimodière Blvd. at the Trans-Canada Hwy.; 257-3359.
- St. Boniface Cathedral, 190 ave. de la Cathédrale; 233-7304.
- St. Boniface Museum, 494 Taché Ave.; 237-4500.
- St. Norbert Provincial Heritage Park, 40 Turnbull Dr.; 269-5377 or 945-6784.
- Seven Oaks House, 115 Rupertsland Blvd. east of Main; 339-7429.
- Seven Oaks Memorial, southeast corner of Main St. and Rupertsland Ave.
- Ukrainian Cultural and Educational Centre (Oseredok), 184 Alexander Ave. E.; 942-0218.
- Upper Fort Garry Gate, south of Broadway off Fort St.
- Western Canada Aviation Museum, Hangar T2 - 958 Ferry Rd.; 786-5503.
- Winnipeg Art Gallery, 300 Memorial Blvd.; 775-7297 or 786-6641.
- Winnipeg Commodity Exchange, 500-360 Main St.; 949-0495.

INTERLAKE REGION

- Ashern Pioneer Museum, 1st St. S.W. just off Hwy. 6, Ashern; 768-2049 or 768-3078.
- Captain Kennedy Museum and Tea House, on PR 238, the River Road Heritage Parkway (east of Hwy. 9 just north of Winnipeg); 334-2498.
- Eriksdale Museum, Railway Ave., Eriksdale; 739-2621 or 739-2666.
- Gimli Historical Museum, Centre St. E. (harbour area), Gimli; 642-5317.
- Hecla Village and Hecla Fish Station, Hecla Provincial Park.
- Kenosewun Centre, in Lockport Heritage Park, Hwy. 44 just east of the Lockport Bridge; 757-2864.
- Little Britain Church, north of Lockport on Hwy. 9.
- Lower Fort Garry, 32 km/20 mi. north of Winnipeg on Hwy. 9; 785-6050 or 1-800-442-0600.
- Lundar Museum, Railway Ave. and Main St., Lundar; 762-5217 or 762-5689.
- Marine Museum of Manitoba, Selkirk Park, Selkirk; 482-7761.
- Moosehorn Heritage Museum Inc., Railway and First Sts., Moosehorn; 768-2087 or 768-2066.
- St. Andrew's-on-the-Red Anglican Church, on PR 238, the River Road Heritage Parkway (east of Hwy. 9 just north of Winnipeg).
- St. Andrew's Rectory National Historic Park, on PR 238, the River Road Heritage Parkway (east of Hwy. 9 just north of Winnipeg); 334-6405.
- St. Peter's Dynevor Church, 5 km/3 mi. north of East Selkirk on PR 508.
- Selkirk Community Arts Centre Inc., 101-250 Manitoba Ave., Selkirk; 482-4359.
- Teulon and District Museum, Teulon; 886-3149 or 886-2792.
- Ukrainian Homestead Museum, adjacent to Winnipeg Beach Recreation Park; 389-4079 or 389-2170.
- V Gross' Doll Display and Gift Shop, 2.4 km/1.5 mi. north of Hwy. 67 on Golf Course Rd., Warren; 322-5346 or 254-4896.
- Woodlands Pioneer Museum, Woodlands; 383-5584 or 383-5867.

PEMBINA VALLEY/CENTRAL PLAINS

- Agriculture and Agri-Food Canada Research Centre, Route 100 and Stephen, Morden; 822-4471.
- Alex Robertson Museum, Alonsa; 767-2101.
- Archibald Historical Museum, northeast of La Riviere; 242-2825 or 242-2554.
- Delta Waterfowl and Wetlands Research Station, at Delta Beach on PR 240.
- Dufferin Historical Museum, south end of Kings Park, Carman; 745-

- 3507 or 745-2235.
- Fort la Reine Museum and Pioneer Village, on the outskirts of Portage la Prairie at the junction of Hwys. 1A and 26; 857-3259.
- 4-H Museum, Roland; 343-2152 or 343-2348.
- Gladstone Museum, in the CNR building, 6th St. at Williams Park, Gladstone; 385-2551.
- Manitoba Agricultural Museum and the Homesteaders' Village, 2.5 km/1.5 mi. south of the junction of Hwys. 1 and 34, Austin; 637-2354.
- Manitoba Amateur Radio Museum, at the Manitoba Agricultural Museum, 2.5 km/1.5 mi. south of the junction of Hwys. 1 and 34, Austin; 637-2354.
- Miami Museum, 3rd St. and Kirby, Miami; 435-2305.
- Morden and District Museum, at the Recreation Centre, 2nd St. and Gilmour Ave., Morden; 822-3406 or 822-5670.
- Morris and District Centennial Museum, at the junction of Hwys. 23 east and 75; 746-2169.
- Musée Saint-Claude, St. Claude; 379-2228 or 379-2156.
- Musée St. Joseph Museum, 6.5 km/4 mi. off Hwy. 75 on PR 201, St. Joseph; 737-2241.
- Pembina Hills Gallery, Morden; 822-6026.
- Pembina Threshermen's Museum, 5 km/3.5 mi. west of Winkler on Hwy. 3; 325-7938 or 822-5369.
- Portage Arts Centre and Gallery, 160 Saskatchewan Ave. W., Portage la Prairie; 239-6029.
- Railway Station Museum, Miami; 942-4632.
- St. Anne's Anglican Church, 3 km/2 mi. west of Poplar Point.
- Star Mound Museum, 3 km/2 mi. west and 1.6 km/1 mi. north of Snowflake.
- Thee Olde Nunnery Cafe and Market, off Hwy. 1 on Hwy. 26, St. François Xavier; 864-2306.
- Thunderbird Nest, 3 km/2 mi. south of The Narrows on Hwy. 68.
- Treherne Museum, 183 Vanzile St., Treherne; 723-2621.

PARKLAND/WESTERN REGION

- Anishinabe Village and Campground, Riding Mountain

National Park; 848-7272.
- Antler River Museum, at the corner of Summit and Ash, Melita; 522-8287.
- Art Gallery of Southwestern Manitoba, 638 Princess Ave., Brandon; 727-1036.
- Auditorium Theatre, 228 Wellington W., Virden; 748-1982.
- Badger Creek Museum, Cartwright; 529-2363.
- Beautiful Plains Museum, west end of Hamilton St., Neepawa; 476-3896 or 476-5101.
- Beckoning Hills Museum, 425 Mill Road S., Boissevain; 534-6544 or 534-6045.
- Binscarth Museum, 19 km/11 mi. south of Russell on Hwy. 83; 532-2223.
- Birdtail Country Museum, Main St., Birtle; 842-3363 or 842-5219.
- B.J. Hales Museum, Brandon University's basement concourse of McMaster Hall, Brandon; 727-9623.
- Carberry Plains Museum, 520 - 4th Ave., Carberry; 834-2284 or 834-2797.
- Chapman Museum, 6.4 km/4 mi. east of Rivers on Hwy. 25 and 6.5 km/4 mi. south; 728-7396 or 728-9801.
- Clack Brothers Museum, 8.8 km/5.5 mi. northwest of Rivers; 328-7330.
- Clegg's Museum of Horse-Drawn Vehicles, 3.6 km/2.3 mi. south of Hwy. 24 near Arrow River; 562-3648.
- Commonwealth Air Training Plan Museum, Hangar 1, Brandon Airport; 727-2444.
- Crystal City Community Printing Museum, 218 Broadway St., Crystal City; 873-2293.
- Daly House, 122 - 18th St., Brandon; 727-1722.
- Dr. Vernon L. Watson Arts Centre, 104 - 1st Ave. N.W., Dauphin; 638-6231.
- Fort Dauphin Museum Inc., 140 Jackson St., Dauphin; 638-6630.
- Frelsis (Liberty) Church, 9 km/5.5 mi. north of Baldur.
- Hillcrest Museum (includes the Agricultural Museum), next to the swinging bridge in Souris; 483-3138.
- J.A.V. David Museum, 414 Williams Ave., Killarney; 523-7325 or 523-8205.
- Keystone Pioneer Museum, 7 km/4.5 mi. east of Roblin on Hwy

5; 937-2917 or 937-2935.
- Manitoba Antique Automobile Museum, on the Trans-Canada Hwy., Elkhorn; 845-2356.
- Margaret Laurence Home, 312 First Ave., Neepawa; 476-3612.
- Miniota Municipal Museum, Miniota; 567-3675 or 567-3683.
- Minnedosa and District Cooperative Museum, 2nd Ave., Minnedosa; 867-5190 or 867-2050.
- Moncur Gallery, at the Civic Centre/Library, Boissevain; 534-2433 or 534-7160.
- Oli Johnson Museum, northwest of Swan River near PR 588; 734-2090 or 238-4379.
- Operation Fire Fly, Souris Airport, Souris; 483-2303.
- Pilot Mound Centennial Museum, Pilot Mound; 825-2035.
- Pioneer Days Museum, 41 Oak Ave. W., Souris; 483-3216.
- Pioneer Home Museum of Virden and Districts, 390 King St. W., Virden; 748-1659 or 748-1694.
- Royal Canadian Artillery Museum, Bldg. A-12, CFB Shilo, 15 km/9 mi. south of Hwy. 1 on PR 340; 765-3534.
- St. Elie Romanian Orthodox Church Museum, 4.8 km/3 mi. north of Inglis on PR 591 near Lennard; 564-2228.
- Seton Centre, 116 Main St., Carberry; 834-2059.
- Sipiweske Museum, west of Glenboro off Hwy. 2; 824-2289.
- Souris Agate Pit, Souris; 483-2561.
- Sparrow's Nest Petting Farm, 4 km/2.5 mi. north of Killarney on government road; 523-8660.
- Spirit Sands and Devil's Punch Bowl, Spruce Woods Provincial Park; 827-2543 or 834-3223.
- Stockton Ferry, near Glenboro on the Assiniboine River.
- Stott Site, Grand Valley Provincial Recreation Park, west of Brandon.
- Swan Valley Museum, 1.5 km/1 mi. north of Swan River on Hwy. 10; 734-3585.
- Swinging Bridge, Souris.
- Tent Town Game Farm, 1.5 km/1 mi. west of Minitonas; 525-4468.
- Trembowla Cross of Freedom Museum, 27 km/16 mi. northwest of Dauphin, off PR 362 on PR 491; 638-9641 or 638-9047.
- Ukrainian Heritage Village, 12 km/8

mi. south of Dauphin and 1 km/0.5 mi. west of Hwy. 10; 638-5645.
- Watson Crossley Community Museum, Grandview; 546-2764 or 546-2250.

NORTHERN REGION

- Boreal Gardens, on the old road between Churchill and Fort Churchill; 675-8866.
- Cape Merry National Historic Site, on the east shore of the Churchill River across from Prince of Wales' Fort, Churchill; 675-8863.
- Christ Church, on Edwards Ave., The Pas; 623-2119.
- Churchill Research Range and Churchill Northern Studies Centre, 24 km/15 mi. east of Churchill; 675-2307.
- Eskimo Museum, Churchill; 675-2030.
- First Catholic Church, The Pas.
- Flin Flon Museum, on Hwy. 10 at the tourist park, Flin Flon; 687-2946.
- Hanging Wall Gallery, 103 Main St., Flin Flon; 687-3294.
- Heritage North Museum, at the corner of Thompson Dr. S. and Mystery Lake Rd., Thompson; 677-2216.
- Hudson Bay Mining and Smelting Co. Ltd. (tours), Flin Flon; 687-2050.
- Inco Ltd. (tours), Thompson; 778-2454.
- Kettle Rapids hydroelectric generating station (tours), on the Nelson River near Gillam; 652-5134.
- Lynn Lake Mining Town Museum, 460 Cobalt Place, Lynn Lake; 356-8302.
- National Exhibition Centre, Leaf Rapids; 473-8682.
- Northern Creations Art Gallery, City Centre Mall, Thompson; 778-5123.
- Norway House (former Hudson's Bay Company inland storage facility), north end of Lake Winnipeg on PR 373.
- Port Nelson, near the mouth of the Nelson River.
- Port of Churchill (tours); 675-8823.
- Prince of Wales' Fort, on the west side of the Churchill River mouth, Churchill; 675-8863.
- Repap Manitoba (pulp and paper mill and sawmill), The Pas; 623-

7411, ext. 3312.
- Sam Waller Museum, 306 Fischer Ave., The Pas; 623-3802.
- Sloop's Cove National Historic Site, 4 km/2.5 mi. upstream from Prince of Wales' Fort, Churchill; 675-8863.
- Snow Lake Art Gallery, 600 Lakeshore Dr., Snow Lake; 358-2533.
- Thompson Art Gallery, 125 Commercial Pl., Thompson; 778-5074.
- Thompson Recreation Zoo, 275 Thompson Dr. N., Thompson; 677-7982.
- Visitor Reception Centre, Bayport Plaza, Churchill; 675-8863.
- Wabowden Historical Museum, Wabowden; 689-2362 or 689-2269.
- Wegg's Post Chimney Site, at Sandy Beach on Setting Lake, near Wabowden.
- York Factory National Historic Site, 8 km/5 mi. upstream on the Hayes River; 675-8863.

EASTERN REGION

- Alf Hole Goose Sanctuary, east of Rennie on Hwy. 44; 369-5232 or 369-5258.
- Anola and District Museum, Anola; 866-2692 or 866-2922.
- Bannock Point (petroforms), just north of Betula Lake off PR 307 in Whiteshell Provincial Park.
- Broken-Beau Historical Society Museum, off Hwy. 44 at Beausejour; 268-1357 or 268-1936.
- Cooks Creek Heritage Museum, at PR 212 and Sapton Road east of Birds Hill Provincial Park; 444-4448.
- Cottonwood Corner Game Farm, 0.8 km/0.5 mi. west of Grunthal on PR 216 and 1 km/0.6 mi. south; 434-6306.
- Dugald Costume Museum, on PR 206 just west of Dugald; 853-2166.
- Fish Hatchery, on PR 312 (Ingolf Road), Whiteshell Provincial Park; 349-2201.
- Immaculate Conception Church and the Grotto of Our Lady of Lourdes, at PR 212 and Zora Rd., Cooks Creek; 444-2478.
- Mennonite Heritage Village, Hwy. 12 north, Steinbach; 326-9661.
- New Bothwell Cheese Factory (tours), New Bothwell; 388-4666.
- Philip's Magical Paradise, 8 km (5 mi.) east of Hwy. 12 on PR 311, Giroux; 326-1219.
- Pine Falls Generating Station, Pine Falls; 474-3233.
- Pine Falls Paper Co. (tours), Pine Falls; 367-2432.
- Pointe des Chênes Museum, west of the forest on Dawson Rd. behind the Villa Youville, Ste. Anne.
- St. Georges Museum, St. Georges; 367-8801 or 367-2927.
- St. Joachim Museum, at the Recreation Ground, La Broquerie; 424-5363.
- St. Michael's Ukrainian Orthodox Church, west of Gardenton.
- St. Pierre-Jolys Museum, 432 Joubert St. N., St. Pierre-Jolys; 433-7226 or 433-7772.
- Sakeeng Museum, Pine Falls; 367-8740.
- Ukrainian Museum and Village, Gardenton; 425-3072 or 425-3501.
- Whitemouth Municipal Museum, on Hwy. 44, Whitemouth; 348-2345 or 348-2641.
- Whiteshell Laboratories of AECL Research (tours), Pinawa; 1-800-665-0436.
- Whiteshell Natural History Museum, at Nutimik Lake on PR 307, Whiteshell Provincial Park; 348-2846 or 348-2203.
- Whiteshell Underground Research Laboratory, off Hwy. 11 and east of Lac du Bonnet on PR 313; 753-2311 ext. 2938, or 1-800-665-0436.

SUMMER FESTIVALS AND EVENTS

What follows is a listing by area of some of the most popular festivals and events that take place during the summer tourist season. For a more complete listing, consult the Manitoba Explorer's Guide or the Manitoba Events Guide, both published by Travel Manitoba. To hear a recorded message that provides current information about events, call 942-2535.

WINNIPEG
June:
- Winnipeg International Children's Festival. Music, dance, mime,

puppetry, and hands-on displays. Features local, national, and international artists.
- Jazz Winnipeg Festival. International, national, and local jazz performers on free outdoor stages and in workshops and concerts.
- Red River Exhibition. Family entertainment, including a giant midway, nightly free-stage shows, and exhibits.

July:
- A Taste of Manitoba (food festival). Over 30 restaurants feature sample portions of food, along with mainstage and busker entertainment.
- Winnipeg Folk Festival. A celebration of music featuring over 200 individual concerts, children's hands-on activities, and the International Food Village.
- Winnipeg Fringe Festival. Theatre performances, including comedy, drama, mimes, and jugglers.
- Blackorama Reggae Festival. A three-day celebration with entertainment, food, and dancing, featuring local and visiting acts.

August:
- Folklorama. This two-week extravaganza showcases exotic foods, entertainment, and cultural displays in over 40 multicultural pavilions throughout the city.

September:
- Ballet in the Park. The Royal Winnipeg Ballet performs outdoor summer shows in Kildonan Park.

INTERLAKE REGION
July:
- Manitoba Highland Gathering (Selkirk). A Scottish festival featuring dance, pipe and drum competitions, sheep shearing and herding, canoe and kayak races, and a Scottish pub.
- Boardwalk Days (Winnipeg Beach). A revival of the glory days of Winnipeg Beach, featuring a parade, games of chance, a midway, and street dances.
- Peguis Treaty Days and Pow-wow (Peguis Indian Reserve). Games, rides, races, drum groups, and competition dancing.

- Triple S Fair and Rodeo (Selkirk). Chuckwagon and pony races, heavy and light horse shows, a rodeo, cattle show, fiddling and jigging.
- Sun Country Jamboree (Gimli). A major festival for country music fans.
- St. Laurent Métis Days (St. Laurent). Voyageur-style fun and games, including square dancing, fiddling and jigging competitions, and traditional Métis costumes.

August:
- Islendingadagurinn (Gimli). A celebration of Gimli's Icelandic heritage, featuring a parade, music, poetry, traditional food, and displays.
- Red River Rendezvous (Lower Fort Garry). Re-enacts the fur trade days with period costumes, games, and voyageur contests.
- Quarry Days (Stonewall). A celebration of Stonewall's heritage as a limestone quarry site.
- Sun Fest (Gimli). An outdoor rock music festival that includes camping, beer gardens, and a midway.

September:
- Ashern Rodeo Days (Ashern). Steer wrestling, bareback riding, calf roping, and barrel racing.

PEMBINA VALLEY/CENTRAL PLAINS
June:
- St. Lupicin Craft Gallery Annual Show (St. Lupicin).
- Carman Potato and Blossom Festival (Carman). Free stage shows, free baked potatoes and French fries, a flea market, and town-wide sidewalk sales.

July:
- Canada's National Strawberry Festival (Portage la Prairie). Three days of entertainment, including nightly street dances, two parades, Aboriginal shows, and a flea market.
- Festival of Nations (location varies). Features the heritage of the south-central region of Manitoba.

- Manitoba Threshermen's Reunion and Stampede (Austin). A parade of old steam and gasoline engines, a rodeo, threshing demonstrations, and bag and sheaf-tying competitions.
- Manitoba Stampede and Exhibition

(Morris). Four days of professional rodeo with chuckwagon and chariot racing, an agricultural fair, exhibits, and a midway.

- Manitoba Sunflower Festival (Altona). Free pancake breakfasts, a farmers' market, Mennonite food, free entertainment, a parade, car show, and street dance.

August:
- Winston Simpson Carman Fiddle Festival (Carman). Fiddle competition, jam sessions, step dancing, and guest artists.
- Wild West Show (Elm Creek). Manitoba's only wild West outdoor theatre.
- Winkler Harvest Festival and Exhibition (Winkler). Free farmer sausage and potato barbecue, stage entertainment, horse shows and rodeo, and trade and craft displays.
- Morden Corn and Apple Festival (Morden). Free corn on the cob and apple cider, free entertainment, a farmers' market, street displays, and a midway.

September:
- Pembina Threshermen's Reunion (Hwy. 3 between Winkler and Morden). An antique parade, threshing demonstrations, old steam engines, and old-fashioned meals.

PARKLAND/WESTERN REGION
June:
- Provincial Exhibition (Brandon). A midway, Budweiser Pro Rodeo, seniors' and family entertainment, kids' world, and summer saloon.

July:
- Parkland Harvest Festival (Rossburn). Chuckwagon and chariot races, quarter-horse and thorough-bred racing with parimutuel wagering, gymkhana, cabaret, and a parade.
- Countryfest (Dauphin). Thirty hours of country music entertainment at the Selo Ukraina site.
- Manitoba Holiday Festival of the Arts (Neepawa). One-week sessions and mini weekend courses in crafts and in the literary, visual and performing arts, for all age groups.
- Prairie Pioneer Days and Folk Fair (Killarney). An old-time dance, a toy show, flea market, antique

displays, arts and crafts, and music.
- Country Fun Festival (Minnedosa). A mini folk festival, a demolition derby, and an agricultural fair.
- Canadian Turtle Derby (Boissevain). Features the international turtle-racing championship, a curling bonspiel, sport tournaments, an antique auto show, and flea market.
- Annual Rawhide and Jellyroll Craft Sale (Wasagaming).
- Northwest Round-up (Swan River). Three days of rodeo, held in conjunction with the Swan Valley Agricultural Society's annual exhibition.

August:
- Canada's National Ukrainian Festival (Dauphin). A four-day celebration of music, dance, foods, and Ukrainian traditions.
- Brandon Folk Music and Art Festival (Brandon). Workshops, a mainstage, children's stage, and arts and crafts.
- Swan Valley Harvest Festival (Swan River). A fiddle contest, bread baking, flour grinding, and other pioneer activities.
- Virden Rodeo and Wild West Daze (Virden). A rodeo with cowboys from Canada and the U.S.

NORTHERN REGION
June:
- Thompson Folk Festival (Thompson). Features professional entertainment groups and musicians from northern Manitoba, children's activities, and a craft village.

July:
- Dip in the Bay (Churchill). A footrace into Hudson Bay by relay teams, plus a parade and other races.
- Historic Carnival (Churchill). Traditional games, live theatre, a dance, special tours, workshops and presentations.
- Flin Flon Trout Festival (Flin Flon). A fishing derby, parade, Queen Mermaid pageant, and the Great Northern Duck Race.
- Thompson Nickel Days (Thompson). Rides, a midway, Native games, the National King Miner contest, a parade, canoe races and mud races.

August:
- Cranberry Portage Arts Festival (Cranberry Portage). Exhibition and sale of northern arts and crafts. Demonstrations and workshops.
- York Boat Days (Norway House). Footraces, water events, and ball tournaments.
- Opasquiak Indian Days (The Pas). Celebrates the culture of the Cree Nation with fiddling and jigging, traditional Native events and foods, a square-dance competition, and canoe races.

EASTERN REGION
June:
- St. Jean Baptiste Day (La Broquerie). Celebrates French culture with a fair, games, horse rides, a beer garden, a social, and an ethnic pavilion.

July:
- Winnipeg Folk Festival (Birds Hill Provincial Park). A celebration of music featuring over 200 individual concerts, children's hands-on activities, and the International Food Village.

August:
- St. Pierre-Jolys Frog Follies (St. Pierre-Jolys). Features the Canadian National Frog Jumping Championships and includes games, sports, dances, and live entertainment.
- Steinbach Pioneer Days (Steinbach). Celebrates pioneer life with interpretive demonstrations, an auction sale, horse show, children's events, and a barbecue.
- Cooks Creek Heritage Day Celebrations (Cooks Creek).

September:
- Paper, Power, Pea and Pickerel Festival (Pine Falls, Powerview and St. Georges). A logging demonstration, market square, parade, beer gardens, and children's events.

SHOPPING

In Winnipeg, certain areas are known for their concentrations of small, owner-operated shops and boutiques.

One excellent place to shop for unique items is The Forks. The Forks Market and the nearby Johnston Terminal offer a wide array of goods, including linens, jewellery, and crafts. In addition, The Forks Market is a good source of fresh produce, gourmet foods, and treats. Within a very short distance of The Forks is the Union Station Market, in the VIA Rail station at the corner of Main and Broadway. It features over 20 small shops. You can find a good farmers' market in St. Norbert, at the extreme south end of the city. A bi-monthly magazine for travellers, Where: Winnipeg, includes lists of shops that sell many specialty items, including art and crafts.

ART AND CRAFTS

The annual Manitoba Christmas Craft Sale, western Canada's largest sale of original work by Canadian craftspeople, takes place in the Winnipeg Convention Centre in late November.

The following is a selective listing of shops and galleries that sell works by Manitoban or Canadian artists and craftspeople. Hours of operation vary, so it is best to phone ahead.

Winnipeg:
- Crafts Guild of Manitoba Museum, 183 Kennedy St.; 943-1190. Pottery, Inuit carvings, and knitted, woven, beeswax and wooden items.
- Craftspace Gallery, 3-100 Arthur St.; 947-0340. Clay, glass, metal, wood and fibre items from a contemporary perspective, predominantly one of a kind.
- David Rice Jewelry, 100 Osborne St. S.; 453-6105. Handcrafted jewellery by David Rice and other artists from across Canada, primarily in gold and sterling silver. Also one-of-a-kind glass, ceramic, paper and fabric objects.
- The Gallery Shoppes, Winnipeg Art Gallery, 300 Memorial Blvd.; 786-6641. Handcrafted jewellery, glassware and ceramics by Manitobans and Canadians. Inuit prints and sculpture. Original paintings by Manitoba artists.
- Leonard Marcoe Studio Gallery, 364 Stafford St.; 475-5895. Contemporary art and crafts by artists

in Manitoba, including paintings, watercolours, ceramics, and sculpture. Many light-hearted items.
- New Prairie Gallery, 201-99 Osborne St.; 284-5091. Specializes in pottery. Also stained-glass items, handmade jewellery, candles, floral arrangements, and handmade cards.
- Northern Images, 2nd level Portage Place; 942-5501. Also 1790 Wellington Ave.; 788-4806. Inuit and Dene art, and local Native art. Soapstone sculptures from the Northwest Territories, parkas, moccasins, and jewellery.
- Shagnapi Studios, 567 Broadway; 774-5454. Art and crafts by Aboriginal Manitoba artists, including sweet-grass baskets, masks, traditional dream-catchers, jewellery, unique clothing, Navaho blankets, books, herbs, and contemporary works.
- Zone Gallery, 603 Corydon Ave.; 453-0658. Contemporary art, including paintings, sculpture, pottery, prints, and jewellery.

Interlake Region:
- Angel Wings and Fairy Dust, 632 River Rd., Lockport; 757-7969. Dried floral arrangements, candles, giftware, wreaths, paintings, stained glass, pottery, jewellery, and Native art.
- Blue Skies Ranch Pottery, 6 km/4 mi. west of Hwy. 8 on the Arnes Road, Arnes; 376-2480. Pottery, sculpture and paintings by Nick Roebuck.
- Craft Post and Art Gallery, 342 - 1st Ave., Arborg; 376-2272. Native art, wood carvings, soapstone, pottery, art cards, prints, and original paintings.
- Selkirk Community Arts Centre Inc., 101-250 Manitoba Ave., Selkirk; 482-4359. Features local artists in both the gallery and gift shop.
- Stonewall Gallery, at the corner of Main and Centre, Stonewall; 467-5319. Contemporary clay and fibre works.

Pembina Valley/Central Plains:
- Grace's Place, Railway St. S., Altona; 324-1918. Country and folk-art crafts in a restored century-old Mennonite village home. Pottery, woodwork, dolls, paintings, and a children's boutique. Also a tearoom.

- Loon Magic Gallery, Winitoba Mall, Winkler; 325-8518. Original paintings and prints, carved emu eggs, and other works by local artists.
- McGills' Country Lane, 2 km/1.2 mi. south of Carman on Hwy 3; 745-3478. Country and Victorian crafts, and homemade jams, jellies and fruit syrups from locally grown fruit.
- My Shack, Winitoba Mall, Winkler; 325-8269. Handmade, authentic Aboriginal leather crafts and beadwork.
- Off the Wall Craft Gallery, at the junction of Hwys. 13 and 3, Carman; 745-3610. Local artisans' products, including woodwork, paintings, stained glass, dream-catchers, "tree spirits," mirror art, and wheat weaving.
- St. Lupicin Craft Gallery Co-op, St. Lupicin; 744-2187 or 744-2764. Jewellery, pottery, stained and blown glass, sculptures and paintings by local and national artists and craftspeople.

Parkland/Western Region:
- Art Gallery of Southwestern Manitoba, Gift Shop, 638 Princess Ave., Brandon; 726-8270. Stained glass and blown glass, pottery, hand weaving, paintings, handmade quilts, candle holders, wooden items, handmade jewellery.
- The Hand Crafter, 298 S. Railway St., Boissevain; 534-2449. Baby mobiles, hangers, woven lawnchairs, pine shelving, and other items made by the mentally handicapped.
- Manawaka Souvenir and Gift Shop, 312 First Ave., Neepawa; 476-3612. Pottery, porcelain, paintings, carved wooden bowls and stained glass by local artists.
- Terry McLean Gallery, 418 - 7th Ave. S., Virden; 748-2475. Original paintings, limited-edition prints, collectors' plates, sculpture and giftware crafted by Terry McLean.

Northern Region
- Eskimo Museum, 242 Laverendrye Ave., Churchill; 675-2030. Sells Inuit art and crafts, and has an excellent book shop.
- Hudson Gallery, 60 Hemlock Cres., Thompson; 778-5074. Original works by northern artists, and limited-edition prints.

- Ma-Mow-We-Tak Friendship Centre, 122 Hemlock Cres., Thompson; 778-7337. Authentic Aboriginal art. Native arts and crafts are also available at the Friendship Centres in Flin Flon and The Pas.
- Murray McKenzie's Studio and Gallery, 111 Churchill Dr., Thompson; 778-7070. Photos by an internationally recognized Aboriginal photographer that focus on the faces of his people.
- Nasselquist Ltd., 83 Main St., Flin Flon; 687-4663. Sells locally crafted abstract copper sculptures known as "Earth Creations." These are also available at the Flin Flon Tourist Bureau and the Flin Flon Public Library.

Eastern Region
- Craft Basket, at First St. and MacArthur, Lac du Bonnet; 345-6080. Crafts by local artisans, including wheat weaving, candles, swags, woodwork, jewellery, dream-catchers, and arrangements created from local flora.
- Essential Bear, 16 Dufferin Ave., Pinawa; 753-2486. Handmade stuffed teddy bears.
- The Gift Horse, Falcon Beach Riding Stables and Guest Ranch, Falcon Lake; 349-2410. Woollens, pottery, wooden items, handmade jewellery, baskets, and fur and leather products.
- Mennonite Heritage Village gift shop, Hwy. 12 north, Steinbach; 326-9661. Floral arrangements, wooden items, pillows, scarves, aprons, and other objects crafted by people from the region.

OUTDOOR RECREATION

PARKS AND NATURAL ATTRACTIONS

For extensive information about provincial parks, consult Manitoba Magic: Provincial Parks Guide, available from Travel Manitoba. Details can also be obtained by calling 945-6784. For information about Riding Mountain National Park, call 848-7272 or 1-800-707-8480 (the park) or 983-2290 (in Winnipeg). A few of Manitoba's natural attractions are listed below.

Winnipeg and Area:
- Assiniboine Forest, on both sides of Grant Ave. east of Chalfont Rd. This oak and aspen forest, with over 3 km/1.9 mi. of nature trails, is home to many species of birds and mammals, including deer and fox.
- Assiniboine Park, Corydon Ave. at Shaftesbury Blvd. Winnipeg's largest park, featuring a zoo, conservatory, English Garden, Formal Garden, Leo Mol Sculpture Garden, and Tudor-style pavilion.
- Fort Whyte Centre, 1961 McCreary Rd.; 989-8355. Includes 80 hectares (200 acres) of forest, lakes, marshes, and self-guiding trails. Habitat for white-tailed deer, red fox, and 27 species of waterfowl.
- Harbour View Recreation Complex, Kilcona Park, 1867 Springfield Rd.; 222-2766. Includes a 9-hole par-27 golf course, miniature golf, driving range, pedal boats, lawn bowling, and tennis.
- Kildonan Park, 2021 Main St. The park borders the Red River and is known for its beautiful trees and gardens. Home of an Olympic-sized outdoor swimming pool and Rainbow Stage, Winnipeg's summer outdoor theatre.
- La Barrière Park, 6 km/3.7 mi. south of the intersection of Waverley St. and the Perimeter Hwy. This park hugs the banks of the La Salle River, and includes picnic sites and walking and cross-country ski trails.
- Living Prairie Museum, 2795 Ness Ave.; 832-0167. This tall-grass prairie preserve is home to more than 200 species of native plants. Includes an interpretive centre.

Interlake Region:
- Hecla Provincial Park, north of Riverton at the end of Hwy. 8. Forest, rugged shoreline, and plenty of wildlife. Features Gull Harbour Resort, a championship 18-hole golf course, marina, beaches, campgrounds, and wildlife viewing tower.
- Narcisse Wildlife Management Area (parking lot 6 km/4 mi. north of Narcisse on Hwy. 17). Thousands of

red-sided garter snakes emerge from limestone sinkholes in late April and early May.

- Netley Creek Provincial Recreation Park, 16 km/10 mi. north of Selkirk on PR 320. Home to Netley Marsh, one of the major waterfowl nesting areas of North America.
- Oak Hammock Marsh and Conservation Centre, north at the junction of Hwy. 67 and PR 220, between Hwys. 7 and 8; 467-3300. This wetland is home to over 280 species of birds and 25 mammals. Thousands of birds can be seen during migration. Includes an excellent interpretive centre.
- Stonewall Quarry Park, at the north end of Main St., Stonewall; 467-5354. Giant lime kilns, an interpretive building, man-made lake, beach, campground, picnic area, and interpretive trails.
- Winnipeg Beach Provincial Recreation Park, Hwy. 9 at Winnipeg Beach. A famous sand beach, restaurants, marina, camping, and excellent windsurfing.

Pembina Valley/Central Plains:
- Beaudry Provincial Heritage Park, southwest of Headingley, accessible from Roblin Blvd. in Winnipeg, or PR 241. Rare remnants of tall-grass prairie and a dense river-bottom forest. Wildlife includes white-tailed deer, raccoons, and beavers.
- Delta Marsh, along the south shore of Lake Manitoba between Hwys. 242 and 430. One of the largest waterfowl staging marshes in North America, this is a world-renowned wetland.
- Island Park and Crescent Lake, Portage la Prairie. This park, in a horseshoe-shaped lake setting, has a deer and waterfowl sanctuary, golf course, tennis courts, picnic sites, and canoeing.
- Portia Marsh, north of Alonsa. Supports hundreds of bird species and over 25 species of mammals. Includes a boardwalk, interpretive signs, and a walking trail that extends into the forest.
- St. Ambroise Provincial Recreation Park, at the south basin of Lake Manitoba. Features a fine sand beach with several campground and picnic areas. The park is a staging area for migratory birds.

Parkland/Western Region:
- Asessippi Provincial Park, at the south end of Lake of the Prairies. The artificial lake is flanked by the valley walls of the Assiniboine and Shellmouth rivers. Fishing, camping, boat rentals, a beach, and self-guiding trails.
- Duck Mountain Provincial Park. Thickly wooded, rolling terrain with dozens of deep clear lakes and a wide variety of birds and animals. Popular for fishing, as well as camping, hiking, boating, horseback riding, and biking.
- International Peace Garden, Hwy. 10 at the U.S. border; 534-2510. This 930-hectare (2,300-acre) garden, dedicated to peace, offers campground facilities, hiking trails, picnic areas, and concessions. Site of the International Music Camp in June and July.
- Oak Lake Goose Refuge, along the south of Oak Lake, 12 km/7 mi. on PR 254. Home to geese, ducks, swans, cranes, and other wildlife.
- Riding Mountain National Park. Boreal forest, aspen parkland, deciduous forest, and open grasslands and meadows. The area is excellent for hiking, camping, fishing, and wildlife viewing. A herd of bison lives in the park.
- Spruce Woods Provincial Park. Contains Spirit Sands, a desert-like area of sand dunes. Home of several plant and animal species that are unique in Manitoba. Hiking trails, camping, a beach, and interpretive programs.
- Turtle Mountain Provincial Park. An area of rolling forested hills and small lakes. Camping, fishing, canoe routes, and trails for horseback riding, mountain biking, and hiking.
- William Lake Provincial Recreation Park, east of Turtle Mountain Provincial Park. Features Turtle's Back Tower, which is accessible via hiking trail and offers a panoramic view of the Turtle Mountains. This area is popular with windsurfing enthusiasts.

Northern Region:
- Bakers Narrows Provincial Recreation Park, 19 km/12 mi.

south of Flin Flon on Hwy. 10. Three beaches, a boat launch, and playground. Ideal for camping, canoeing, and fishing.
- Churchill area. Polar bears, beluga whales, seals, caribou, over 200 species of birds, and more than 350 species of plants. The aurora borealis (northern lights) are spectacular.
- Clearwater Lake Provincial Park, at the junction of Hwy. 10 and PR 287. Includes "the caves" (huge slabs of rock broken off the dolomite cliffs) on the south shore of Clearwater Lake. The lake is one of the clearest in the world. Excellent fishing, plus swimming, boating, hiking, overnight lodging and camping.
- Grass River Provincial Park, on Hwy. 39. This wilderness of lakes and evergreen forest is home to woodland caribou, moose, wolves, bald eagles, and waterfowl. Ideal for canoeing and fishing. Includes camping facilities and lodges, and a self-guiding trail.
- Paint Lake Provincial Recreation Park, at the junction of Hwy. 6 and PR 375. Located in precambrian boreal forest, this park offers good camping and fishing, a beach area, and a marina.
- Pisew Falls, on Hwy. 6 between Wabowden and Thompson, south of Paint Lake. Manitoba's second-highest waterfall.
- Wekusko Falls, 24 km/15 mi. south of Snow Lake on Hwy. 392. Good camping and fishing, a beach area, and a lodge.

Eastern Region:
- Atikaki Provincial Wilderness Park. A true wilderness, including rugged forest, rock outcrops, wild rivers, and calm lakes accessible only by air or canoe. Highlights are Shining Falls and prehistoric rock paintings.
- Birds Hill Provincial Park, 24 km/15 mi. north of Winnipeg on Hwy. 59. Oak and aspen forests, native prairie wildflowers, deer, and waterfowl. Also walking trails, a paved bicycle trail, riding stable, beach, campground, and picnic sites.
- Buffalo Point, a peninsula on southern Lake of the Woods. Sand beaches, a boardwalk, excellent fishing, trails, camping, a modern resort, and tame white-tailed deer.

- Grand Beach Provincial Park, on the east shore of Lake Winnipeg. Powdery white sand beaches and dunes as high as 8 metres/30 ft. Excellent for swimming, fishing, and windsurfing. Good self-guiding trails, a campground, and an outdoor amphitheatre.
- Nopiming Provincial Park. Features towering granite outcrops, over 700 lakes, and stands of black spruce. Wildlife includes woodland caribou in season. Campgrounds and several fly-in or drive-in fishing lodges.
- Sandilands Forest Centre, 2.5 km/1.5 mi. south of the junction of Hwys. 1 and 11; 453-3182. This site contains a black spruce bog and eastern deciduous and jack-pine forests. Includes a suspension bridge, self-guiding trails, and a forest museum.
- Tall-grass Prairie Preserve, 3.2 km/2 mi. east of Tolstoi on PR 209, on the north side of the highway. Over 2000 hectares (4,950 acres) of rare tall-grass prairie are protected here. Home to over 150 plant species, as well as deer and moose.
- Whiteshell Provincial Park. Includes rushing rivers, tranquil lakes, Rainbow Falls, petroforms, a goose sanctuary, and a fish hatchery. West Hawk Lake is popular with scuba divers. Resorts, fishing lodges, campgrounds, marinas, golf, and excellent hiking.

BEACHES

Dozens of Manitoba beaches are suitable for swimming. Some of the best and most popular beaches are listed here.
- Clear Lake, at Wasagaming in Riding Mountain National Park.
- Delta Beach, at the south end of Lake Manitoba on PR 240.
- Falcon Lake, in Whiteshell Provincial Park.
- Grand Beach, in Grand Beach Provincial Park. This beach has been named as one of the top ten in North America.
- St. Malo Provincial Recreation Park, 50 km/30 mi. south of Winnipeg, east of Hwy. 59.
- Spruce Woods Provincial Park at Kiche Manitou Campground.
- Steep Rock Beach, on the east side of Lake Manitoba near PR 239.

- West Hawk Lake, in Whiteshell Provincial Park.
- Winnipeg Beach, 76 km/47 mi. north of Winnipeg on Hwy. 9.

CANOEING AND KAYAKING

The Manitoba Recreational Canoeing Association's resource committee provides route information for a number of canoe routes. Contact the Manitoba Recreational Canoeing Association, Resource Committee, Box 2663, Winnipeg, MB, R3C 4B3; phone 925-5078 and ask for the MRCA.

Hydrographic charts, topographic maps, and illustrated maps of several canoe routes can be purchased from the Department of Natural Resources, Land Information Centre, 1007 Century Street, Winnipeg, MB, R3H 0W4; 945-6666. A comprehensive map catalogue is available. Pre-payment is required.

SAILING

Extensive information about sailing and sailboarding can be obtained from the Manitoba Sailing Association, 200 Main Street, Winnipeg, MB, R3C 4M2; 925-5048. Hydrographic charts and topographic maps are available from the Department of Natural Resources (see "Canoeing and Kayaking" above).

Visitors to Manitoba can charter keelboats for cruising on Lake Winnipeg. Sailboards and dinghies can be rented in Winnipeg and cartopped or trailered to the many lakes surrounding the city.

FISHING

The Travel Manitoba publication Manitoba Fishing & Hunting Adventures provides information about fishing opportunities in various regions of the province. Included in this guide are extensive listings of fishing lodges, outfitters, and air charter services. Manitoba Lodges & Outfitters: An Adventure in Nature is a catalogue that lists the prices of packages at selected lodges.

Some of the province's better fishing lodges and resorts are listed in the "Lodging" section of this guidebook (see pp.172-175). Please see Elkhorn Resort (Parkland/Western region); Aikens Lake Wilderness Lodge, Inverness Falls Resort, and Jessica Lake Lodge (Eastern region); and Big Sand Lake Lodge, Knee Lake Resort, Nejalini Lake Resort, and Nueltin Fly-In Lodges (Northern region). For additional information about lodges, outfitters, and vacation packages, contact the Manitoba Lodges and Outfitters Association, 23 Sage Crescent, Winnipeg, MB, R2Y 0X8; 889-4840.

Details about the province's fishing regulations are published in Travel Manitoba's Sport Fishing Guide. You must purchase a Manitoba sport fishing licence if you will be engaging in any aspect of sport fishing during your visit. Non-residents under the age of 16 do not require licences, but they must fish with a licence holder and their catch must be applied to that person's limit. A non-resident under 16 who wishes to have a separate limit must buy a licence.

Sport fishing licences are sold at most hardware and sporting-goods stores, fishing centres, and lodges. Not all vendors carry non-resident licences. Licences may also be purchased by mail. For more information, contact the Department of Natural Resources, Box 22, 1495 St. James Street, Winnipeg, MB, R3H 0W9; 945-6784.

A Manitoba sport fishing licence is not valid in Riding Mountain National Park. For details about fishing licences and regulations in national parks, contact Parks Canada, 45 Forks Market Road, Winnipeg, MB, R3C 4T6; 983-2290.

Angling maps, hydrographic charts, and topographical maps may be purchased from the Department of Natural Resources Land Information Centre (see "Canoeing and Kayaking" above).

GOLF

The Manitoba Explorer's Guide includes a comprehensive table that details the facilities offered by each of Manitoba's 118 golf courses. The following is a selective listing of some of the better courses in the province.
- Brandon Community Recreation & Sports Center (18-hole), 34th St. and

McDonald Ave., Brandon; 729-2177.
- Carman Golf Club (18-hole), Carman; 745-2366.
- Clear Lake Golf Course (18-hole), Wasagaming, Riding Mountain National Park; 848-4653.
- Falcon Beach Golf Course (18-hole), Falcon Lake, Whiteshell Provincial Park; 349-2554.
- Halcrow Lake Golf & Country Club (9-hole), The Pas; 623-7551.
- Hecla Island Golf Course (18-hole), Hecla Provincial Park; 1-800-267-6700 or 279-2072.
- John Blumberg Golf Course (9- and 18-hole), 4540 Portage Ave., Winnipeg; 888-8860.
- Kingswood Golf & Country Club (18-hole), La Salle; 736-4079.
- Larters at St. Andrews (18-hole), St. Andrews (near Lockport); 334-2107.
- The Links at Quarry Oaks (18-hole), Steinbach; 326-4653.
- Minnewasta Golf & Country Club (18-hole), Morden; 822-4992.
- Portage la Prairie Golf Course (18-hole), Island Park, Portage la Prairie; 857-6177.
- Selkirk Golf & Country Club (18-hole), Selkirk; 482-5911.
- Snow Lake Golf Club (9-hole), Snow Lake; 358-2744.
- Thompson Golf Club (9-hole), Moak Lake Rd., Thompson; 677-3250 or 778-5537

CAMPING

Riding Mountain National Park and many of Manitoba's provincial parks have campground facilities. There are also many privately owned campgrounds in the province. The Manitoba Accommodation & Campground Guide, published by Travel Manitoba, lists more than 200 campgrounds and indicates the services offered by each

To reserve a site at Wasagaming Campground in Riding Mountain National Park, call 1-800-707-8480.

From mid-May until the end of August, you can reserve sites at many of the most popular government-operated provincial campgrounds by using the Dial-A-Site reservation service. Call between 9am and 4pm Monday to Thursday, except on statutory holidays. The participating campgrounds and their Dial-A-Site

phone numbers are listed below. A minimum length of stay applies to Dial-A-Site reservations; the numbers in parentheses represent the minimum stay (in consecutive nights). For more information about campgrounds in provincial parks, call 945-6784.
- Asessippi Provincial Park (3); 564-2473.
- Bakers Narrows Provincial Recreation Park near Flin Flon (2); 687-3037.
- Birds Hill Provincial Park (3); 224-0075.
- Falcon Beach, Whiteshell Provincial Park (2); 349-2231.
- Grand Beach Provincial Park (3); 754-3759.
- Gull Harbour, Hecla Provincial Park (2); 378-2945.
- Kiche Manitou, Spruce Woods Provincial Park (3); 827-2458.
- Rainbow Beach Provincial Recreation Park near Dauphin (2); 638-9493.
- Wellman Lake, Duck Mountain Provincial Park (3); 525-4832.
- West Hawk Lake, Whiteshell Provincial Park (3); 349-8247.
- Whitefish Lake, Porcupine Provincial Forest (3); 734-3429.

HIKING

The Parks Branch of the Department of Natural Resources supplies free hiking trail maps for most of the provincial parks in Manitoba. Call 945-6784. The map of the Mantario Hiking Trail can be purchased from the Department of Natural Resources, Land Information Centre, 1007 Century Street, Winnipeg, MB, R3H 0W4; 945-6666.

Information on hiking in Riding Mountain National Park is available by contacting the park office at 848-7275 or by writing to Riding Mountain National Park, General Delivery, Wasagaming, MB, R0J 2H0.

The Manitoba Walking and Hiking Guide by Ruth Marr is an excellent resource that features more than 230 routes, from easy strolls to invigorating hikes and backpacking adventures. Copies can be obtained by contacting Fifth House Publishers, 620 Duchess Street, Saskatoon, Saskatchewan, S4R 1H3; 306-242-4936. The book is also available through bookstores or from the Department of Natural Resources Land Information Centre (see address above).

Listed below are a few of the more interesting trails in the province.

• Ancient Beach Self-guiding Trail, Grand Beach Provincial Park. This 2.5 km/1.6 mi. trail loops around an ancient beach that was part of the great inland lake that covered most of southeastern Manitoba 8,000 years ago.

• The Caves Self-guiding Trail, Clearwater Lake Provincial Park. Halfway around this 0.8 km/0.5 mi. trail you'll come to "the caves," deep crevices that formed when rock masses split away from the shoreline cliffs.

• Cedar Bog Self-guiding Trail, Birds Hill Provincial Park. A 3.5 km/2 mi. trail that passes through grasslands and an aspen forest, and descends to an unusual, cool, damp bog with a stand of eastern white cedar.

• Gorge Creek Trail, Riding Mountain National Park. This challenging, scenic, 6.4 km/4 mi. trail descends the Manitoba Escarpment. The trail is not a loop. If possible, have a vehicle waiting at the lower end.

• Harbour Trail, Hecla Provincial Park. A 5.5 km/3.4 mi. loop around the northern point that defines Gull Harbour. The trail passes through tall spruce trees and offers superb views of Lake Winnipeg and nearby islands.

• Mantario Hiking Trail, Whiteshell Provincial Park. A strenuous 60 km/37 mi. trail that winds through meadows, across rivers, along lake shores, through jack-pine forests, and up onto high lookout ridges.

• Pine Point Self-guiding Trail, Whiteshell Provincial Park. The first loop of this 9.6 km/6 mi. trail leads to Pine Point Rapids on the Whiteshell River, and the second loop follows the river to Acorn Falls and Viburnum Falls.

• Spirit Sands Self-guiding Trail, Spruce Woods Provincial Park. This trail passes through extensive sand dunes that form a "desert." The return trek to the dunes is approximately 5.9 km/3.6 mi.

• Turtle's Back Hiking Trail, William Lake Provincial Recreation Park. A trail leading from William Lake to one of Turtle Mountain's highest points, where a tower offers a spectacular view. The most direct route to the summit is 5 km/3 mi. return.

BICYCLING

Riding Mountain National Park has long back-country trails, and mountain bikes can be rented at the Wasagaming townsite. The Pine Ridge Bicycle Trail in Birds Hill Provincial Park near Winnipeg is a 7.2 km/4.5 mi. paved trail designed for cycling.

A cyclists' map of Winnipeg, a booklet titled Pedalling in the Prairies, a "Manitoba by Bicycle" brochure, and a mountain-bike trails brochure are available from the Manitoba Cycling Association, 200 Main Street, Winnipeg, MB, R3C 4M2; 925-5083.

A very detailed book that is recommended for cyclists visiting Manitoba is Manitoba Outdoor Adventure Guide: Cycling by Ruth Marr. It is available from the same sources as the Manitoba Walking and Hiking Guide (see "Hiking" above).

The Canadian Cycling Association's Complete Guide to Bicycle Touring in Canada is also recommended. It is available through bookstores.

HORSEBACK RIDING

Information about horseback riding can be obtained from the Manitoba Horse Council, 200 Main Street, Winnipeg, MB, R3C 4M2; 925-5115.

CROSS-COUNTRY SKIING

Trail maps are available from the Manitoba Cross Country Ski Association, 200 Main Street, Winnipeg, MB, R3C 4M2; 925-5037.

Cross-country ski maps for trails in provincial parks are available on-site or from the Parks Branch, Box 52, 1495 St. James Street, Winnipeg, MB, R3H 0W9; 945-6784.

ALPINE SKIING

For information about alpine skiing in Manitoba, contact the Manitoba Alpine Ski Association, 200 Main Street, Winnipeg, MB, R3C 4M2; 925-5112.

POLAR BEAR AND WHALE WATCHING

The Manitoba Explorer's Guide includes a list of tour operators that specialize in wildlife packages of various kinds, in all regions of the province. Some of the companies that offer polar bear or whale-watching tours in the Hudson Bay region are listed below.

- B&B Scuba, 2-1333 Niakwa Road, Winnipeg, MB, R2J 3T5; 257-3696. Scuba diving and snorkelling in Churchill River mouth and Hudson Bay with the beluga whales. One-week tours start in July and August and must be pre-booked.
- Churchill Nature Tours, Box 429, Erickson, MB, R0J 0P0; 636-2968. Beluga whales in July and August; polar bear safaris in October and November. All-inclusive packages from Winnipeg.
- Churchill Wilderness Encounter, Box 9, Churchill, MB, R0B 0E0; 675-2248 or 1-800-265-9458. Polar bears and beluga whales. Daily tours, and all-inclusive package tours for groups.
- Dymond Lake Air Services Ltd., Box 304, Churchill, MB, R0B 0E0; 675-8875. Aerial sightseeing tours of the Churchill area for polar bears, caribou, and other wildlife.
- Frontiers North, 774 Bronx Ave., Winnipeg, MB, R2K 4E9; 949-2050 or 1-800-663-9832. Beluga whales, polar bears, Arctic tundra.
- The Great Canadian Travel Company, 273 Donald St., Winnipeg, MB, R3C 1M9; 949-0199 or 1-800-661-3830. Specialists in beluga whale watching and polar bear tours.
- Great White Bear Tours, Box 91, Churchill, MB, R0B 0E0; 675-2781 or 675-2460. Escorted photography tours in a specially designed 12-passenger vehicle.
- Kaskattama Safari Adventures Ltd., 170 Harbison Ave. W., Winnipeg, MB, R2L 0A4; 667-1611. Tours in the Cape Tatnam Wildlife Management Area.
- Sea North Tours Ltd., 39 Franklin St., Box 222, Churchill, MB, R0B 0E0; 675-2195. Tours in boats that are hydrophone-equipped for listening to beluga whales. Also

seal and polar bear viewing.
- Seal River Heritage Lodge, Box 1034, Churchill, MB, R0B 0E0; 675-8875 or 1-800-665-0476. Eco-tourism in a remote wilderness lodge setting. Whales, seals, polar bears, caribou, wolves.
- Tundra Buggy Tours Ltd., Box 662, Churchill, MB, R0B 0E0; 675-2121 or 1-800-544-5049. Guided polar bear tours aboard the Tundra Buggy. You can sleep among the bears in a lodge at "Polar Bear Point."

BIRD-WATCHING

The Manitoba Explorer's Guide includes a list of tour operators, some of whom specialize in bird-watching excursions.

Some of Manitoba's best areas for bird-watching are listed among the "Parks and Natural Attractions" above. The Birder's Guide to Southwestern Manitoba, published by the Brandon Natural History Society, identifies several excellent routes for bird-watchers in that part of the province. Churchill gift shops carry The Birder's Guide to Churchill by Bonnie Chartier, published by the American Birding Association. Birds of Oak Hammock Marsh is available from the Department of Natural Resources, Land Information Centre, 1007 Century Street, Winnipeg, MB, R3H 0W4; 945-6666.

ABORIGINAL HISTORY

Leo Pettipas has compiled the following lists of sites in Manitoba that are important sources of information about Native history. The museums are the principal ones that contain archaeological collections and displays of Aboriginal material culture. The provincial commemorative plaques pertain in whole or in part to pre-contact Aboriginal themes.

PLACES

- Assiniboine Riverwalk near The Forks, Winnipeg. Interpretive panels provide information about

traditional Native use of the river.
- Emerson Travel Information Centre, Emerson. A wall-size painting by Cree artist Donald Monkman depicts the earliest peopling of the Red River Valley.
- Lockport. The Kenosewun Visitor Centre and a provincial commemorative plaque detail the area's long Aboriginal history.
- Netley Creek Provincial Recreation Park. Features a small interpretive structure that includes a panel describing facets of the Aboriginal history of the district.
- Oak Hammock Conservation Centre. Includes a display of pre-contact cultural history, featuring artifacts, graphics, and text.
- Riding Mountain National Park. The Visitor Centre and the Anishinabe Village and Campground offer displays on ancient Aboriginal history and an ecotourism living experience from an Ojibwa perspective.
- St. Norbert Provincial Heritage Park, Winnipeg. Interpretive panels along the Rivière Sale Self-guiding Trail provide information on the earliest peoples of the Red River Valley.
- Star Mound Hill and Star Mound School Museum Park, near Snowflake. Thought to be the former site of a Hidatsa village, the park now includes a display of Native artifactual material from the area.
- Stott Site, west of Brandon. Once the scene of large-scale bison runs, the site now features a reconstructed buffalo pound, Native encampment, viewing stand, interpretive panels, a provincial commemorative plaque, and a self-guiding trail.
- The Wall Through Time at The Forks, Winnipeg. Interpretive panels present the cultural and natural history of The Forks.
- Whiteshell Provincial Park. Contains numerous petroforms, including those at Bannock Point near Betula Lake which are readily accessed by trail.

MUSEUMS

(Please see "Attractions," pp. 179-183, for locations and phone numbers.)
- Antler River Museum, Melita.
- Binscarth and District Gordon Orr Memorial Museum, Binscarth.
- Birdtail Country Museum, Birtle.
- Duck Mountain Forest Centre, Duck Mountain Provincial Park.
- Eskimo Museum, Churchill. Carved from the Land, a book by curator Lorraine E. Brandson, is based on the museum's collection and archives.
- Fort Dauphin Museum, 140 Jackson St., Dauphin.
- Heritage North Museum, Thompson.
- J.A.V. David Municipal Museum, Killarney.
- Manitoba Museum of Man and Nature, 190 Rupert Ave., Winnipeg.
- Miami Museum, Miami.
- Miniota Municipal Museum, Miniota.
- Moncur Gallery, Boissevain.
- Morden and District Museum, Morden.
- Morris and District Centennial Museum, Morris.
- Oli Johnson Museum, Big Woody, near Swan River.
- Pilot Mound Centennial Museum, Pilot Mound.
- St. Boniface Museum/Le Musée de Saint Boniface, 494 Taché Ave., Winnipeg.
- Sam Waller Museum, 306 Fischer Ave., The Pas.
- Sipiweske Museum, Wawanesa.
- Stonewall Quarry Park, Stonewall.
- Swan Valley Museum, Swan River.
- Transcona Historical Museum, 141 Regent Ave. W., Winnipeg.
- Watson Crossley Community Museum, Grandview.

SPECIAL TRAVEL SERVICES

VISITORS WITH DISABILITIES

For general information about the services available in the province, contact the Independent Living Resource Centre, 201-294 Portage Avenue, Winnipeg, MB, R3C 0B9; 947-0194. Easy Wheeling Manitoba lists hotels, motels, campgrounds, parks, recreation sites and points of interest where parking and entrances are accessible. It is available free of charge from Travel Manitoba or the

Canadian Paraplegic Association, 825 Sherbrook Street, Winnipeg, MB, R3A 1M5; 786-4753.

If you have a parking permit for persons with disabilities, you are encouraged to bring it to Manitoba so that you may park in any space marked by the "symbol of access."

FURTHER READING

Aboriginal History:
Putt, Neal. *Place Where the Spirit Lives: Stories from the Archaeology and History of Manitoba*. Pemmican.

Anthologies of Fiction and Poetry:
Duncan, Mark, ed. *Section Lines: A Manitoba Anthology*. Turnstone;
Tefs, Wayne, ed. *Made in Manitoba: An Anthology of Short Fiction*. Turnstone.

Flood of 1950:
Bumsted, J. M. *The Manitoba Flood of 1950: An Illustrated History*. Watson & Dwyer.

Grey Owl's Books (Archibald Belaney):
The Adventures of Sajo and Her Beaver People. Macmillan;
The Men of the Last Frontier. Macmillan;
Pilgrims of the Wild. Macmillan;
Tales of an Empty Cabin. Macmillan.

Louis Riel:
Flanagan, Thomas. *Louis `David' Riel: `Prophet of the New World'*. University of Toronto Press;
Howard, Joseph Kinsey. *Strange Empire: Louis Riel and the Métis People*. James Lewis and Samuel;
Riel, Louis. *The Collected Writings of Louis Riel*. University of Alberta Press;
Siggins, Maggie. *Riel: A Life of Revolution*. HarperCollins;
Stanley, George F. G. *Louis Riel*. McGraw-Hill Ryerson.

Lower Fort Garry:
MacDonald, Graham. *A Good Solid Comfortable Establishment: An Illustrated History of Lower Fort Garry*. Watson & Dwyer.

Manitoba Legislative Building:
Baker, Marilyn. *Symbol in Stone: The Art and Politics of a Public Building*. Hyperion.

Natural History:
Teller, James, ed. *Natural Heritage of Manitoba: Legacy of the Ice Age*. Manitoba Museum of Man and Nature.

Northern Manitoba:
Johnson, Karen L. *The Wildflowers of Churchill and the Hudson Bay Region*. Manitoba Museum of Man and Nature;
Lithman, George, et al., eds. *People and Land in Northern Manitoba*. University of Manitoba Dept. of Anthropology;
Taylor, Robert. *The Edge of the Arctic: Churchill and the Hudson Bay Lowlands*. Windermere House.

Royal Winnipeg Ballet:
Dafoe, Christopher. *Dancing through Time: The First Fifty Years of Canada's Royal Winnipeg Ballet*. Portage & Main Press;

Social History:
Shilliday, Gregg, ed. *Manitoba 125: A History. Volume 1, Rupert's Land to Riel. Volume 2, Gateway to the West. Volume 3, Decades of Diversity*. Great Plains Publications.

Winnipeg General Strike:
Bumsted, J. M. *The Winnipeg General Strike of 1919: An Illustrated History*. Watson & Dwyer;
Durkin, Douglas. *The Magpie* (a novel). University of Toronto Press;
Smith, Doug. *Let Us Rise: A History of the Manitoba Labour Movement*. New Star;
Sweatman, Margaret. *Fox: A Novel*. Turnstone.

Photo Credits

Legend: Top - T; Centre (Left & Right) — CL, CR; Bottom - B

John Bykerk — pp. 2T; 12; 19B; 22T&B; 35T; 61T; 68B; 108T; 111B; 113T&C; 126T; 127T; 134T; 148T; 151T, CL & CR; 154B; Back cover, B; **David Firman** — pp. 25B; 26T; 29; 41B; 47; 54B; 66B; 91T; 103T&C; 104T; 118T; 119B; 120T; 124B; 125B; 129; 138T&B; 143; 144; 145; 166T; **Distinctive Dimensions** — p. 86T&C; **Gimli Icelandic Festival** — p. 89T&B; **Glenbow Archives** — pp. 2C; 41T; 45; 57; **Mike Grandmaison** — Front cover, T; pp. 3C; 9; 13T; 14B; 17T; 18B; 26C; 27T&B; 30T; 31T; 32T&C; 54C; 65; 75C; 78T; 80B; 107B; 114B; 116C; 122T&B; 132T; 133; 134B; 137T&B; 139T; 152C; 158; 163T&B; 164T&B; 165B; 168T; **Donna Henry** — pp. 16B; 38; 79B; 156T&B; 157C&B; **Henry Kalen** — Front cover, CL&CR; pp. 2B; 3T,C&B; 13B; 14T; 15B; 16T; 17B; 18T; 19T; 23T; 30B; 31B; 32T; 33; 36; 40B; 43; 46; 48; 52C; 53C; 54T; 62T; 67T&B; 71T&B; 72; 74B; 75B; 76T&B; 77T; 78B; 80T; 82T&B; 85B; 86B; 87T&B; 88B; 90B; 92T&B; 93T&B; 94T,C&B; 95; 97T&B; 98; 100T&B; 101T&B; 103B; 104B; 105T,C&B; 106T,C &B; 107T; 108C&B; 109T&C; 110; 111T; 112T,CL,CR&B; 113B; 114T; 115T,C&B; 116T&B; 117; 118B; 119T; 120B; 121T&B; 123; 125T&C; 126C&B; 127CL&CR; 128T&C; 130T&B; 131T&B; 132B; 135; 137CT&B; 138C; 139B; 140T,C&B; 142; 146; 147T&B; 148B; 149T&B; 150T&B; 151B; 152T&B; 154T&C; 162T&B; 163C; 165T&C; 166B; 167T,C&B; 168B; Back cover, TR&CL; **Manitoba Culture, Heritage and Citizenship** — pp. 34T&B; 35B; 37T&B; **National Archives of Canada** — p. 50T; **Prairie Theatre Exchange** — p. 83; **Provincial Archives of Manitoba** — pp. 20; 28T,C&B; 40T; 41C; 42B; 49B; 50B; 55T,C&B; 56T,C&B; 58T&B; 59; 60; 61B; 63; 64; 68C; **Dave Reede** — pp. 1; 3C; 49T; 53T; 66T; 99; 109B; 127CR; 139C; Back cover, TL; **Royal Ontario Museum** — p. 42T; **Royal Winnipeg Ballet** — Front cover, B; pp. 70; 84T&B; **Saskatchewan Archives Board** — p. 44; **Harv Sawatzky** — pp. 15T; 23B; 24T; 30C; 51; 52T&B; 74T; 75T; 77B; 79T; 155T&B; 156C; 157T; 159T&B; 160T&B; Back cover, CR; **Robert Taylor** — pp. 3C; 21; 23CL&CR; 24B; 25T; 26B; 39; 128B; 155C; **University of Manitoba Department of Archives and Special Collections** — pp. 53B; 62B; **University of Winnipeg** — p. 85T; **Western Canada Pictorial Index** — pp. 68T; 69T&B; **Winnipeg Folk Festival** — pp. 73; 81; 90T; 91B; **Winnipeg International Children's Festival** — p. 88T

Maps courtesy of: **The Forks Renewal Corporation (GRANDESIGN)** — p. 96; *The Winnipeg Free Press* (in conjunction with **Travel Manitoba**) — pp. 4-7; 102; 124; 136; 141; 153; 161.

Formac Publishing acknowledges the support of the Canada Council and the Nova Scotia Department of Education in the development of writing and education in Canada.

Canadian Cataloguing in Publication Data
Manitoba
Includes index.
ISBN 0-88780-322-9
1. Manitoba — Guidebooks. 2. Manitoba — Description and travel. I. Morton, Marilyn.
FC3357.M36 1995   917.12704'3   C95-950173-8   F1062.M36 1995

Formac Publishing Company Limited
5502 Atlantic Street
Halifax, Nova Scotia B3H 1G4
Printed in Canada

Distributed in the United States by:
Formac Distributing Limited
121 Mount Vernon Street
Boston, Mass. 02198